This is a book that should have bee[n] [...] we used to joke that if there is such [...] would like to return to life as an air f[...] about their easy life because we kne[w] [...] [wa]sn't true. She is the most independent of women, accomplishing all the functions of a wife and mother with skill, compassion, and grace. A military wife is the most admirable of all God's creatures.

—Colonel Jerry Ellington, USAF (Retired)

Shirley passionately writes how her husband's job demanded that she be his partner in decisions so he could meet his work demands. To be open-minded, accepting, and willing to change at a moment's notice are but a few challenges for a military wife. All women will relate to the sacrifices she made.

—Betty Baumgartner, army wife, artist, author

What a great idea! Wish I'd thought of it first. Finally, someone speaks for the thousands of us who shared the air force career of fighter pilots for whom we were honored to stand in second place to their love of country and flying!

—Jean Russ, widow of General Robert Russ, USAF

Shirley Forgan is not only "credible" about her recollections and recounts of the Forgans' air force career—truly a shared endeavor—but she in her own right is an incredible lady. I know firsthand from where she speaks and writes—her *heart!* To write this book is further example by Shirley of the resolve, courage, and commitment it takes to be, or comes from being, a partner in the military family. Job well done, Shirley!

—Colonel John R. Haydon Jr., USAF, MC (Retired)

Shirley has revealed the distaff side of military life with discerning perception. She enables the reader to share her sundry moments by describing her wonderful adventures. She has talent for organization, friendship, and making a home for her family under sometimes hectic circumstances. As a commander's wife, Shirley knew the importance of meeting the needs of the people in her husband's unit. She was exemplary in her air force wife role.

—June Eddins, air force wife

Shirley Forgan's life as an air force wife is documented in an unbroken series of events—some serious, some humorous, some successful, while other escapades, although not successful, are written for your enjoyment. Her life with an air force fighter pilot is heightened as his career soars. Shirley captures it all and makes sense of a complicated and convoluted journey.

—Colonel Anthony I. Skur Jr., USAF (Retired)

What a fun read. The book sounds just like Shirley. She's everyone's friend, she'll travel anywhere, she loves to be right in the middle of what her sons (and grandsons) are doing, and she has to be busy, busy, busy. Shirley took a tough job and made it fun. She didn't let the burdens weigh her down. And that's the way she lives in civilian life too.

—Christi Dotter, retired teacher

Earning My Wings

March 2016

To Dee & Sac

with great memories

of Zaragoza Air Base, Spain.

Enjoy MY "war stories" not HIS

God Bless our military

and their families!

Shirley Forgan

Earning My Wings

ADVENTURES OF AN AIR FORCE WIFE

SHIRLEY DOBBINS FORGAN

TATE PUBLISHING & *Enterprises*

Published by Tate Publishing & Enterprises, LLC
127 E. Trade Center Terrace | Mustang, Oklahoma 73064 USA
1.888.361.9473 | www.tatepublishing.com

Tate Publishing is committed to excellence in the publishing industry. The company reflects the philosophy established by the founders, based on Psalm 68:11,
"The Lord gave the word and great was the company of those who published it."

Book design copyright © 2010 by Tate Publishing, LLC. All rights reserved.
Cover & Interior design by Chris Webb

Published in the United States of America

ISBN: 978-1-61663-311-0
1. Biography & Autobiography / Personal Memoirs
2. Biography & Autobiography / Military
10.05.07

Dedication

To my husband, Dave, our sons, Bruce and Todd, and the United States Air Force who provided the stories that made my journey from 1957 to 1989 one of joy, sometimes sorrow, but always an adventure.

To all military wives/mothers who are the strong ties that bind their families together in a tumultuous lifestyle.

Acknowledgments

My thanks and total gratitude:

To my husband, Dave, for tolerating late or do-it-yourself dinners while I traveled down memory lane on the computer and for his contribution of factual material. He pleasantly surprised me with, "It's good. I can hardly put it down."

To my dear Canadian friend, Frances LaVigne Henderson, who helped edit sentence structure, grammar, clarity, and vocabulary. She was also a cohort in many of the adventures.

To our bridge-playing friend and poet, Hollis Davis, for creative advice and organizational recommendations and for teaching me the importance of "hooking" and "flowing."

To Dave's fellow fighter pilot, Bill Bagwell, who contributed to my story his memories of military life in Japan.

To Todd, my computer guru, without whom I would have been in "la-la land" due to my lack of computer knowledge. And to Bruce for assisting in the photograph requirements.

To Kay Wood, friend and freelance editor—she earned every penny.

For giving generously of their time and expertise to proofread the final draft, I thank dear friends Christi Dotter and Patty Greenwood.

And last but not least, my appreciation goes to Tate Publishing and Enterprises for taking a chance on a first-time author. They were always supportive, attentive, cooperative, and prompt in their responses. They patiently worked with me through the complicated journey of producing the best book possible. I was blessed to be on their team.

Table of Contents

Foreword

War stories normally recount defining moments in one's life, those unforgettable experiences that leave indelible imprints but also ultimately define the person and who they are.

This is Dobbie's (Shirley's) story, her great adventures, *her* defining moments. She's transformed from a carefree working gal to a military spouse, whisked thousands of miles across the ocean to begin a new life in Japan, a country struggling to regain its feet.

At first, one could mistake this as yet another story about living and raising a family in a foreign land. But such is not the case. The military spouse is much more—an equal partner in carrying out the nation's national security mission and shouldering heavy responsibilities as social hostess to streams of foreign dignitaries; "making do" without what is routinely available in the U.S.; being provider and protector during long mission absences of one's spouse; yet, through it all, being gracious beyond description, representing the best that America offers, white gloves and all.

What is it that makes military spouses so strong and resilient despite difficult and adverse situations? This is a book about that special lifestyle as spouses become terrific team players, wearing far more hats than their husbands in roles of wife, lover, mother, leader, confidant, and motivator—whatever is needed—with a grand smile. Dobbie (Shirley) tells a great story, rising to the occasion again and again, with entertaining descriptions and a sparkling personality—plus her good heart.

Readers will finish this book realizing that the military spouse is the critical member keeping it all together, living according to the values that built America and sustain our country today, a great go-getter, a practitioner of stick-to-it-tiveness, and a constant improviser that makes things happen.

The nation reaps a valuable return on investment from these gallant spouses serving selflessly so that the military mission can go forward. America owes an incalculable debt of gratitude to Dobbie (Shirley) and the hundreds of thousands now serving, plus the millions who have gone before. There are many brave women on active duty in the military today (their male spouses keeping the home fires burning); however, this story is about Dobbie's generation of courageous wives.

Each military spouse makes a significant difference; every military spouse is an American hero in her (or his) own right.

General Michael P.C. Carns, USAF (Retired)

My wife, the author.
I gave her a ring; she married me.
I gave her a house; she made a home.
I gave her my love; she bore two sons.
I took her around the world; she faced the challenges.
I gave her security; she gave me devotion.
Dave

Introduction

Much has been written about the military—history, leaders, battles, wars, people, places, losers, winners, heroes, courage, and bravery. Few books, however, have been written about the true unsung hero, the military wife. Two familiar sayings in air force circles are: "The toughest job in the air force—an air force wife," and, "If you want a job done right, ask an air force wife."

My husband's aunt encouraged me to journal my experiences through our air force years, but I was too busy being a wife, mother, and "team player" in the military. Though I never kept a journal, I did keep meticulous photograph albums that I have used to jog my memory. Because my friend Frances continually provoked me to write the book, she is to blame for my failure to clean the house, cook dinners on time, walk the dog, and get enough sleep. Once started, I was on a writing roll.

This is the story of one family's life in the military—sad moments, happy times, and hilarious incidents—always an adventure and a challenge. The job of a military wife is not for sissies. It requires a special kind of woman, willing and able to make countless sacrifices. One cannot name a career field that is more demanding on the family with its perpetual moves, frequent separations, undersized and cramped base houses with your choice of white walls and beige carpet or beige carpet and white walls, and a changing landscape of relationships.

Together for thirty-one of thirty-three and a half years of his air force service, Dave and I lived in nine states (with three repeats) and four foreign countries. We moved twenty-two times. Our two sons each attended nine different schools. All this for a small paycheck, distressed furniture, boxes full of continually altered curtains, well-worn suitcases, high long-distance phone bills, and an ever-present curiosity about the place and length of our next assignment. On the upside, we were privileged to meet an assortment of dignitaries, including a king and two queens, and came away with many lifelong friends from all over the world and a wealth of memories.

Was it easy? *No.* Exciting? *Definitely.* Rewarding? *Absolutely.* Civilian friends asked, "How do you do it? How do you cope?" Air force families have a great support system and take care of each other. When asked about the changing role of the commander's wife, I advised, "Whatever you do, always look after your people."

Assigned sponsors at each new duty base communicated with us before we arrived. Even the teens had a correspondence program. The various military units have welcome and farewell socials, and wives' clubs are available for connections to greet and help newcomers during transition. We are intense about meeting and making friends because time is too short—*the next assignment is always just around the corner.* Retired friends say they miss most the support system and the camaraderie. I agree.

Looking back, I ponder about our favorite assignments. For a variety of reasons, many earn my vote. My husband's vote goes to those assignments that allowed him to be in the cockpit, doing his favorite work: *flying.* We highly prize our acute awareness of patriotism, sacrifice, and "worldly education."

I invite you to experience "wild blue yonder" travels, thrills, and adventures in this memoir of an air force wife.

A True Military Wife Is Someone Who...

1. Can put eight rooms of furniture into a five-room house
2. Has twenty pairs of draperies, and none of them fit the living room windows.
3. Can emerge sane from one motel room after spending two weeks over Christmas with four kids who all have the chicken pox.
4. Can, in one week's time, pick up a houseful of furniture, pile four kids, two dogs, a cat, three hamsters, a bird, and six suitcases into a station wagon, drive all the way cross-country, and still greet her husband with a smile. (From desperation, I would think.)
5. Doesn't even blink when she gets to England and finds out their household goods are in Japan.
6. Has all of her kids born in different states (She gets extra points for different countries).
7. Answers in Spanish when you speak to her in Japanese.
8. Pulls out her ID card when she goes into supermarkets.
9. Is faintly suspicious when she sees the same doctor in the hospital twice in a row!
10. Knows where and what Minot, North Dakota, is—and fears it!

Reflections

December 1958

What am I doing at twenty thousand feet over the Pacific Ocean, headed for a strange land, entrusting my life to a man I barely know—although just six short weeks ago he was declared my legal husband? I promised to love and obey, but do I really want to live a lifestyle of protocol and authority contrary to my upbringing? It's too late to run home to Mommy.

Dinner has been served and cleared, most of the lights are turned off, and I hear some snores and snorts around the cabin. I close my eyes but can't sleep. Inside this four-engine, propeller-driven aircraft, I have nineteen hours to reflect on how I got here.

Only eighteen months ago, after graduating from Oklahoma State University, I arrived in "Big D" (Dallas, Texas), June 1, 1957. My '49 Ford was loaded with my clothes and prize possession: a black and white fifteen-inch TV, a graduation present from my parents. I was eager to be on my own, living an exciting life in the big city. *Look out, world. Here I come.*

Pool Floozy to Bridal Belle

Dallas, Texas; McAlester, Oklahoma
June 1, 1957-December 1958

I located Kings Terrace Apartments, found my new roommate, Judy, at the complex's swimming pool, and immediately changed into my bathing suit to join the other "pool floozies." The pool, I was to discover, is where we would spend almost every weekend. From after work on Friday until we hit the sack Sunday night, we consumed beer, hamburgers, hot dogs, pizza, and reconnoitered the male population.

On day one, while basking in the sun, I observed a red '56 Chevy Corvette and a white '57 Ford Thunderbird drive in and park. Fascinated with sporty cars, I was "at attention" even before the four big, handsome hunks disembarked and headed our way. Had I died and gone to heaven? Poking Judy from her sun-induced sleep, I inquired who the "gods" were and learned they were jet fighter pilots training at Perrin Air Force Base in Sherman, Texas, forty-five minutes north of Dallas. I was later accused of asking, "Which one owns the Corvette?"

Like many student pilots, they converged on "Big D" every weekend to chase the Dallas-based American, Braniff, and Delta Airlines stewardesses. Kings Terrace and other apartment complexes were near Love Field (the only Dallas airport at the time), so I lived in the midst of three hundred stewardesses. The competition was stiff. "Red Corvette" was one of six Perrin pilots who rented an apartment in Kings Terrace for weekends, which helped me keep track of him at the pool during the next two months. My other two roommates told me I didn't have a prayer to get a date with "Red Corvette" because he had been dating an American "stew" for several months. I took the challenge, and little did "Red Corvette" know that he was going to be the target for my affections. However, I put my fantasy on hold and focused on my first priority: finding a job.

The two sex machines in Dallas 1957

Pool Floozy learning how to become the perfect Air Force wife

I had completed the requirements for an elementary education degree in three and a half years, including two summer sessions, but student teaching forty-one fourth graders tried my patience and challenged my ability to teach. I decided I didn't like teaching. Second semester of my fourth year at Oklahoma State, I took four business courses—shorthand, typing, office machines, and filing—spending most of my time with my fraternity pin mate and enjoying social life with little academic challenge. After paying for all those education courses, my father was unhappy I became a secretary. I considered it an easier job—better hours, higher pay, and more glamorous than being an old maid schoolteacher.

Dallas was considered a prime city for a good job at one of the oil companies. After a week of interviewing, taking shorthand and typing tests, and hearing, "Don't call us, we'll call you," I was called. I had an appointment with Mr. Teeple at Magnolia Petroleum Company in the tallest building in the city at the time. Pegasus, the flying red horse, highlighted the building's roof.

Mr. Teeple noticed a biology course on my transcript and thought it would be helpful in the job. I doubted I remembered anything from Biology 101 but heartily agreed with him. I was hired for a secretarial position in the Insurance Department Workman's Compensation Section for $325 a month—$25 more a month than a teacher's salary.

The months of June and July passed, and the first weekend in August, while I was basking in the sun at the pool as usual, "Red Corvette" swam over to where I was sitting on the edge of the pool. He was so handsome, over six feet tall, athletic, muscular physique, brown crew-cut hair, and eyes so dark brown they were almost black. He said, "Hello, my name is Dave Forgan." Not understanding the last name, I asked him to repeat it. He said, "It's organ with an F in front." He continued to get my attention. I told him my name was Dobbie. He asked me to repeat it, and I said, "It's obbie with a D in front." He laughed, and the "formal" introductions were complete.

Now here's the scoop on my nickname "Dobbie." During my senior year of college, I knew a fraternity boy whose last name was Dobbs. My last name was Dobbins. We college students habitually called each other by last names, so we became "Dobbs and Dobbs." When I met Judy, my future Dallas roommate, she picked up on the nickname and called me "Dobbie." (At times in my marriage, it was altered to "Gawddammitdobbie!") I was known almost exclusively by the nickname for the next twenty years until I got tired of being called Doobie, Dotie, Darbie, Dottie, Dobie, and explaining the origin.

My stew competition was out of town, so I tried keeping Dave's attention by flirting unmercifully—didn't get me very far. He soon went on to other interests at the pool.

That night I had a date to a party. In those days, every weekend was a party, and apartment doors were left open for anyone to enter, drink, dance, survey the opposite gender, and exit. Well, who should enter this party-apartment but "organ with an F in front" and his friend Bo—without dates. I called Judy, home early from a boring date, and urged, "Come quickly, 'Red Corvette' and his friend are here, and I overheard them say they're going to a party at 4942 Statler Terrace." (This apartment later became known as the "4942 Club" for its renowned parties.)

Judy arrived, and I dumped my date (shame on me) as we escaped out the back door. I was hot on the trail of "organ with an F in front!") Judy and I slipped into 4942 where guests were guzzling beer and dancing. To my dismay, Dave danced with Judy as I talked and danced with Bo while keeping an eye on Dave. Finally, we switched partners, and I had my chance. About 4:00 a.m., Dave asked if I wanted to see the sun rise on Dallas. I wondered if this was similar to watching submarine races or chasing rabbits at night on a golf course (excuses to park, kiss, and grope), but he was *serious*.

We walked toward his place with me thinking, *Uh-oh, here*

it comes—*"Would you like to come up to the apartment?"* However, we went directly to his car, which, unfortunately, was blocked in by another car. When Dave tried to guide the other car out of the way, it got away from him, knocking him to the ground. He tore his pants and skinned his knees, and the car banged into his roommate's Volkswagen. Oh well, on to the beautiful sunrise. (Dave did confess to his roommate the next day.) I focused on being "cool" since Dave was two years older, and I didn't want to appear silly and immature at the ripe old age of twenty-three years. Dave was a perfect gentleman. The sun rose. He drove me home, walked me to my door, said goodnight, and left. So much for impressing him.

After breakfast the next day, Judy and I made the usual trek to the pool to drink beer and see what or who was interesting. Sitting on the side of the pool, I gripped the edge as Dave swam over to me. Hooray, I hadn't been dumped, or maybe he had nothing better to do since his stew was still out of town. We discovered *Annie Get Your Gun* was playing at a theater and made a date for the evening show. I spent the afternoon getting ready for the date of my life. I gloated to my doubting roommates! I had a date with the inaccessible Dave Forgan.

For this significant date, I wore a fitted, cotton, black dress with a large white collar, black patent pumps, and, of course, the always-correct white gloves. Dave was impressed with the white gloves. Finally, I had made a good impression.

We double-dated for the theater then returned to our apartment complex. Dave asked me up to his apartment, and I again thought, *Uh-oh, here it comes. I've been invited to see his airplane pictures.* He introduced me to another student pilot, asleep under newspapers on the floor. I wondered when and where Dave would make a pass, but he deposited himself in a chair in the living room, I sat on the sofa, and we talked! The roommate at our feet slept right through it. Dave finally walked me home and gave me a quick kiss goodnight. Once again I thought, *Well, that's that.*

The next weekend, I invited Dave to accompany me to my

sorority sister's wedding in Durant, Oklahoma, wanting to impress everyone with this good-looking fighter pilot in a red Corvette. To my dismay, his car was in the repair shop. I showed up with my good-looking hunk in my '49 Ford. We had a nice time, and several acquaintances inquired about my new beau, and I made the most of my bragging rights.

The following weekend, I went to Tulsa to be a bridesmaid in another sorority sister's wedding. My still-in-college pin mate met me there. Once we were alone, I nervously returned his fraternity pin, breaking the news that I had met someone else. It was a shock. He assumed we were getting married since we had looked at rings.

Judy became unhappy with our two roommates, so we parted their company the first of September and rented a one-bedroom apartment near Southern Methodist University (SMU). Dave called to say he had previous plans for the weekend. I assumed stew was back in town; however, he stopped by our apartment Sunday evening on his way back to Perrin AFB, and we continued seeing each other every weekend after that. Good-bye, stew. I was swept off my feet by my knight in shining armor—a lieutenant piloting a shiny F-86D! We enjoyed each other's company, along with other pilots and their dates, having fun at the pool, seeing movies, and eating lots of hamburgers and pizzas.

After flying over my home turf, McAlester, Oklahoma, on one of his flight training missions, Dave asked, "Are there any paved streets in that town?" I was indignant! One weekend in September, I took this candidate for marriage home to be scrutinized by family and friends. We drove into town and made the first turn to my neighborhood—yup, a dirt road full of potholes. The little red machine was almost swallowed up. Not only did his car get everyone's attention, Lt. Forgan made a good impression too. Mother wanted to know where I'd rented him. He was handsome, had nice manners, which Mother liked, and had played college football, which Daddy liked. We spent Saturday afternoon with my parents and their friends, the Smiths, watching the televised OU football team clobber their opponent, as usual. Then someone suggested going to Little Rock to see the Oklahoma State-Arkansas game. The six of us piled into Dr. Smith's car, requiring me to sit on Dave's lap for the four-hour drive. This was the most intimate position we had been in yet. Didn't bother me.

Passing a sign for the Ouachita Mountains, we got a big laugh when Dave said, "These O Wah Cheeta Mountains aren't very big." (He had graduated from the University of Colorado where the Rockies dominate the skyline.) Had there been room, I'd have fallen off his lap laughing; however, all in good humor, we corrected his pronunciation of the Oklahoma Indian name, "Wash i taw." He said some city folks up north thought we still fought Indians in what was formerly Indian Territory. I considered my little town of eleven thousand people pretty civilized, but Dave was from Chicago—even larger and more cosmopolitan than my new, big world of Dallas.

Dave passed muster (military talk for inspection). Mother didn't have a critical thing to say about him—a first. My girlfriends liked his looks, and my parents' friends' children liked his car. Test number one passed!

After graduation from Advanced Pilot Training at Perrin AFB, Dave spent five days with Judy and me in Dallas. By this time, Dave and I were smooching it up, but he was still always the gentleman. I didn't miss a day of work; he met me downtown for lunch every day. After work one day, we went to dinner and the movie *Around the World in Eighty Days*. Dave saw it; I slept through half of it.

We had dated eight weekends and five days when, at the end of September, Dave drove to his home in LaGrange, Illinois (a suburb of Chicago). He made reservations for me to fly there for the weekend to meet his parents. *Ah ha! He does like me!* But I had to pay for the airline ticket. Was he cheap or was he testing me to see if I was serious? I didn't care because I had a feeling this was serious and worth it. When I asked Mr. Teeple about taking Friday off, he said he would ask his boss. On my lunch hour, I paid for the ticket and bought a new dress and returned to the office only to see Mr. Teeple's sad face. His boss had refused my request. I had played by the rules and was too honest to call in sick. Dumb me.

"Sweet boss" said he would talk to "big jerk boss" when "big" awoke from his nap. Big boss was getting ready to retire, and I didn't understand why he'd care if "Miss New Secretary" wanted one day off. Called into his office, I sat stiffly in front of his desk, not sure what to expect. I got the third degree, felt on trial, and was reduced to tears. "Yes, this man is probably going to be my husband. He is leaving for Japan and wants me to meet his parents. No, I will never again ask to have a day off." Request granted. Thanks to "sweet boss" for his support and understanding.

I spent a nervous weekend with Dave's parents. They were nice but had a more formal lifestyle than I was accustomed to. They ate dinner every night in the dining room—his father in shirt and tie, carving the meat and serving our plates. By contrast, my daddy usually was still in his work overalls at "supper," and Mother controlled the food, the service, and the kitchen—sacred domain for Italian women. (My mother was first generation Italian in her family born in the U.S.) Dave took me to downtown Chicago on Saturday night to roam famous Rush Street. Famous? I had never heard of it. Restaurants and bars—geeze, this was even bigger than Dallas—and you could buy drinks by the glass. Couldn't do that in Dallas. No prohibition here—nor many Baptists.

I returned to Dallas, assuming we had passed test number two. Promising to write letters, we went our separate ways. Dave drove the red machine to San Francisco to be shipped to Japan. (The military allows each active duty member to ship one personal car overseas and back at U.S. Air Force expense.) He departed from California's Travis AFB to the 40th Fighter Interceptor Squadron at Yokota Air Base in Japan for his first permanent assignment after flight training.

I continued working at Magnolia through the fall, winter, and spring and dated lots of guys, but all paled in comparison to "Jet Jockey Forgan." Judy and I moved again to Redwood Apartments on the other side of the SMU campus (move number three)—another party area after a quiet two months.

Correspondence between Dave and me became intimate and serious. My communication went from weekend activity, pool gossip, the weather, to "I miss you," and "I love you." His letters were full of flying stories, his buddies, tales of Japan, to "I miss you too" and "I love you too," and finally, "I think we should get married." When he finally asked me to marry him, I said, "Absolutely!" He wrote my parents a lovely letter, requesting permission to marry their daughter (I said he had good manners), and, of course, they were delighted I had finally found someone they heartily approved of. I sent him a picture of an engagement ring I liked. He sent it to his parents, and they took it to their jeweler friend. Dave repeatedly suggested that I visit his parents, but I kept making excuses. I had increased my bank account balance to $200 and didn't want to deplete it buying an airline ticket. At his insistence, I finally flew to LaGrange the weekend of April 26, 1958, once again paying my own way. To my surprise, Dave's father presented me with a ring and "engaged" me to his son by proxy. Tears clouded our eyes. They gave me a pearl drop necklace, and a white orchid corsage was delivered from Dave's two aunts. We called Dave in Japan—all of us overjoyed with happiness and love—then my future in-laws took me to dinner to celebrate.

I flew back to Dallas where Judy picked me up at the airport in my car. I kept my white gloves on to hide the ring. She didn't ask, and I didn't tell. In the apartment, I removed my gloves, flashed the ring, and we screamed and hugged.

Several stews had captured air force pilots for marriage, and my friend Nancy needed new roommates. Judy and I moved into the renowned "4942 Club," a two-bedroom apartment (move number four). Shortly after we moved in, an eviction notice appeared in the mailbox for all four occupants, three who had already departed. I tried to persuade the manager to reverse her decision, but she wouldn't budge. She sternly conveyed that Judy and I could stay, but Nancy had to go, leaving Judy and me to find two more roommates or, with Nancy, move again—which is what we did the end of May, going back to Kings Terrace where this whole story began. Five moves in one year.

Nancy had dated an AF pilot the previous year who was assigned to Phalsburg, France. With our guys overseas, Nancy and I didn't let any grass grow under our feet. We hung out with Paul and Dave #2. Dave #2 had a boat, and I liked to water ski. Even after Dave and I got engaged, the four of us—Nancy, Paul, Dave #2, and I—continued to spend weekends together. Dave didn't understand why I wasn't home all weekend writing letters to him. He told me that of my forty-five letters, only fifteen were written on weekends and only four of those at night. What was I doing? Well, I wasn't about to tell him. Didn't he have better things to do than count my letters?

Dave and I finally scheduled our wedding for October 18, 1958. In July, the office gave me a farewell party and a beautiful, large silver tray. I was not replaced, which hurt my feelings. Had I been kept around for Monday morning entertainment as I recounted my weekends' activities? Did Mr. Teeple keep me employed out of the goodness of his heart? Or was the new hire, Ann, qualified to do my job and hers? Probably all of the above!

I purchased my wedding gown in Dallas for a whopping $145, a lot of money in 1958. It was too ostentatious, but I felt like a fairy princess without a magic wand. The new girl at work, Ann, lent me her wedding veil for "something borrowed," and she and Nancy were my bridesmaids with Judy being my maid of honor. Since Dave's friends were scattered around the country, he asked his dad to be best man and the husbands of two of my McAlester friends and a pilot still at Perrin AFB to be ushers and groomsmen.

I worked until August then went home to finish wedding

plans. My meager belongings—mostly clothes, my fifteen-inch black and white TV, and pots and pans purchased from a needy but cute young salesman were stuffed into my '49 Ford as I headed north to Oklahoma, returning after fourteen months. It had been a crazy, undisciplined year of "sowing my oats"; it was time to transform into a wife and take on serious responsibilities. I was twenty-three years old.

Wedding October 18, 1958, McAlester, Oklahoma

The Wedding and Honeymoon

Preparing for the special event was fun but also a little stressful. Mother was the epitome of organization, and I had few decisions to make. Bless their hearts—my parents went all out for their only child; I was spoiled and never asked the cost. I'd been a bridesmaid several times; now it was my turn to be the bride. The invitations were mailed, I was honored at several bridal showers, and the gifts stacked up. We would begin married life with silver spoons in our mouths—literally. Writing thank-you notes kept me busy—an obligation Lt. Forgan escaped because he was in Japan. It was the first of many household chores he would escape—sly one!

The week before the wedding, I picked up Dave in Dallas where he had flown from Japan. His parents arrived four days before the wedding, and on their first night in McAlester, we had dinner at my parents' house. For this get-to-know-the-in-laws night, Mother dispatched my maternal Italian grandparents—who'd arrived by train from California—to old Italian friends for the evening. About nine o'clock they called, ready to come home. Daddy retrieved them, and it was obvious Grandpa had had too much Italian vino. He was quite jovial. Mother insisted he was tired and needed to go to bed, but he ignored her. He wanted to celebrate the forthcoming marriage of his only granddaughter. He entertained us with the story of their wedding, when he borrowed $2 for the license and they partied for four days—a typical Italian wedding celebration. On their fiftieth wedding anniversary, Grandpa had stood on his head in the middle of the living room floor to demonstrate his youth and masculinity.

During the evening, the liquor inventory was depleted, so Daddy made a phone call. Ten minutes later, the doorbell rang and more booze was delivered. Amused, Dave's dad exclaimed, "My god, we've returned to prohibition!" The "bootlegger" conveniently lived two blocks from our house, one block outside city limits.

The ceremony would be at the First Baptist Church, where I had been baptized and taught not to drink, smoke, dance, or play cards. Boy, was I a sinner according to their doctrine. Dave and I had premarital consultation with the preacher, who stated, "Of course, it will be a double-ring ceremony." Dave replied, "No, it won't," leaving the preacher speechless. Dave deemed it unnecessary to explain that climbing in and out of a jet fighter plane required placing his hand in a kick step on the side of the plane. If a finger with a ring on it got caught in the spring-loaded door, it could rip off a finger. I questioned why he couldn't remove the ring before flying, but he theorized that a ring wasn't required to prove he was married. Couldn't argue with that.

We also debated serving champagne at our reception. Dave sternly declared he had never been to a wedding reception without champagne, but I had to stand firm, stressing this was a Baptist shindig, so there could be no booze at the rehearsal dinner or reception. Dave huffed and puffed, but I won the battle. With a stroke of luck, though, the preacher canceled his rehearsal dinner attendance, so our celebration began at the Isle of Capri Italian Restaurant in the nearby Italian community of Krebs—with alcoholic beverages and a happy Forgan clan!

Dave's Aunt Grace and Uncle Fred, Aunt May, and the godparents drove to McAlester from Chicago. His Aunt Peg arrived by private plane (nice to have rich friends), and my aunt Dodie came from Fort Worth. This show was getting on the road.

My prewedding hours were tranquil. I slept late and visited with Ann, Judy, and Nancy when they arrived from Dallas. I unwrapped more gifts and talked to Dave on the phone. He was busy polishing the soles of his shoes black per my mother's strict instructions. She had read this prevented light-colored soles from being a distraction when the groom knelt at the altar. I'm surprised Dave acquiesced to her request, but since my parents were paying for the wedding, I guess he felt compelled to obey and stay on the good side of the in-laws.

Dave's mother said it was the happiest wedding she had ever seen. All went according to plan, or Mother would have had someone's head. Everyone survived on cake and punch without champagne at the reception in the Aldrich Hotel ballroom. We changed into our getaway outfits and departed with rice in our hair, mouths, and clothes.

Daddy lent us his car for our honeymoon, and we drove forty-five minutes to Muskogee (Dave pronounced it Mus´ ko gee—still having trouble with Indian names) to spend our wedding night at a motel. Earlier that day, Dave had taken over a bottle of champagne to be chilling in the bathroom sink. It wasn't exactly first class, but he finally got some champagne. In the bathroom, I changed into my wedding-night nightie while Dave put on his pajama bottoms. His dad jokingly had attached a big safety pin to the fly. The next morning at breakfast, the waitress commented, "You must be newlyweds." Surprised, I asked how she guessed. She said it was our happy faces. Were we that obvious?

We drove to Hot Springs, Arkansas, for a three-day stay. The gist of the name didn't occur to us until Dave's dad later joked about hot bedsprings. Between lovemaking, sleeping, and romantic dinners, Dave taught me the mechanical parts of an airplane—just what every bride wants to hear on her honeymoon. He was frustrated as I kept calling the empennage the espionage.

We drove to LaGrange to spend time with Dave's parents since he had been gone for a year. They honored us with a cocktail party (no lack of booze in that town), where I met the rest of the family and friends and tried to remember who went with what wedding gift.

On our wedding day, a friend of Dave's in Japan was supposed to submit the concurrent travel paperwork, enabling me to return to Japan with Dave. The fellow fouled up and sent us a telegram announcing his failure. We hurried back to McAlester, and I took Dave to the Oklahoma City airport for his solo return.

He called me from Japan with instructions to go to Tinker Air Force Base in Midwest City near Oklahoma City to arrange for my transportation to Japan—and to not let them tell me no. Daddy drove me to the transportation office where for two hours they told me no. I didn't understand their reasoning and military jargon but understood them to say because I wasn't married when the lieutenant was assigned overseas that I didn't qualify for transportation. We drove back to McAlester with me weeping all the way. The next day, on the sly, Daddy went to U.S. Speaker of the House of Representatives Carl Albert's office. (Political influence in the military was a no-no.) Mr. Albert's office mailed a letter to Tinker kindly requesting any assistance. A week later Tinker called, offering me transportation via ship—seventeen days at sea and arriving after Christmas. Dave decided if I couldn't get there before Christmas, he would pay my airfare. I don't know where he got the $500—his paycheck was less than $400—but pay my way he did.

Mother and her friend drove me to Dallas to my former apartment and roommates. Mother was so distraught over leaving me that her friend literally had to pull her away. More Italian emotion! I was excited; she was hysterical!

When my luggage was weighed at the airport the next day, I learned there was a maximum weight allowance. Needing clothes for the next two months until our household goods arrived, I carried a leather coat with several dresses hidden inside it, a hatbox containing one hat with numerous items packed around it, a makeup bag, and a handbag. All my possessions weighed more than I did. My suitcase was a bit overweight, but it cost only $5 extra, a small amount to pay on each leg of the trip. Little did I know.

I flew from Dallas to Los Angeles, almost missing my next flight to San Francisco. I was running for the gate when the hatbox fell open and the items spilled out. The attendants hollered at me but held the gate to the plane open while I frantically collected everything off the floor. I made it on board and collapsed into the seat, my stress bucket overflowing.

Arriving in San Francisco on Saturday, I took a taxi to the famous Mark Hopkins Hotel, where Dave suggested I stay. He persuaded me to go to the Top-of-the-Mark bar overlooking the city. "Little Okie from Muskogee" went to the top but was so intimidated, I looked around and returned to my room. Staying in San Francisco three nights, I had one nice dinner in the hotel's lovely dining room, one dinner across the street at the other famous Fairmont Hotel, and then casually dined in the coffee shop the third night. I chatted with taxi drivers outside the hotel, watched TV, and called the parents and the in-laws. Boy, was I lonely. I went to see *Houseboat*, starring Sophia Loren and Cary

Grant, at the movie theater in the Fairmont—the most fun I had in San Francisco. Too bad.

Monday, I took a taxi to the Japanese Consulate to get my passport and visa and decided to walk back to the hotel. It was an exhausting climb up a steep hill, as I wore stylish, pointed-toe, spiked-heel shoes. No wonder I have bad feet.

Tuesday, I left for Japan via Hawaii. At the airport, I was told my luggage was overweight. "Yeah, I know. Here's another $5." I was stunned when told excess luggage weight going overseas was $5 a pound, and it would cost me $75. They weighed everything but my handbag, wouldn't accept a check, and I had no spare cash. My inherited Italian tears began to fall. A kind Japanese man suggested I take the balance of his weight allowance since he was traveling light. I gratefully accepted and solicited a couple more "lightweight" passengers. The airline accepted this, and I paid cash for the balance only to Hawaii where I would repack.

After an eight-hour, propeller-plane flight to Honolulu, I opted for a two-day rather than a two-hour layover. I was going to be married all my life. I might never again be in Hawaii. I found a big box at the hotel, packed it with clothes, and lugged it to the post office, enabling me to meet my weight allowance. Hawaii looked just like in the movies, only I was disappointed in the small size of Waikiki Beach. I took a city tour and relaxed the rest of the time, trying to drain my still overflowing stress bucket.

Two days later, I left for Tokyo on Pan American Airlines. We had one refueling stop at Wake Island, but it was dark when we landed, so I couldn't see a thing. My mind returned from long hours of reflections as I began to face reality. It had been a long, stressful journey, and I started getting nervous as we approached the airport in Tokyo. Was this really happening to me? Was it all a dream? If Dave wasn't there to meet me, what would I do? Having said, "I will," this little girl from "Big Mac" (McAlester) was about to take the second biggest step of her life. Was I up to it?

Good-bye, CONUS (Continental United States).
Ko nichiwa (hello), Japan.

Holy Shitake!

Yokota Air Base, Japan
40th Fighter Interceptor Squadron
December 1958-February 1960

After my long flight, we touched down to sweet ground in the land of the rising sun. When I exited customs, there was my six-foot, two-inch, round-eyed husband standing tall among a scurrying throng of little Japanese people. I couldn't miss him. Dave had arranged a special night for us at Tokyo's famous old Imperial Hotel. Alone in our room, my dear, new husband looked at me longingly; however, after nineteen sleepless hours, I collapsed on the bed and immediately fell asleep. He woke me several hours later to go to dinner, and our honeymoon began again.

The next day, we bumped through potholes and dodged motor vehicles and pedestrians on our way to Yokota Air Base—a one-hour, thirty-five mile ride on dirt and gravel roads, narrow and crowded (like everything else). In most countries, people drive on the right; in England and a few other countries, they drive on the left. The Japanese seemed to drive on *both* sides. When a Japanese male got in or on something with a motor, he transformed into a Samurai or Kamikaze. Few Japanese vehicles had mufflers, so the din was overwhelming. If they couldn't make enough noise with their engines, they leaned on their horns. Emission control devices didn't exist, and low octane gas was mixed with oil. The combustion produced large, lingering clouds of smoke. Virtually all Japanese homes were heated with charcoal-burning hibachi pots, which, combined with vehicle pollution, produced an eye-burning smog. To combat this irritation, many Japanese wore surgical masks outdoors—the children called them "booger bags." I can clearly recall the strong, offensive aroma of Japan as we drove into the countryside from the city. It was a mixture of "night soil" (human fertilizer), automobile smoke, and smog.

Fighter pilot's wife

First home in Japan - 600 square feet of plywood and plaster

My fighter pilot

The small village of Fussa was adjacent to the base, and beyond that was farmland and mountains. The farms were tiny by American standards, and every inch was cultivated. At the corner of each little field was a small concrete box where "night soil" was collected; it came from any available source. Benjo ditches with running water lined the roadways and were used for toilet facilities by the Japanese *and* their animals, adding to the Japanese aroma. We never became accustomed to seeing both sexes use the benjo ditches. Off base public restrooms were also problematic for most Americans. Commonly, men used urinals on one side of the room, and ladies squatted over holes in the floor in stalls on the other side. However, the Japanese people were very tenacious and hardworking. At that time, the late 1950s, they were still rebuilding their economy and worked ten to twelve hours a day, and most had second jobs. They had little to work with and wasted nothing.

Dave was apprehensive about my acceptance of our little off-base house in the rice paddies. When we approached the six hundred square feet of plywood and plaster, I forced myself to say, "Hey, it's all right. What do we care? We're on our honeymoon." An Oscar-winning performance. I was happy my friends back in the U.S. couldn't see it.

The house had no insulation; therefore, the windows were covered with plastic to contain the interior heat in the winter and the cool air in the summer. Thankfully, we had the comfort of a window air-conditioning unit. Installed on a wood rack outside, a jet plane's gas tank containing kerosene was connected by copper tubing to an indoor potbelly stove to heat our small abode. The military provided us with some austere furniture. In the bedroom, a double bed, two nightstands, and a dresser left little room to walk around. In the tiny kitchen, I was able to cook and wash dishes without taking a step in any direction. The bathroom walls, floor, and tub were covered with one-inch white tiles, and a white sink and white toilet with pull-chain flush added no color to the stark, sterile room. To get hot water, we had to light the hot water heater. Once we forgot to turn it off, and it boiled over, dripping condensation from the ceiling into the living room like a sprinkler system gone awry. The *bungalow* (using the word loosely) had a second bedroom, which we used for storage, including the hard top for the red machine. The gravel streets in the little neighborhood were narrow and muddy most of the time thanks to frequent rains. As a result, Americans quickly adopted the Japanese custom of removing shoes when entering a home.

A few days after our arrival, we attended the squadron's Christmas holiday party, where I was officially welcomed. The military constantly hails and farewells as people come and go. Dave was flying the F-86D, assigned to the 40th Fighter Interceptor Squadron, commanded by a lieutenant colonel, and I was thrilled when the commander asked me to dance. I was on exhibit, everyone eagerly sizing up the new bride the handsome fighter jock had married. I must have passed the test because everyone was very nice to me.

Before long, I experienced the "hotsi" bath for the first time and was totally intimidated. I instructed Dave to face the wall while I stripped off my clothes and sat on a little wooden stool. A young, female Japanese attendant in a skimpy bathing suit washed me with soap and water and rinsed me with a bucket of water. Then I climbed into a big tub of *hot* water to "marinate" while Dave went through the ritual of getting washed. (It was considered very unsanitary to wash and soak in the same tub. Makes sense!) After I turned into a prune, Dave took my place in the hot tub, and I was directed onto a massage table. When it was Dave's turn, the little attendant *walked* on his back, using her toes and feet to massage, while I watched in wide-eyed fascination. I informed Dave two was company, but three was a crowd. Thereafter, at the inns or hotels, we had romantic evenings enjoying the warmth of the traditional hotsi baths—in private. Large pools were available where numerous Japanese families soaked and swam in the nude together, but my Baptist upbringing kept me too modest to participate in these community "outings." I like my bathroom privacy.

Subsequently, I became involved in wives' activities, and on many weekends Dave and I drove into Tokyo for dinner, entertainment, and sightseeing. The Japanese were fascinated with my bleached blond hair, and they always wanted to touch it. The red machine was also an attraction. Whenever we returned to our parked car, we found it surrounded by spectators.

There were few places to go for entertainment other than a pizza place directly outside the base gate and a few sushi houses in the area. Other than entertaining in our homes, most of the social life, including numerous squadron parties, occurred at the officers' club. It fed the bachelors, catered to ladies' events, and was always busy at night offering a variety of entertainment. The bar was large, slot machines were everywhere, and both were well used. Dave immediately placed the officers' club off limits for this new bride unless he accompanied me. Full-time Japanese maids and babysitters for the families were a cheap commodity. He had observed too many wives with too much spare time hanging out at the club, drinking and gambling.

Television entertained children on base; however, the Japanese program selection was limited—either Godzilla-type horror shows or Samurai warrior films with early versions of kung fu. U.S. westerns or cartoons with Japanese subtitles or language dubbed in provided comic relief.

Bridge-playing was a popular pastime. When we crowded two tables of players into our small living room, we rotated seats. Those sitting near the potbelly stove got too hot and switched to the other table to cool off. I soon learned to increase my bridge knowledge because my new husband hated to lose. The pilots played bridge while they sat twenty-four-hour alert on the flight line, and Dave was accustomed to winning.

Our first argument occurred two months after my arrival. At a couples' bridge night, I made a super *faux pas* in bidding my cards. Unfortunately, it was during a lull in the conversation when all was quiet. Dave's loud exclamation, "Gawddammit, Dobbie!" reverberated around the room. I was reduced to tears on the drive home and promised I would learn to play bridge better if he would try to be more patient. I purchased a bridge book at the Base Exchange (BX) store, so half the promise was kept. I learned to play better bridge; Dave never became more patient. Years later, our younger son, Todd, jokingly commented that until he was thirteen, he thought my name was "Gawddammit Dobbie." Funny remark at the time, but it tells you something about Dave's short fuse.

Shopping was interesting. The U.S. government paid the military members in paper "military script," which we called monopoly money. It was legal only on base, so we exchanged it for Japanese yen when shopping off base. We bought our food at the always-crowded base commissary. The only available milk was reconstituted powdered milk mixed with jellied butter fat, which came from a central dairy plant that supported all the military bases in the area. A Japanese baker provided one type of bread that was absolutely tasteless. Vegetables were grown at a special military-owned farm that did *not* use "night soil," and meat arrived frozen from the U.S.

The other place to shop on base was the BX. It was small, and when something new arrived, there was a near riot before it quickly sold out. Since BX clothing was limited, we used Japanese tailors and seamstresses. Sears Roebuck and Montgomery Ward catalogs were standard items in every little American "shack" in the Far East.

Off-base shopping was a challenge—always crowded and everyone seemed to be in a hurry. The shops were neat, tiny, and stacked wall to wall, floor to ceiling with wares. Inexpensive prices made it a shopper's paradise. Husbands said they were going broke with their wives "saving" them so much money. Bamboo items, cameras, cloisonné, coral jewelry, dolls, fans, glassware, lacquer ware, lanterns, porcelain and pottery, pearls, silks, tortoise-shell products, wood-block prints, and curios were good buys. I did my best to contribute to Japan's economy. It was my duty. We bought a set of china dishware for twelve for 7200 yen ($20.00). Restaurant dinners ranged from 500 to 1,500 yen ($1.50 to $4.00). Taxi fare was 60 to 100 yen for the first two kilometers with 20 yen extra for additional 400 to 570 meters, which translated to 17 to 28 cents for the first 1.3 miles and five cents extra for 433 to 542 yards.

We soon bought our first furniture—a large, three-piece sectional sofa that required a living room with two connecting walls, nine feet from each corner. It took up half the room, but we had the required wall space. That sofa made Forgan history—strip poker was played on it; baby urine and vomit stained it; the boys jumped on it and made forts from the cushions; extra guests slept on it. Years later, when I couldn't decide whether to recover the sofa or buy a new one, an upholsterer told me the sofa could be dragged behind a truck for two blocks and not be fazed. Therefore, the sofa remained in the family and has frequently been recovered. When we moved to the Dallas area forty-four years later, our older son, Bruce, inherited the famous, fabulous, flexible Forgan sofa.

Like my mother, I started cooking big meals at noon; however, my new husband wanted only a sandwich with chips for lunch. I was trying hard to be a typical fifties housewife, wearing dainty little aprons, dusting, and vacuuming every day. Since there wasn't much to clean, I spent my spare time learning to cook. I did the wash by hand, in the kitchen sink, which wasn't easy. Copying Mother, I washed on Mondays, ironed on Tuesdays, attended wives' functions on Wednesdays, grocery shopped on Thursdays, cleaned on Fridays, slept late on Saturdays, and devoted Sundays to writing letters. I have always been a faithful letter writer—to friends, parents, aunts, uncles, and everyone enjoyed our news.

It wasn't all social as we made some charitable contributions too. The squadron sponsored a young Japanese girls' orphanage. On our visits, the little girls swarmed over us like bees, pulling on our arms, hugging our legs, tugging at our clothes, and playing with the ladies' jewelry. Of course, they always wanted to touch my blond hair. The squadron men painted the entire facility and planted flowers, and families contributed more help on their own time.

The big event of the year was Christmas. The squadron purchased clothes, toys, and candy for all the little ones, and we had a big party at the orphanage. Their various reactions were amazing to watch. One child sat down immediately and played with her doll; another took all her presents and ran back to her bed and storage bin to put everything away, as if fearful someone would take them if they weren't hidden. They sang Christmas carols in Japanese and "Silent Night" in English.

It was difficult not to fall in love with those snotty-nosed little girls. They tugged at our heartstrings. Dave was the squadron volunteer in charge of the orphanage activity our last year there, and we made several visits on our own time. When we went to say good-bye, the Papasan and Mamasan invited us into their private living quarters, which was rarely done, and presented me with a beautiful hand-embroidered Hopi coat. I was touched by their offering.

I volunteered to assist an English class in a Japanese junior high school, a one-hour train ride into the mountains. The students needed to hear American pronunciation since Japanese cannot say our Rs, Ls, and Fs. When I entered the classroom, the students respectfully stood, bowed, and said, "Guud mawning, Meesas Hogan." In spite of my corrections, their pronunciation of my name never changed. They taught me some Japanese words and giggled, hands over their mouths, upon hearing *my* pronunciation.

Dave and I took several sightseeing trips around Japan, trying to absorb their culture, from topless girly shows to Kabuki. The Kabuki drama, which originated in the seventeenth century, is in reality a type of melodrama with one outstanding difference: men play all the female roles. (They had "cross-dressing" before it was exploited.) We stayed at Japanese inns and followed their customs, removing our shoes before entering. We sat on the floor, slept on the floor, and ate our meals at small tables on the floor. Our favorite Japanese food was sukiyaki—slices of tender beef, vegetables such as spinach, onions, mushrooms, and bean curd cooked in soy sauce and light wine, and the ever-present bowl of rice. We also liked tempura—shrimp dipped in batter and deep fat fried. We avoided raw fish.

We took time to enjoy the beautiful sights—temples, statues of Buddha, gardens, festivals, and shrines. Travel in this pleasant land of cherry blossoms and polite bows also had problems: ever-present crowds, low doorways (hazardous for six-foot two-inch Dave), smelly fish, widespread road construction, left-side-of-the-street driving, language barriers, and awkward results from the Japanese belief that it's impolite to say no. You never knew if your question was answered correctly. "Is this the way to the shrine?" "Hai" (Yes). But we didn't find the shrine. "Is this the women's benjo (bathroom)?" "Hai" (Yes). Wrong, it was coed. We learned to avoid asking yes or no questions because the answer was always "Hai."

Ann and Tommy McLoughlin lived near us, and we became good friends. He was a fighter pilot in Dave's squadron, and they were also newlyweds, hailing from New York City. Ann told me stories of growing up in a cold water flat in Manhattan and never leaving New York City before coming to Japan. I shared about small-town living in Oklahoma, which she thought was populated only with Indians and cowboys. (Well, she was close.) We were both in culture shock.

Tommy and Dave pulled night alert on the flight line for a week once a month. Ann was afraid to stay alone, so I stayed all night with her, setting the alarm for an hour before our hubbies were due back. I sleepwalked home and jumped into bed, pretending to have been there all night. Tommy and Dave never suspected; we never got caught.

Other good friends, Kathy and Tony Skur, had boys, ages four, three, and two. Kathy had her hands full with these rambunctious little guys. On one occasion, she sent them into the men's restroom at the BX, and when they didn't return, she sent someone to check on them. The man came out laughing, as all three boys had removed their clothes and were stark naked! Kathy did not think it was funny and ordered a GI to get back in there, dress the boys, and shoo them out the door. He did as he was told. The boys playfully burned all of Kathy's hats in their potbelly heating stove and once removed all the doors in the house (not too difficult considering the construction) as well as the refrigerator door. Dave said the only time he ever saw Tony mad was when he threatened to bring the boys a toolbox for their birthdays.

One of Dave's bachelor friends dated a Japanese waitress at the officers' club. Her nickname was Punkie. They had a little house in the mountains for their weekend retreats and invited Dave and me for dinner one night. Punkie had prepared sukiyaki, and as the bachelor, Dave, and I sipped sake (rice wine), Punkie drank rum and coke. A culture lesson in reverse!

Dave's tour of duty in Japan was drawing to a close in February 1960, after serving one-half of a bachelor tour overseas (one year) and one-half a married tour (one and a half years).

He had initially intended to complete his two-year commitment to the air force and then return to Marshall Field Department Store in Chicago. He was on military leave of absence from the store after having worked there six months before entering active duty. However, we decided we liked the military lifestyle, and he loved the flying. He applied for indefinite status, which meant he relinquished his separation date and signed on to stay in the air force indefinitely. His mother was not happy about this decision. She worried about the flying dangers and wanted him to come home to Chicago. Dave decided he would rather be a "fly boy" than a "rag man."

The Japanese paid a lot of money for American cars, so Dave thought he could get a good price for the Corvette, a rare car in Japan. Shortly before our departure, someone contacted him, and he drove into Tokyo to meet the possible buyer. A Japanese "sugar-daddy" wanted to buy the sexy car for his sexy, movie star girlfriend. The sale didn't transpire, so Dave shipped the car back to the States for us to pick up when we arrived in San Francisco.

When asked his preference for a new stateside assignment, Dave indicated his three choices: fighters, fighters, and fighters— on the east or the west coast. He received his new assignment: a radar controller on a radar site outside Fordland, Missouri, in the middle of the U.S. So much for declaring choices. We left Japan reluctantly, leaving good friends, fun times, and cheap living. We had lots of sad farewells; however, we looked forward to the land of round eyes, better housing, and no language barrier. We remained in contact with many couples from that first assignment and have been blessed to renew our friendships over the years. Those who have passed away remain in our fondest memories.

Ah, memories…
Sayonara.

Beach Bums

Panama City/Mexico Beach, Florida
Tyndall Air Force Base
Weapons Controller School
March 1960-July 1960

We stayed in Honolulu on our return to CONUS to relax, take a breather, and ease into the culture shock of a higher cost of living, wearing shoes indoors, and everyone speaking English. I quickly removed my shoes and walked barefoot through the lush, green grass—so different than Japan's predominant rocks, gravel, dirt, and cement. Around midnight the first day, we found a hamburger joint and devoured good ole' American burgers with French fries that weren't bitter like Japanese potatoes. We rented a car and drove around the island, viewing sugarcane fields, surfers on the north shore beaches, and rural farming. We visited the American National Cemetery—a stirring experience. All those white crosses honoring our military generated moments of silence. Dave treated me to dinner and dancing at the beautiful Royal Hawaiian Hotel, the famous pink hotel on Waikiki Beach. It rained every afternoon, and I understood why everything was so green.

After five relaxing days, we flew from Hawaii to Travis AFB, near San Francisco, on a C-121 cargo/passenger military plane. Because a storm was brewing, we circled the base before landing—circled and circled and bounced and bounced. Many passengers were airsick, and since it was a military plane with no carpeting, the "stuff" flowed up and down the corrugated metal floor. My fighter pilot husband with an iron-coated stomach sat there and ate the remainder of his box lunch. I almost threw up watching him. I got greener and greener. Because he believed motion sickness was all in one's mind, Dave commanded I not regurgitate my lunch. Lucky for him, we landed before my "mind" was in his lap.

We collected the Corvette, shipped earlier, and drove south to the Los Angeles area to visit my Italian relatives. Dave had met my grandparents at our wedding, but now he met two aunts and an uncle. They were somewhat intimidated by how big he was. I'd never seen them so quiet. Grandmother was normally quiet around outsiders because of her broken English, but jolly old Grandpa wasn't bothered—supplied with Italian wine, he communicated with anyone.

It was really scary remembering to drive on the right side of the street after driving on the left in Japan. Making a left-hand turn at an intersection was confusing. We tended to turn into the left lane, facing oncoming traffic. Amazingly we didn't have a head-on collision. From California, we drove to Ent AFB in Colorado Springs, Colorado, where Dave tried—unsuccessfully— to change his assignment. We continued our cross-country trek to LaGrange, Illinois, to visit Dave's parents. On the way from Illinois to Oklahoma, we located Fordland, Missouri, our next assignment—a town so small it was difficult to find on a map. The countryside was pretty, and I emphasize the word *country*. We did not look forward to living in this area. After visiting my folks and friends in McAlester, Oklahoma, we drove to Tyndall AFB in Panama City, Florida, where Dave would attend school to become a radar controller. During that long drive across the country, we came to appreciate the diversity of America's "spacious skies, amber waves of grain, purple mountain majesties, and fruited plains, from sea to shining sea."

We found housing on Mexico Beach, a fourplex right on the beach. It housed a Royal Canadian Air Force (RCAF) couple

(Frances and Jim LaVigne), two RCAF bachelors, a USAF couple with a baby, and us. After settling in with the few living necessities we had shipped for temporary duty, my days consisted of getting up, eating breakfast, and lying on the beach with my new friend, Frances. She was seven months pregnant, so we scooped a big hole in the sand for her tummy so she could sunbathe her back. I went inside for lunch, watched *As the World Turns*, and then returned to sunbathing for the rest of the afternoon. When the fellows arrived from school, they joined us on the beach. Tough life, but someone had to do it!

We had lots of cookouts and shared dinners. I was careful to always be decently dressed because the two bachelors kept running into our apartment to use our binoculars to gawk at some babe walking down the beach. Since we had the only TV, they also tended to make themselves at home. Why didn't I keep the door locked? One evening, Dave and I tiptoed around the end of the complex to the car, put it in neutral, and pushed it up the street before starting the engine—*to go out for the evening alone.*

Jim and Frances joined our ever-growing list of lifelong friends, sharing many escapades together. For the next twenty-two years, they would visit every place we lived, with the exceptions of Missouri, Kansas, and Spain. Jim was always the life of the party, and Frances continuously would drag me to shop in every available store around the world. I could actually write a book about the Forgans' and LaVignes' adventures.

Dave completed Weapons Controller School in three months, and we drove to Fordland, Missouri. Dave did not look forward to his new job—staring at a radar screen—and I was reluctant to consider the assignment as anything but boring. I was so tanned from the Florida sun, Dave joked I might not be served in restaurants while traveling with him across the South, where in 1960 segregation still ruled. There were strict rules preventing "colored" folks being served in restaurants; separate facilities were provided for "colored" and "whites" in all public buildings.

From beachcomber to landlubber…

Fordland Where?

Fordland Air Station, Missouri
Ground Control Intercept Radar
July 1960-November 1960

We drove through the little town of Fordland—twenty-nine miles east of Springfield, population 302, no indoor plumbing—and found the radar facility situated on a little hilltop in the country. We were depressed. Dave's indefinite status in the air force might become more definite—like "Get out now!" The family housing for enlisted and noncommissioned officers was on one street, ending with a circle of nine houses for officers. Recently built and very austere, our new 1,200 square feet quarters looked like a palace compared to our six hundred square feet "shack" in Japan. It had a living room, a kitchen and dining area, and three bedrooms and two bathrooms down the hall. Lots of space.

Our meager household goods from Japan were shipped to us from storage, as well as our belongings still in McAlester. It was fun unwrapping wedding gifts again. "Oh, remember this? Oh, I forgot we had that." The honeymoon was over; it was now time to get domesticated. In Springfield, we purchased our second pieces of furniture—matching Danish-style bedroom and dining room suites, made of teak veneer. We slept in that double bed until 1989 for 29 years. It served us well.

Mother and Daddy came for a visit, and Dave bought special steaks to grill. We had never grilled steaks when I was growing up; being Italian, Mother cooked everything with tomato sauce, butter, and garlic. Daddy's first mistake was ordering his steak well done (Dave likes his *rare*). Then, when served the expensive piece of meat, my dear father asked for catsup. I thought Dave would choke.

The few of us assigned to the radar site really had a good time. In the evenings, the adults chased the kids off the croquet course set up in the center of the traffic circle and played some crazy games, making our own fun. One month after we arrived, the commander was notified that the radar site would be closed. Great planning—all those new houses, one never even occupied. The radar was immediately shut down, and the next four months were spent closing the site. That didn't require much, so a daily softball game was organized with enlisted men and NCOs playing against the officers. The commanding officer, a major, had a field phone strung out to the fence, and time-outs were signaled for his calls. The government planned to ship the liquor inventory from our officers' club to another radar site, but the men decided to hell with that. We all did a pretty good job of depleting the supply before heading to our next assignments.

I had been trying for several months to get pregnant—without success—so I visited a Springfield doctor. He advised Dave to come in for a sperm count and told me to go home, put on a sexy nightgown, light candles, and seduce my husband. Dave was somewhat hesitant about getting his "manhood" measured, and his worry was all for naught. I was with child. The realization hit me when I started suffering the agony of morning sickness—morning, noon, and night. I was not quite as thrilled about motherhood as I had expected to be.

After only four months at Fordland, Dave was reassigned to the radar site at Olathe Naval Air Station, Kansas. It was a mystery to me why the navy had an installation in the middle of the U.S. The nearest large body of water was Lake of the Ozarks in Missouri.

We drove to Olathe to look for a rental house. I threw up constantly, was in a bad mood, and got more depressed by the minute over the meager selection of homes, seriously doubting my endearment to military life. After unsuccessfully searching all day, we drove to nearby Gardner Lake (no evidence of the navy on this small body of water). It was surrounded by little cottages, mostly used for weekend fishing getaways. Rounding a curve, we stumbled upon a new, large home with a builder's sign out front. I told Dave the house would never be for rent as it was obviously custom built. But he called anyway. Sure enough, an older couple, the Jenkins, had built it to accommodate visits from their eighteen grandchildren. Because he'd just had lung cancer surgery, Mr. and Mrs. Jenkins weren't prepared to move. They consented to rent it to us, took us "under wing," bought us a refrigerator, carpeted the living room, and later installed a fence out back when our little, very active firstborn started walking. Mr. Jenkins even built a wooden toy box for Bruce.

We returned to Fordland and prepared to move to what I considered a higher level of civilization, not knowing how very lonesome I would be in that lovely new house on the lake. Our small inventory of household goods was packed, we loaded the car with overnight needs and all the liquor we could carry from the defunct officers' club, and drove two hours to Gardner Lake, Kansas, to meet the moving van at our new home. I threw up all the way.

Short stay in "Show Me" state...

Lonely in the Land of Oz

Gardner Lake, Kansas
Olathe Naval Air Station
Ground Control Intercept Radar
November 1960-October 1962

Things were looking up. We had progressed from living in six hundred square feet in Japan to 1,200 square feet in Missouri to approximately two thousand square feet in Kansas. The lake house had a dining room, a kitchen, three bedrooms, two baths, a large recreation room, and a nice living room with a fireplace. In addition to our three-piece sectional sofa, we had a cherry-wood chair with matching table and a mosaic and brass coffee table we'd purchased in Japan. Dave's old maple bedroom suite and a crib set us up nicely for houseguests and a new baby.

Dave worked shift hours, which we both hated. I was lonely because no one was around during the week, and the weekend residents were mostly old people who fished for hours. Boring. I cleaned the house every other day and watched TV. I needed a hobby, but in a few months, I would definitely have one: taking care of a baby.

Even though Dave's primary mission was not flying, he had to maintain flying proficiency and collect flight pay. To get his flying time, he drove thirty minutes to Richards-Gebaur AFB, varying between weekends and weekdays since he worked shifts. We were delighted to discover a family there we had known in Japan, and I frequently stayed with Helen and their teenagers when Glen and Dave flew cross-country missions in the two-seater T-33 plane.

We were lucky to discover Judy and "Boomer" Roberts in Kansas City. Judy's mother had played bridge with Dave's mother in LaGrange, Illinois, and both moms pressed us to meet. The Roberts finally invited us for dinner and bridge, and another lifelong friendship began. They eventually had two sons and one daughter (I failed to get her "how to make a girl" recipe!).

Farther along in my pregnancy, we had to sell the sexy red machine. When I pushed back the seat to make room for my tummy, I couldn't reach the gas pedal. As the new owners drove it away, I cried. That car was responsible for bringing Dave and me together. We replaced it with a new '61, two-door, white Chevrolet Bel Air and an old '51 Chevy clunker for Dave to drive to work. Purchased for only $150, it gasped its last breath before we moved from Olathe, and we left it sitting under the trees, full of spiders and squirrels.

During my tummy-growing days, we visited my parents in McAlester. A bachelor friend from Tinker AFB near Oklahoma City came to see us over the weekend and mentioned his brother, Bruce. Dave and I reacted immediately with "That's it!" Our baby would be Bruce Dobbins Forgan, my maiden name in the middle. Although I did not want to nickname my children—Dick for Richard, Joe for Joseph—Bruce was stuck with a nickname. When our second child said "Bruce," it came out "Boo." Bruce is still known as "Uncle Boo."

Since we were too far from a military medical facility, I had the option of going to a civilian doctor for prenatal care and delivery. A doctor was recommended, and I figured with nine kids of his own, he was an expert. He seemed nice until delivery time; then he turned into a demanding monster. He could "make" babies, but he certainly couldn't deliver them—or so I thought at the time.

Right on schedule, I began cramping one afternoon and washed and waxed the kitchen floor. I later heard that a surge of energy hits when labor begins. Old wives' tale? Nature's way of preparing you for the work delivery requires? Who knows? I realized, "Uh oh, this is it! Here comes baby number one." In the middle of the night, during a tremendous thunderstorm, I couldn't sleep and was cramping badly, so Dave took me to the hospital. I thought they would give me something for the pain and I'd be more comfortable. Wrong. Seven other expectant mothers appeared on the scene in different stages of labor, from moaning to screaming. It was ominous. The nurses said storms always brought on labor—another old wives' tale? I didn't really give a damn. "Just give me something for pain. Now!"

I was on a gurney in the hall for hours with several other laboring mothers until a nurse finally rolled me into a semi-private labor room with Carlotta. Her husband had been killed in a car wreck when she was two months pregnant, so she went through this ordeal with only her mother beside her. Carlotta banged the wall with her fist to the rhythm of her contractions, and I just cursed a lot. Dave took turns holding our hands, wishing he were somewhere else. Finally, after ten hours of agony, I was wheeled into the delivery room—an all white, stainless steel, inner sanctum. The nice doctor with nine kids yelled at me to push, and I yelled back that I *was* pushing.

Bruce's due date was May 9, in between my May 3 birthday and Mother's Day the next week. I thought it would be nice if he arrived on one of those two days, a special honor for Mommy, but Bruce did his own thing, arriving with the help of forceps at 2:30 p.m. on May 6, 1961. He weighed seven pounds, twelve ounces, was nineteen inches long, and had a beautifully-shaped head covered with soft, blond hair shaped to a widow's peak on his forehead. All his little parts were perfect—and some not so little—and he had a bruise on his cheek from the forceps.

Dave was exhausted after all *his* work and stress during *my* fourteen hours of labor. He finally went home, rested, and got ready for his promotion to captain party that evening—one of my absences from several of his promotions. After the party, Dave walked into our house, saw muddy footprints on the stairs, and couldn't believe that he, "Captain Neatnik," had been so careless. At the top of the stairs, he saw the TV was missing and realized we'd been robbed! The back door was pried open, and the vacuum cleaner, my jewelry box, some blankets, and a .22 pistol were gone; the squirrel-shooting rifle left on our bed had been overlooked. It appeared someone was setting up housekeeping. Dave called the police, but no suspects were ever found.

The next day, Dave sneaked a bottle of champagne into the hospital. He visited all the new mothers, pouring champagne in everyone's water glasses. I immediately threw up after I drank mine. While everyone thought he was so cute, I thought, *Hey, come here and pay attention to me. I'm the important one who just delivered your son.*

A couple days later, we took Bruce to his first of many homes, nervous about the responsibility for this new little human being, who cried, ate, peed, and pooped—not necessarily in that order. I was unprepared when I changed his diaper for the first time. I forgot to cover him and he sprayed me and the sofa. It was the first—but not the last—time he pissed me off. Mother, bless her heart, came to help. She was a Godsend, especially when we couldn't take the crying anymore—mine or Bruce's. After she returned to her quiet, peaceful home in McAlester to recuperate, the other grandparents came to view their new grandson. My mother-in-law informed me I looked as if I'd been pulled through a knothole. I think she got mixed up as to who was pulled through what.

I devoted most of my time to caring for this mysterious bundle, who was a real handful. He cried a lot. Maybe he had colic. Maybe I didn't feed him enough. When he was three weeks old, Maggie and Major Hinkley from our squadron in Japan come through town on their way to a new assignment. They stayed at our house, and we put their three teenagers in a motel.

I was a little overwhelmed, trying to prepare meals and take care of Bruce. He cried constantly. Maggie asked where his pacifier was, and I told her I didn't believe in them. She took a rubber nipple from an empty baby bottle, stuffed it with cotton, taped the back, and stuffed it in Bruce's mouth. Heavenly silence. Peace and quiet. The next day I bought pacifiers for every day of the week. I was ready to give him anything!

Since I still didn't like the sight of children plugged up with a pacifier, I gave it to Bruce only at sleep-time until he was about nine months old. I was told that to wean him from it, I should cut a piece off the end and gradually keep cutting until he had to hold it in his mouth with his teeth. The first hole I cut was too big—when he put the pacifier in his mouth, he was able to stick his tongue in the opening. He pulled it out, looked at it, frowned, and threw it on the floor. I started over with another pacifier with smaller cuts. One night, I found the pacifier on the floor by his crib, Bruce was sound asleep, and that was the end of the pacifier. He favored a little terrycloth bunny that he faithfully cuddled and slept with. After the pacifier disappeared, he chewed the floppy little bunny ears and eventually reduced them to one-inch stubs. That bunny resides in a cedar chest in our home with many other family heirlooms.

Bruce's first Thanksgiving was highlighted with his picture in the local newspaper, sitting on the kitchen counter beside a ready-to-cook turkey. He had a fork in his mouth and was prepared to dig in. My parents drove from Oklahoma to spend the holiday with us. Dave's parents returned for Christmas, which they continued to do the rest of their lives, unless we were out of the country or health problems prevented their travel.

When the in-laws departed after Christmas, we drove to Maxwell AFB, Montgomery, Alabama. Dave was a student at Squadron Officer School (SOS) there for fourteen weeks, the first of three military education schools an officer was encouraged to attend. We lived in a horrible cockroach-infested trailer. We could actually hear them in the kitchen at night after we went to bed. When I turned on the light, the pink kitchen sink was brown with the nightly roach invasion. I had the place pest-controlled immediately. When the outside temperature dropped, so did the trailer temperature. It was so cold inside that at night I dressed Bruce in terrycloth pajamas, enclosed him in a zip-up sleeping bag, and covered him with baby blankets. I checked him several times during the night to make sure he was covered and felt his cold little nose. He got a good night's sleep; I didn't!

Before we left Kansas for Alabama, Bruce (at eight months old) was walking across his playpen. Because of the intimate (I use that description sarcastically) size of the trailer, he could walk the entire length and width inside, holding on to pieces of furniture or the wall. He quickly learned he didn't have to hold on to anything, and my days of chasing him began. For fourteen weeks, Dave studied and I chased Bruce and attended wives' functions. The base had a marvelous babysitting nursery, and I took Bruce there frequently so they could chase him. Each Wednesday was "Games Day" when the military students and instructors played volleyball, soccer, and flicker ball—a new game. The games were supposed to teach officers how to work as a team. It was a "family day," mothers brought their children, and we all enjoyed picnics. Had fun. No one could believe our little ankle-biter, running all over the place, was only eight to nine months old! The instructors were ready to recruit him for some of their athletic teams. Observing some of the nonathletic officers, I agreed Bruce would have been an asset.

Dave finished the fourteen-week course and was named a distinguished graduate. All that studying paid off. As a result, he was requested to return to the school as an instructor. Glory be, his ticket out of GCI (radar controller)! After the fun activities with other officers and their families at Maxwell AFB, I dreaded returning to my lonely existence in Kansas—Dave working shifts and my conversations restricted to baby talk as I sat in the fenced yard with feisty little Bruce investigating every corner of his confined space, mowing the yard with his little toy mower and crawling up, down, and all around the lawn furniture.

After returning to Gardner Lake to await paperwork for the

new assignment to Maxwell AFB, Dave received a phone call from Air Defense Command personnel saying he was being reassigned to a radar site on the farthest island in the Aleutian Islands chain. One could spit on Russia. Dave's job was to make sure Russia didn't "spit" on us. He responded, "No, no, no! I am waiting on paperwork to go to SOS!" He made several frantic phone calls and succeeded in keeping his ticket out of GCI.

During this stagnant period of time, when Bruce was only ten months old, I turned up pregnant again. No morning sickness this time, but at almost three months, I started spotting blood. The doctor ordered me to stay flat on my back in bed. Yeah, right, like I could do this with a ten-month-old running around. I called a military wife, the only friend I had nearby, and she came over to care for Bruce until Dave got home. I started bleeding too much, so the doctor suggested I come to his office. An elderly neighbor lady who had previously babysat Bruce came over, and Kay and I prepared to drive to the doctor's office.

Before leaving, I called base operations at Richard-Gebaur AFB where Dave was flying and told them, "*After* my husband lands, please tell him I have an emergency and am on my way to the doctor's office." We had been "brainwashed" to *never* do anything that could jeopardize our husbands' mental condition when he was flying. Stupid guys at Base Ops radioed him in the air, telling him I had an emergency. He landed the plane as quickly as he could and flew his car at Mach 1 toward home. Kay and I met him heading in the opposite direction and waved him down. I transferred to Dave's car, and we raced to the doctor's office.

The doctor informed us that I had already lost the fetus, but while on the examination table, I passed the placenta. Standing by my side, Dave nearly passed out. Staying overnight in the hospital for observation, I was sad to lose the baby but had been nervous about taking care of two children only nineteen months apart.

Awaiting our desired move to Montgomery, we took trips to Oklahoma and Illinois to impress everyone with our adorable and brilliant first child. I had several high school friends, married and still living in McAlester with their families, and it was always fun to visit there.

Before we departed Gardner Lake for our next adventure, Dave's dad retired from Western Electric Co. in Illinois. They came for a short visit on their way to Sarasota, Florida, where they would spend their retirement years.

The new orders finally arrived, and in October 1962, after two years at Olathe Naval Air Station/Gardner Lake, we were packed and moved to Montgomery, Alabama. I looked forward to a great new assignment with many couples our age with young children and busy, fun-filled days. Little did we know we were headed into a hotbed of racial unrest in the Deep South.

Down the yellow brick road…

Little Dixie

Montgomery, Alabama
Maxwell Air Force Base
Squadron Officers' School
Air Command and Staff College
October 1962-July 1966

In Montgomery, we rented a motel room with a kitchenette while we looked for a house, and Bruce soon produced another "mother-training" drama. One day at the motel swimming pool, where Bruce and I whiled away a lot of time, I turned to speak to another mother. She began to stammer and point to the pool. Turning around, I saw Bruce floating facedown in the water. Fully dressed, I jumped into the pool and pulled him out. I placed him on the edge of the pool, and as I tried to climb out, he jumped back in. It was the beginning of many traumatic "Fearless Forgan" episodes.

Dave was too "junior" to qualify for base housing; therefore, we bought a house ten miles from the base in a pleasant-looking neighborhood. Situated on a big yard (more room for Bruce to run and for me to chase him), it had three bedrooms, two bathrooms, a living room, a dining room, a kitchen, and a large play area for Bruce off the kitchen. The Hall family lived next door, and their twelve-year-old, Patrice, became our designated babysitter. I begged Dave to fence the backyard, but according to him, we could afford only a chain-link fence, which he wouldn't have. Better for me to lose my sanity than to have a tacky fence?

Two days after we moved in, while unpacking boxes, I suddenly missed Bruce. Uh oh, here we go again! I ran outside and found him two houses away, playing in the backyard inside a five feet tall chain-link fence. I knocked on their door, introduced myself, and thanked the mother for putting my little boy in their backyard to play with her little boy. She looked surprised and explained, "I didn't put him there. He climbed over my fence." Bruce was seventeen months old!

Meeting that neighbor gave me my first taste of questionable southern hospitality. She asked where we were from, and when I told her my husband was from the Chicago area, she grimaced. I quickly added, "I'm from Oklahoma!" She smiled with approval that I was from the South, even though somewhat west. We lived in Montgomery three and a half years, and we never met the family across the street, even though their two kids frequently played in our yard. One day, I counted fourteen youngsters of various ages in our backyard—the neighborhood playground.

We had super good times with our military friends and families at Maxwell AFB. Our husbands were captains and instructors in the school. We all had young children, and our daily lives were very integrated. SOS consisted of three classes a year, each fourteen weeks long. Most of the student-officers brought their families. It was my responsibility to look after the wives who accompanied their husbands in Dave's section, to help them be happy and organized. At the beginning of each class, we invited everyone in Dave's section to our house for cocktails and a casual buffet dinner to get acquainted. It was my initial training for many future social duties.

I am sorry to relate that southern racial bias existed at the time. If a black student officer was assigned to your section, you were not allowed to have him in your home—even though he or she was serving the country. If black students were included, socials were held on base. Prior to our arrival, an instructor had ignored the "rule." His southern civilian neighbors reported him to the police, and he was arrested. His family moved away until he finished his assignment. Sad. I am happy to have lived long enough to witness a halt to this grave injustice.

Base policy did not allow ladies to wear slacks in the BX or commissary. Another injustice. Many foreign military students were attending Air University at Maxwell AFB, and the "rulemakers" wanted the American wives to make good impressions. ("We've come a long way, baby!") However, there was no policy for Hassani, the Iranian student in one of Dave's classes, who wanted me to help him purchase sexy underwear for his wife in Iran. This same student declared that as long as he was at Maxwell, he "wasn't married" and proved it by having his own little harem. I refused to assist him in any manner and told Dave, "Tell Hassani to take his request to one of his 'girlfriends.'"

In the meantime, we were having a devil of a time getting Bruce to sleep. We decided one night to let him cry it out—*for two hours*. He was exhausted and so were we. Finally, silence reigned. Then we heard a thump and ran to his room to find he had tried to climb out of his crib and landed on his head. We carried him to the living room and stood him up. He walked around a little wobbly. When he seemed all right, we put him back to bed. Then we heard him vomit and realized he probably had a concussion. We raced to the emergency room, and while waiting for the doctor, Bruce tore the chained writing pen off the doctor's desk. It was difficult to convince the doctor that an hour earlier this kid had been loopy.

We took him home with instructions to wake him every two hours to make sure he was sleeping and not unconscious. After trying so hard to get him to sleep, now we had to wake him up! The doctor also recommended we put Bruce in a regular bed to prevent his climbing over the railing and killing himself. We did so; however, it increased our workload, continuously returning him to his bed.

Bruce and Todd – my adorable twosome,
Montgomery, Alabama 1963

Bruce and Todd with Santa Claus,
December 1966, Midwest City, Oklahoma

Bruce 5th grade & Todd 3rd grade,
Mount Holly Springs, Pennsylvania, 1966

Bruce high school graduate 1979 and Todd high school graduate 1982

Proud Mom with her two big sons

After three months in Montgomery, I conceived for the third time. No morning sickness. I felt great! During the pregnancy, little monkey Bruce climbed onto the kitchen countertop, opened the bottle of my prenatal capsules, and spread them across the counter. He'd bitten into one, but I didn't know if he had swallowed any. The pediatric clinic was concerned about the extra iron I was taking being hazardous to a toddler and said to bring him in immediately. They pumped his stomach while I sat in the hall and cried, blaming myself.

My belly was getting so big everyone predicted Forgan twins. There were no ultrasounds in those days, but I was relieved when the doctor told me he heard only one heartbeat. When I was seven months along, a new military couple moved into a house on the corner, and being the good military wife, I took them a casserole for dinner. She took one look at me and asked if my due date was imminent. I went home, cried, and called Mother to come before the due date because no one thought I was going to make it until then. I was lucky to have a loving and supportive mother to help during my times of need. I don't know how my father managed without her because he couldn't boil water.

In September, Mother flew to Montgomery about two weeks before my delivery date. She felt so sorry for me, waddling around the house, trying to get in and out of chairs. My back hurt, and I couldn't get comfortable in bed. I wanted to be slim again. We attended a formal function at the base the twenty-seventh, and Mother was upset that I went out for the evening. I had been feeling rather crampy all day, but there was no way I was going to the hospital early again. I danced and drank martinis—no one told us in those days that it wasn't healthy to smoke or drink during pregnancy. When we got home around 1:00 a.m., Dave wasn't feeling well, showing signs of getting a cold. He went to bed, suggesting I not go to the hospital so he could get a good night's sleep. So *he* could get a good night's sleep? I had no sympathy.

I supplied myself with a *Reader's Digest* and a pack of Marlboro cigarettes and rested on the sofa a couple hours before I fell asleep. Shortly thereafter, Mother shook me awake, asking what was wrong. Perturbed with her for waking me, I sent her back to bed, but about 4 a.m., I woke Dave. Seeing me in obvious pain, he notified the hospital we were on the way. We didn't even know where to go—unlike the first time when we made practice runs and had my bag packed. I stayed in the car while he found the maternity Quonset hut.

After examining me, the nurse immediately called the doctor to say I was pushing and he'd better arrive ASAP. I don't suppose he was happy about being called out at five o'clock in the morning. Dave planned to head home because he still wasn't feeling well (poor fellow), but the nurse told him by the time he got back from registering me, we would have a baby.

They rushed me to the delivery room. The doctor sauntered in and ordered Demerol, which knocked me out like a light. Fifteen minutes later, I heard the cries of my newborn. Now that was the way to deliver. I asked, "Is it a girl?" and heard, "No, but he weighs nine pounds!" I nearly fell off the delivery table. No wonder I'd been so uncomfortable the last three months. Baby number two entered the world one day earlier than his due date; he was born on Dave's birthday, September 28. "Happy Birthday" because that was the only gift I had for my husband.

When Dave finally returned home, my worried mother met him at the door. He assured her I was fine but was embarrassed to tell her how much Todd Macmillan (middle name after Dave's Scottish side of the family) weighed. Mother cried. My Italian mother cried a lot—sad, happy, scared, mad, whatever, the tears flowed. Todd and I came home from the hospital the next day. Except for losing a lot of "frontage," I didn't feel like I'd delivered a baby. The doctor said I was capable of having a twelve pounder. I said, "No, thank you. This is it!" I was terrified I'd have six boys attempting to have one girl.

Todd was a perfect "big" baby. He slept and ate. Boy, did I feed this one. He drank eight-ounce bottles of milk in no time. I was skeptical and concerned about Bruce accepting Todd, but he patted his new baby brother on the head, like "nice doggy," and ran outside to play. So much for being jealous. Daddy came for a short stay, and as he and Mother prepared to leave for Florida, President Kennedy was assassinated in Dallas. Everyone remembers where he or she was at that momentous occasion. I was feeding Todd when the news hit like a ton of bricks, and we stayed glued to the television for days.

Todd started crying a lot, which was unusual for him. When Mother bathed him the morning she and Daddy were to leave, she mentioned how large Todd's testicles were! I inspected, exclaiming, "Holy cow." I immediately took him to the pediatrician, who diagnosed an inguinal hernia and scheduled surgery. It tugged at our heartstrings to see our helpless two-month-old baby rolled into the operating room. Todd recovered quickly from this first bump in the road.

As did most of the military wives, I hired a "colored" maid who cleaned our house, ironed, and took care of the boys every Wednesday. If we arrived home late, Ruth bathed and put the boys to bed. She didn't mind as long as we took her home; she was scared to ride the bus after dark. Ruth did all this for $3.50 a day, which I thought was obscene, so I raised it to $5. Other new wives did the same. "Oldtimers" didn't like being forced to pay more, but they too increased the pay.

Ruth had seven children of her own, but Bruce challenged even her. One day I was down the street at a Tupperware party when a stranger rang the doorbell. Bruce was in her station wagon; she had found him about two blocks away. The postman, very familiar with our little "gadabout," told her where he lived, but she wouldn't leave him with the maid. Ruth told her where I was, and she brought Bruce to me. I had to drag him out of her car. He had a penny and was going to the store, come hell or high water. Ruth felt horrible, but we understood. The little fellow could disappear in the blink of an eye.

Before Bruce was four years old, he had his stomach pumped and suffered a concussion. Then he had two cuts on his head requiring stitches, a cut foot requiring stitches, a cut on his forehead not requiring stitches, a bee sting, and a "goose egg" on his forehead from a wayward golf ball. Even though there were ten other kids standing around, it hit Bruce—of course. He was an accident waiting to happen. Added to his misery and mine were chicken pox, measles, and mumps. Dave stabilized the swing set into the ground—accident prevention—since Bruce rode the seesaw on it back and forth so hard he nearly tipped over the whole thing. I predicted that if Bruce lived to be six years old, it would be because somebody upstairs was watching over him. Obviously, we weren't doing a very good job of it.

When Bruce was around three years old, he slipped out of his bedroom early in the morning. I woke up to find him outside playing. To deter that wandering streak, Dave reversed the doorknob on Bruce's bedroom door with the lock on the outside so we could lock him in. Hearing him trying to get out woke me, and I quickly rescued him before he found something "interesting" to do in his bedroom.

He found something interesting to do all right—but in the neighbor's garage, which had an extra refrigerator. Bruce helped himself to a dozen eggs and "bombed" their garage ceiling and walls. I cleaned up the mess and swatted his behind. Lucky for me, our neighbors had four older children and were very understanding. What a little athlete we had! Besides throwing eggs, Bruce could throw a plastic ball in the air and with a plastic bat hit it over the roof of our house. Daddy thought we had a future major leaguer, and so did we.

Todd was a happy little guy and so much easier to manage than his brother. He charmed everyone with great smiles, displaying wonderful dimples so deep you could plant tulips in them. (He's still a charmer, but with a different audience). When he was five months old, we'd prop him into a sitting position on the sofa, and he'd flop over, giggling. Bruce would shake his brother's jump seat—with Todd in it—causing Todd to laugh and laugh. It didn't take much to entertain him.

I swore I would chain our second son to the playpen and not let him walk early, but at ten months, Todd quite readily was up and walking. Bruce would leave the yard to play with friends down the street, and I feared Todd would follow him. The difference between the two boys? I ordered Todd to stop at the edge of the yard, and he'd stand on that border calling, "Boo, Boo, come back!" He never left the yard without permission.

Todd had no childhood illnesses and only one accident while in Montgomery. He fell off his tricycle and split his upper lip on the inside of his mouth. The base pediatric clinic tried to stitch the split together because he was chewing on the hanging tissue.

The most disgusting thing that Todd did as a toddler was hard on me—not him. He had a ball! One day after his nap, he removed his dirty diaper and painted his new furniture with the poop. I had to use a toothbrush and disinfectant to remove his "paint job" from the furniture's crevices. I almost didn't forgive him for that episode, but he smiled at me so innocently, displaying those deep dimples. Who could stay mad?

Patty and Dave Germann were in our same SOS unit, and we became very good friends. Their daughter and son were similar in age to Bruce and Todd and occasionally played together. Ila and Bo Marshall, who were in our first squadron in Japan, were also in our unit and lived only five houses away. Their two little boys were great playmates for our sons. We three couples celebrated many good times—birthdays, holidays, official socials, and parties for no special reason. My photo album is crammed with Germann, Marshall, and Forgan pictures. The husbands were friends, the wives were friends, and the children were friends. Such fond memories of the camaraderie we shared in Montgomery.

Not so fond a memory is the civil rights eruption. The march from Selma to Montgomery made history. Dave called to say the march was culminating at a park in town and to stay home to avoid possible danger. Of course, that only piqued our interest. Ila and I gathered our four boys in her car and drove to the area, curious to see what was happening. As we approached the park, it took two hours to wearily navigate two blocks through heavy traffic. We escaped as soon as we could, returning home to watch it on TV. Some brave mothers left their families at home and drove for days to participate in the march. Men came from everywhere; many got into altercations, some injured, others killed. The police behavior with attack dogs and water hoses was outrageous. How sad such a revolution was necessary to remedy the "laws of the South." It all started in Montgomery with courageous "colored" lady Rosa Parks, who refused to move to the rear of a bus. Time has passed, some healing has occurred, and although racial discourse still exists, history has been made with the election of an African-American as U.S. president.

Each summer we made the traditional trips to visit grandparents. In McAlester, we enjoyed my former high school friends and their families. During the day, we chalked up pool time with the kids, and at night, we attended adult-only socials while my parents enjoyed babysitting. We went to Florida to see Dave's parents, but it wasn't as much of a vacation for me. While spared the chores of housecleaning and cooking, I still fed, bathed, dressed, and entertained the boys. Playing at the beach helped occupy our time.

One of our most memorable trips was also the scariest experience of my life—in a T-34 plane Dave checked out from the Aero Club at Maxwell. This was a propeller-driven trainer, which he had flown in his early student-pilot days, a single-engine plane with two cockpits, one in front of the other. I became the copilot in the rear. Had Dave told me he nearly washed out of flying school trying to pass that level of training—he had difficulty landing it—I would have taken a raincheck on the trip. On his last check ride, he wrote up some malfunctions on the plane that needed attention before our departure date. Dave's parents took care of the boys while we were gone. I'm not sure who had the scariest experience: them or us.

The day of our departure Dave concluded from preflight that we barely had enough instruments to manage the trip. The plane-to-ground radio worked only when he disconnected me; his fuel gauge worked but mine didn't; my oil pressure dial worked but his didn't. As for me, ignorance was bliss. I settled in my seat, strapped in, put on my earphones, and pretended to be Amelia Earhart. Cruising along at about five thousand feet, I enjoyed the 360-degree views through the all-glass canopy. Clouds began descending lower and lower around us, forcing Dave to request an IFR (Instrument Flight Rules) clearance, meaning he had to fly by instruments (not visual) to rise above the clouds. This was against Aero Club safety rules. Why I don't know and probably don't want to know. We climbed to about nine thousand feet, and I was still fat, dumb, and happy, enjoying the ride and the beautiful, puffy, white, cotton-ball clouds.

Then the excitement began! I heard the engine go *putt, putt, sputter, sputter* and then nothing. It was like the sound of one hand clapping—the quietest nothing I had ever heard. The only sound was my heavy breathing. I gripped the sides of the cockpit so hard my knuckles turned white, and while my life did not pass before my eyes, I remember thinking, *This is it. We're leaving two sons without parents.* In the front cockpit, I could see Dave flipping maps around, trying to locate a landing place while looking for a hole in the clouds to glide through. I didn't know we were over mountains we couldn't see and passing through the clouds might bring us face-to-face with a mountain peak. *Splat!*

The last thing Dave tried—the first thing they taught him in flying school—was switching to the second gas tank in case the first tank was empty. He had reasoned we couldn't possibly be out of gas since we'd been airborne only about forty-five minutes, but he switched tanks anyway. I've never heard a sweeter sound in all my life than that engine starting up, purring us on our way. Dave reconnected me to the radio intercom, explained what happened, and assured me we were fine. When we landed for our first gas stop, he had to pry my fingers from the sides of the cockpit.

We continued to Washington, D.C., where we visited a couple days with dear friends from our first squadron in Japan, Ann and Tommy McLoughlin. Their family had grown to four children: Kathy, born in Japan when we were there, and later Tom and twins Mary and Mark. Ann stayed home with the children, and Tommy took us sightseeing. Seeing our nation's less-than-beautiful capitol was disappointing, but thanks to Lady Bird Johnson's efforts years later, many flowers were planted, giving the whole D.C. area a lovelier appearance.

Our plane had been leaking oil, so the Aero Club at Andrews AFB loaned us a T-34 to continue our trip to Long Island, New York. They worked on ours while we were gone, trying to solve the problem. Flying their plane was like transferring from a dilapidated, old Model A Ford to a classy Cadillac. I felt much safer.

We cruised up to Long Island to visit Nancy, my former Dallas roommate, her husband, Irv, and their two little boys. Irv had completed his three-year commitment to the air force, returned to Dallas to compete for Nancy's affection, and became a pilot for American Airlines. They took us to the World's Fair in New York, which was awesome.

When we climbed back into our airplane to leave, I played Amelia Earhart again, looking "cool," hoping to impress them. We headed south, landed at Andrews AFB, and exchanged planes. Soon after departure, oil began spraying on the canopy, which, unfortunately, had no wipers. Dave managed to land in mountainous Asheville, North Carolina, where a fire truck waited at the end of the runway. Our plane was smoking so badly they thought we were on fire. Dave called the Aero Club at Maxwell and told them in no uncertain terms what they could do with their T-34. They sent a pilot in a Navion, a two-seat, four-person plane with another pilot on board with a case of oil. The second pilot "hopped" the piece of junk back to Montgomery, landing frequently to refill oil, and we rode safely home in the Navion. I never flew with Dave again until 1976, a short flight over our base in Zaragoza, Spain, when I had a white-knuckle grip on the side window and his leg.

Dave completed his three years as an instructor at SOS and transferred to the next level of military education, the Air

Command and Staff College, also at Maxwell AFB. Because he had been an instructor in SOS, he was able to waive the first half of the one-year school and attended the second half. To his credit, he was a distinguished graduate as he had been in SOS. While at Maxwell, he also received his Master of Science in Business Administration from George Washington University. He chalked up many hours of flying time on weekends with cross-country flights in the T-33, a jet trainer; in fact, at his SOS farewell party, one of the pilots said, "Now that Dave is leaving, more flying time will be available for the rest of us." Some of the wives didn't like their husbands to be gone on weekends, but I relished the freedom. The boys and I could eat hot dogs, peanut butter and jelly sandwiches, go to bed when we wanted, and watch our own TV shows.

In the sixties, the Vietnam conflict was in full swing, and more pilots were needed. "Lucky" Dave was selected to return to the cockpit for his next assignment. He would spend four months training in the F-105 fighter plane in Wichita, Kansas, before heading to Southeast Asia for a combat tour. We sold the house and, except for a small temporary shipment to Wichita, had most of our things packed for storage. Dave sold the junker car he'd used at Montgomery to a used car dealer for $75—proof of its condition. The next morning, the junker was parked in a neighbor's yard—the one we'd complained about to the city with tall grass, garbage and bottles on the drive, and junkie cars parked around the house. The joke was on Dave. Our worthless neighbor worked for the used car dealer.

We stayed a week in a Montgomery motel, and Dave's parents came from Florida to say good-bye. We were leaving what was to be Dave's longest assignment in nearly thirty-four years in the air force: three years and nine months. Bruce made a final visit to Maxwell's ER for stitches—the result of Todd's swinging a shuffleboard stick into the back of his head. This began a long tradition, or "curse," of one of the boys getting hurt when we left or arrived at a place. I held my breath each move, waiting for the next crisis.

Bye, y'all.
Come back, ya heah.

In July, we left the heart of Dixie and drove to McAlester to visit my folks and vacation nearby at Lake Eufaula—swimming, boating, and playing with the boys. After a few days, my parents happily volunteered to keep the boys at their house, which allowed Dave and me some special time alone at the lake. Afterwards, Dave went to Fairchild AFB in Washington state for survival training for three weeks while the boys and I survived in Oklahoma. When he returned, we traded in our '61 Chevy Bel Air for a new, red and white '66 Chevy Caprice, our first air-conditioned car. We drove to Wichita, Kansas, where Dave would train to fly the F-105 at McConnell AFB. Bruce and Todd were five and three years old.

Three years and five years

Temporary Duty to Waiting Wife

Wichita, Kansas
McConnell Air Force Base
Replacement Training Unit (F-105)
July 1966-November 1966

We arrived in Wichita in July 1966 and rented a furnished house near an elementary school, where Bruce entered kindergarten number one. In September, we celebrated Todd's third birthday and Dave's thirty-third. We led a quiet life while in Wichita. Todd still took afternoon naps, and when Bruce came home from morning kindergarten, sometimes he would fall asleep too. I enjoyed the quiet time. On weekends, we went sightseeing and swimming, had picnics, and enjoyed time with Daddy. His weekends were free since he flew only during the week.

Dave was training to fly the F-105 at McConnell AFB in preparation for a combat assignment in Southeast Asia. There were no two-seater training planes, so each pilot was on his own. Dave had flown the smaller F-86 fighter and the T-33 trainer for several years. In comparison, the F-105 was a big monster—so big and so fast on landing that on his first flight Dave said it took four tries to get it on the ground. He joked about thinking they'd have to shoot him down. He usually kept his crises to himself, since Bruce kept me busy with his crises. I didn't need any more.

I planned to live in Midwest City outside Tinker AFB, near

Oklahoma City, while Dave was in Southeast Asia. I could participate in the officers' wives' club activities, and access the BX, commissary, and medical facilities (frequently needed thanks to Bruce). My parents were just under two hours away in McAlester. I drove from Wichita to Midwest City and found another house to rent, this time unfurnished. Dave requested our stored household goods to be shipped to our new address. We had no good-byes, checked Bruce out of kindergarten, packed our few meager belongings, and left. A short story for a short stay.

We're no longer in Kansas, Toto.

Midwest City/McAlester, Oklahoma
Dave: Korat Air Base, Thailand/469th Tactical Fighter Squadron
November 1966-December 1967

The boys and I drove to Midwest City to meet the moving trucks, one from storage in Montgomery and one from Wichita. Dave moved into Bachelor Officers Quarters at McConnell AFB until he finished his transitional training. As I tried to coordinate the efforts of the movers, a neighbor's dog bit Todd on the leg. We spent several hours at Tinker AFB's ER, reluctantly leaving the moving company employees on their own. The neighbors had to put their dog in quarantine for thirty days, which didn't put me on their new, good-neighbor list; however, they weren't on mine either. Several days later, checking the inventory sheet, we discovered Dave's tools and fishing equipment were missing. Either the truckers or employees at the storage warehouse in Montgomery had stolen them. Because the movers were alone at the house while I was at the hospital, I'm surprised that's all that was missing. My stress bucket overflowed from the day's events.

I immediately enrolled Bruce in his second kindergarten. It was easier for me to unpack and settle with only one child at home. Todd entertained himself with empty boxes and toys and didn't get in my way. When I visited Bruce's kindergarten, I was stunned. A staggering number of children were in the class, and the teacher controlled them like the Gestapo. I guess it prevented chaos, but I felt sorry for the little tykes when she ordered, "Freeze!" and they had to stop in their tracks. Scared even me.

The boys were excited about the season's first snowfall. After living in "Little Dixie," where kids went barefoot all winter, Bruce and Todd considered snow a trick of nature that offered a new kind of playtime. I purchased coats, gloves, boots, hats, and sweaters for them, and they threw snowballs, built a snowman, and made snow angels. I stayed busy drying wet socks, coats, and pants, rubbing cold hands and feet, and making oodles of hot chocolate to warm their cold little tummies.

Dave finished his training at McConnell AFB in mid-December and joined us in Midwest City. Both sets of parents came to celebrate Christmas, but the atmosphere was somewhat tense, anticipating Dave's departure for Southeast Asia.

Bruce contributed some humor to the Christmas holiday. The boys shared a bedroom with Bruce on the top of bunk beds. Shortly after they'd gone to bed Christmas Eve, I heard a crash in their bedroom. I ran into their room and found Bruce sprawled on the floor. He said he heard Santa Claus on the roof, and he fell out of bed, trying to look out the window. Whew. No injury—only disappointment that he missed seeing Santa Claus. He went back to bed, but sleep was a long time coming; he was afraid he'd miss Santa again.

The grandparents went home, and we cherished January together before Dave had to leave. He was assigned to Korat Air Base, Thailand, to fly combat missions over North Vietnam, the most heavily defended area in the history of warfare. The F-105 was nicknamed "The Thud" because of its large size and the sound it made crashing into the mountains around Hanoi. Unfortunately, too many planes and pilots were lost. Sadly, I kissed Dave good-bye at the Oklahoma City airport the end of January 1967 and sat in my car for a long time, crying, with horrible thoughts that

I might not ever see him again. I was very lonely and emotionally drained when I returned to our house in Midwest City.

I attended a wives' club luncheon at Tinker but felt like an outcast. My civilian neighbors weren't friendly. I was not a happy camper. I called Mother and cried, "Find me a house to rent; I want to come home." Easier said than done. The boys and I drove to McAlester one weekend and searched for something to call "home" for a few months; however, there was nothing decent to rent in the little town. I finally found a suitable house for sale and called the owners in Louisiana. I gave them a big sob story. My husband was in Southeast Asia, defending our country, and our two little boys and I had no place to live. I shed a few tears, and they acquiesced in sympathy and rented with the understanding that if the house were to sell I would move out. I considered this a good option, as the boys and I could always move in with my parents for any remaining time in McAlester.

Mother returned to Midwest City with us to help me pack most of our household goods. This saved money. The government had already paid for our move to Midwest City; this one was my responsibility. Cooking breakfast one morning, I splattered hot grease onto my left hand, and it was my turn to go to the emergency room. I spent the rest of the day in bed, knocked out from painkillers. Thank you, God, for my mother. She continued packing until I was able to help again. The movers loaded us up, and once again, after another three short months, the boys and I moved to another new address. I was happy to free Bruce from that prison-like kindergarten number two. It was the end of February.

Our little three-bedroom house in McAlester was surrounded with neighborhood children—plenty of playmates for Bruce and Todd. It was only four blocks from my parents, but Mother thoughtfully didn't dominate our time. Sometimes when she saw me starting to "climb the walls," she said, "Okay, boys, come spend the night with Nonna ("grandmother" in Italian) and Grandpa." What a break. I'd have a bourbon and water, put my feet up on the coffee table, eat a peanut butter and jelly sandwich for dinner, and watch TV without interruptions or demands on my time. The boys loved going to their house where they had so much unrestricted fun.

Nonna introduced them to "pea fights" (flipping peas at each other with spoons). Retrieving them one day, I found everyone covered with whipped cream. A "fight" with spray cans was in progress. Nonna gave them sheets of cardboard to slide down the second floor wood stairs on their bottoms—*bumpity, bumpity, bump*. She straightened coat hangers, attached a string with bacon stuck on a safety pin, and took the boys to catch crawdads in a ditch.

Grandpa had a lengthy station wagon, and the kids loved riding in the back, shouting at Grandpa to stomp on the brakes so they'd slide forward the length of the back end. No safety precautions in those days. Grandpa co-owned and managed a slot car racetrack, and he spoiled his grandsons with slot cars of their own and dimes to race them. It was a well-managed operation by my father, who insisted all the children be on their good behavior. Many parents in town were grateful for a safe, fun place for their children to spend leisure time. It also kept Daddy out of Mother's hair and away from her constant nagging. Everyone was happy. Bruce and Todd have fond memories of Nonna and Grandpa.

Bruce entered kindergarten number three—nice children, nice teacher. However, the teacher was concerned that he didn't socialize or interact very much with the other kids. She thought he didn't make the effort to be friendly because he figured he would soon move again. I didn't agree with her. That was just Bruce's personality. He's always been somewhat of a loner.

Several of my high school girl friends still lived in McAlester, and in the summer, we spent many hours with them and their children at the pool. These same friends took turns inviting me to the country club's monthly dinner and dance nights. So I wouldn't be a wallflower, their husbands were very nice to dance with me. I also played a lot of bridge at the country club. Staying busy kept me from getting lonesome.

Surprisingly, there were eight "waiting wives" in McAlester. Two were sisters several years my junior, but I had known their oldest sister in high school. Some wives lived in apartments, some with their parents, but I was the only one who had a house. Every Friday night was designated "Happy Hour at Shirley's." We cooked dinners (burning a lot of steaks learning how to grill), played bridge, or just talked. The military lifestyle is different from the civilian world, with its own language, and it was a joy to be on common ground and talk military with other wives. Susan's husband was flying the F-100 in South Vietnam. Judy's husband was flying the T-28 in Thailand (a very secretive assignment). One husband was an entomologist in the army, and the others served in various jobs in the army and marines.

In the summer, we flew to Sarasota, Florida, to visit Grandma and Grandpa Forgan. There wasn't much to occupy the boys' time in Sarasota, and we got bored. So we took a time-out and flew up to Montgomery, Alabama, to visit our good friends Ila and Bo Marshall and Patty and Dave Germann, who were still stationed at Maxwell AFB, and the children all had fun playing together again.

After being gone a month, we happily returned to McAlester. The daughter of my parents' best friends was getting married in August and asked Bruce to be the ringbearer. We were concerned how he would handle his role. He just might throw the pillow bearing the ring up in the air at the last minute and take off. We borrowed a white suit with short pants and a Peter Pan collared shirt, and Bruce wore white knee socks with black shoes. He was absolutely adorable and played his part perfectly. I was so proud of him. We partied at the bride's parents' house after the reception, and I let the boys stay up as long as they could. Todd fell sleep on a bed sometime during the evening, but Bruce was still going strong at 1:00 a.m. I was exhausted, so I finally bundled them up and took them home.

Bruce and Todd had their sixth and fourth birthdays in May and September. Bruce entered first grade in September 1967, his

EARNING MY WINGS

fourth school in a year, and Todd started preschool. At last, I was alone part of the day and enjoyed the peace and quiet. Poor Bruce, by the time he learned a new address and phone number, it changed. I had always taught him our seven-digit phone numbers, the new one in McAlester being 423-0956. His teacher told him he was wrong—in McAlester, it was GA3-0956. Knowing that GA is 42 on the phone dial, I asked her, "What's the difference if it's GA or 42? Isn't the point to know your number to call in an emergency?" Understanding? No. Narrow-minded.

I put an eight-by-ten-inch photo of Dave on the chest of drawers in the boys' bedroom. When they said their prayers at night, we always asked God to take care of Daddy flying his plane and to bring him home safely. After they went to sleep, I checked on them and always found the picture facedown. I never knew why—unless they were scared by a face staring at them in the dark. I asked about it when they were older, but they had no recollection.

We were exempt from accidents on arriving in McAlester; however, Todd had two traumas. Sometimes he walked around bent over, and at night he had his little hand down his pajamas with a tight grip on his private parts. The doctor discovered Todd had another hernia. Bless his heart, he was hurting but never said a thing! He had a second hernia operation—other side, and at a later date had his tonsils out. He was a little trouper through both operations.

While I fought my own battles on the home front, Dave flew as many missions as often as he could, aiming for the magic number of one hundred missions over North Vietnam—the price of a ticket home. After nine months, he was getting close. One day I was on the phone with my friend's sister, Patricia, and the operator interrupted, saying there was an emergency call from overseas. We immediately hung up as I whispered, "Please don't ring! Please don't ring," but obviously, I was the one being called. If Dave were killed in action, the military would send an officer to notify the widow—no phone call; however, the call could mean

Dave had been injured, shot down, or captured. In 1967, there were a lot of those visits and calls around the country. I nearly jumped out of my skin when the phone rang, and *it was Dave.* Tired of continuous busy signals (no call waiting in the sixties), he told the operator to break in on the conversation—it was an emergency. He was celebrating at the officers' club, having just finished his one hundredth mission. He could head for home any day. I could hardly talk I was crying so hard.

In the meantime, Patricia, knowing the call was for me, notified my parents and my friend Virginia, her sister. I was still sitting on the floor, wiping away tears, when I saw Mother race to the sliding glass doors on the side of my house. She was white as a ghost. Daddy was close behind her, looking very somber. I grabbed them, hugged them, and told them everything was all right. Dave was fine, and *he was coming home.* We all cried for joy and relief. The doorbell rang, and I opened the door to find Virginia, stiff as a statue and stone-faced. She came out of the trance hearing the good news and relayed it to Patricia, who sat in the car with their kids bundled up, aroused from their naps to race to my house. They all came in for a few minutes, heard more details, and then everyone left. We were all emotionally drained.

Dave called me when he arrived in San Francisco. His roommate was killed the day he left. Aquilla Britt was flying to Tan Son Nhut Air Base in South Vietnam to receive special recognition and receive his third Silver Star for Gallantry in Action. In landing, he collided with a C-123 (cargo plane) on the runway—after all the dangers he had faced and survived! Aquilla's wife lived in the San Francisco area, and Dave called her to express his deepest sympathy. Many years later, I visited the Vietnam Memorial in Arlington, Virginia, found Aquilla's name, and made a pencil rubbing of it. I framed the rubbing, pictures of "the wall" and me pointing to his name, and brochure information and gave it to Dave for Christmas. It had special meaning to him and brought tears to his eyes. He and Aquilla had experienced the horrors of war together. *My* hero came home with a Silver Star for Gallantry, three Distinguished Flying Crosses, and seventeen Air Medals, but more importantly, *he came home.*

Halloween, October 31, 1967, I met Dave at the airport in Oklahoma City and started crying the minute he exited the jetway. He didn't understand my tears of relief. Women! Men! We drove home and went to the neighbor's to get Bruce and Todd. Dave knelt on the sidewalk, and they ran and jumped into his arms as if he'd never left. However, that first night when he suggested it was the boys' bath time, I realized he'd not been there telling me what to do for nine months; it would be an adjustment having the "boss" home again. I hosted a welcome-home party for Dave at the officers' club at the Naval Ammunition Depot on the outskirts of town, and Jack Lane took him to an OU football game in Norman. He was back to civilization. Figuring the odds, of the eight husbands of the waiting wives in McAlester, I wagered one wouldn't make it. Dave was next to last to come home, and then we nervously awaited the return of Susan's husband. They all made it back.

Todd, Dad, and Bruce
– HE'S HOME!

Dave – 100 missions in the F-105 over North Viet Nam 1967

Dave's next assignment was to the Pentagon, where he was assigned to air force headquarters as an action officer (future plans for fighter planes)—long hours of "pushing papers." After a couple weeks resting in McAlester, he drove our car to Virginia and started to work. I flew in to search for our second house to buy. We purchased a two-story, three-bedroom, two-and-a-half bath home with a partially finished basement that made a great playroom. Cost: around $30,000—the same house now sells for almost $450,000. Groan! It was located in Springfield, Virginia, Kings Parks Subdivision—well maintained, family oriented, lots of activities, a community swimming pool, and an elementary school within walking distance. Dave and I had met at Kings Terrace Apartments and now would reside in Kings Park Subdivision, keeping up the regal address. The Pentagon was normally a thirty-minute drive from Kings Park, but during rush hour, it was an hour-and-fifteen-minute nightmare. I avoided rush hour.

It was very exciting to think about living across the Potomac River from our nation's capitol. I was eager to see the monuments and important buildings, to study our history, and to experience the political events. (I later discovered that babysitters were nonexistent on weekdays, so I was stuck at home until Todd entered first grade.) Even reading *The Washington Post* newspaper was exciting. It was a little scary to think about driving in heavy traffic and rush hour, but what an interesting place to live for the next several years. In seventeen months, the boys and I had lived in three different places; it would be pleasant to put down roots again.

The packers and movers showed up again, but this time it was on the government's bill. I sent the final rent payment to the homeowners in Louisiana, thanking them for renting their house while my husband was off to war. The boys and I moved in with my parents for three weeks before flying to Washington International Airport to become Virginians. My McAlester civilian friends couldn't understand how I coped with such a nomadic lifestyle, but I loved it and all the experiences that came with it. I couldn't understand why they didn't get bored living in the same town and house for years, seeing the same friends, doing the same thing day after day, but I admit their lives were simpler and much less stressful. It takes all kinds to make the world go round.

Bye all you "Okies."
Thank you for taking good care of us while Dave was gone.

Fort Fumble

Springfield, Virginia
The Pentagon
December 1967-July 1971

We moved to Springfield on December 15, 1967, and began our well-practiced box unpacking. It was easy and fun to find an appropriate place for everything in the spacious new house. I kept the boys out of school because only a week was left before the Christmas holidays. They helped arrange their room and, after school hours, met all the kids in the neighborhood—plenty of playmates and babysitters for Bruce and Todd. Bruce managed to get in fights with some of the boys, but their mothers were cooperative; we just marched our sons home for a time-out when the occasion called for it.

We had been there only one week when Dave called from work to say he'd missed the bus and I had to come get him. I panicked! I hadn't driven outside the local neighborhood. It was nine o'clock at night, and the boys were in their pajamas, but we piled into the car, and I prayed for God to help me find the way. Luckily, the boys were tired and didn't provoke me. I was already scared we might get lost. I made all the right turns, survived the "mixing bowl" since the traffic wasn't heavy that time of night, and pulled up to the Pentagon's River Entrance. Dave pried my hands from the steering wheel and drove us home. I felt I'd just finished my first combat mission and deserved a medal. Dave couldn't understand what all the fuss was about. He said, "You made it, didn't you?" Easy for him to say. Freeing us from transportation problems, Dave purchased a second car, a yellow '66 Corvair convertible. We had a tendency to buy cars that started with a C—Chevy Corvette, Caprice, and Corvair.

Shortly after our arrival, Bruce provided the traditional accident. Todd was riding his tricycle on the sidewalk across the street with Bruce standing on the back. When Todd hit a crack, Bruce flew over his head and skidded down the concrete on the right side of his face. It resembled raw hamburger meat. He got a lot of attention the first day of school after the holidays. Half of his face was one large, crusty scab.

We weren't completely settled when Dave's parents came for Christmas, nine days after we had moved in. Groan. How did I do it? We found the boxes marked "Christmas decorations" and set the scene for the holiday. I unpacked the silver, china, and crystal for Christmas dinner, but there were no curtains at the windows or pictures on the walls. A card table and chairs sufficed in the kitchen eating area for the time being.

We started a new tradition that first Christmas in Springfield. In the downstairs playroom, we put a Christmas tree totally decorated by the boys. Dave's mother had made some little animal tree ornaments from felt and sequins and a tree skirt with a sequined "choo choo" train. The boys added strung popcorn and cranberries, colored construction-paper chains, and anything seasonal they made in school, Sunday school, and Scouts. Santa Claus deposited his gifts from the North Pole under this tree on Christmas Eve. In the living room, we decorated a second tree and surrounded it with all the gaily-wrapped family gifts to be opened Christmas morning after the boys discovered what Santa had left. We kept the new tradition alive even after the boys discovered Santa's identity—putting their "toys" under their tree and family gifts under the "nice" tree.

After the holidays, the grandparents returned to Florida, and I continued getting settled and decorating the house. Bruce joined his new first grade class and, poor kid, learned another address and phone number—the fourth in a period of one year. Todd stayed home because preschool wasn't available, and he had several neighborhood playmates to keep him entertained.

Kings Park community provided many activities for the children, including big Fourth of July celebrations with fireworks and parades. In 1968, Bruce won first place for his bicycle decorated with red, white, and blue crepe paper and little American flags. Todd and his two best friends dressed as the "Spirit of 1968" for the parade. Todd was an air force pilot, Scotty a sailor, and Steven a soldier. Adorable. We had super birthday parties, always doing something special and different. It was a fun and stable time for the boys.

The exception to the fun was Dave's terrible work hours at the Pentagon. We never knew when he was coming home—hours or several days late. He never saw the sun during the week, leaving home before sunrise and returning after dark. Sometimes he called around four or five o'clock to say he was locking his safe and heading home. Then he called an hour later to say he was still there. After another call from him, still at work, I fed the boys and got them ready for bed. If Dave wasn't home by nine o'clock, I ate by myself. I was usually asleep on the sofa by the time he got home. Our neighbors couldn't comprehend Dave's work hours, as the civilian husbands were all home between five and six o'clock. I admit I was jealous of their schedule. Dave's coworkers were outstanding officers, who all worked difficult, long hours. They must have done something right because three of them, including Dave, retired as generals.

Soon after our arrival, I had to learn my way to the commissary. Several military installations were in the area, but I chose the closest one. The harrowing experience was an all-day excursion to Cameron Station (an army installation) come rain, snow, or summer heat and humidity. After Bruce went to school, Todd and

I made the dreaded weekly trek to the commissary. We drove thirty minutes and then waited another thirty minutes for a parking place. Women almost came to blows over parking spaces. After I finally parked, I deposited Todd in the nursery next door. I shopped an hour or more then pushed the loaded cart to one of twenty-three cash registers with about fifteen customers in each line—at least another thirty-minute wait. (I soon learned not to go on payday when lines were even longer.) After checking out, our groceries went in numbered crates, which were placed on a moving belt that transported them outside to a covered pick-up area. I retrieved Todd and then got in the slow-moving line of cars headed to the pick-up area. After another thirty minutes, attendants working for tips stuffed my groceries into the car trunk. Heaven forbid if a mistake occurred and you didn't get all your groceries or you got someone else's. You did without or had a surprise for dinner.

To lessen the trials and tribulations of commissary shopping, three of us air force wives devised a game plan. We each did our own big shopping and bought eggs, milk, and perishables for the other two. This required each of us to make the dreaded trip only once every three weeks. We had a combined ten children among us. It was a sight to behold—a grocery cart filled with twelve half-gallons of milk, plus two other loaded carts. Customers probably thought we were dealing in the black market or feeding civilian neighbors, but no one ever questioned us. It was time-consuming to shop for three families, go home to put away perishables, deliver groceries to the other two houses, then return home to put away the rest of the groceries—an all-day undertaking. Keeping three separate lists was vital for distribution. By the time I finished, I was too tired to fix dinner, but I could look forward to freedom from the commissary battlefront for the next three weeks.

Fall of 1968 Bruce entered second grade and Todd started kindergarten. Todd was placed in an afternoon class, but I had him reassigned to mornings since he still took afternoon naps. I didn't think he was mature enough to begin kindergarten, but Virginia law required him to be in school if he turned five before October l, and his birthday was September 28. The school said if he didn't "blossom," he could repeat kindergarten, which I certainly opposed since he was starting school with two neighborhood buddies.

One day Bruce and a classmate walked into our house with the ugliest puppy I have ever seen. She stood on the floor and shook. She was the runt of the mother's sixth litter. Mom dog was a short-legged, fat, smooth-haired, beagle-looking mix. Puppy was a long, skinny, nearly hairless legged, shaggy, Heinz "157" varieties terrier mix—must have taken after dad dog. I reluctantly commented how cute she looked but told Bruce to return her with the don't-call-us-we-will-call-you message. The next week when I took our boys horseback riding, Bruce's classmate brought her back, and Dave couldn't say no. Her name was Hazel; she lived sixteen years; her looks never improved. A friend always remarked upon entering our house, "Do something with that dog; she hurts my eyes." I resented that remark because Hazel was family! The old saying "I can talk bad about my kids, but no one else can" also applies to family dogs. Hazel traveled all over the world with us, and when we moved, I'd suggest to the boys that they walk the dog to meet new neighborhood kids. They wouldn't do it and said they were embarrassed to be seen with her. For shame.

The famous Hazel "ugly dog"

One of the most exciting events during this tour was attending President Nixon's inauguration in January 1969. Friend Patty Germann drove down from Pennsylvania, four of us gals bundled up in sweaters and coats, and Dave deposited us early in the morning close to the capitol. We huddled together to stay warm, waiting hours with the large crowd for the ceremony to begin. Afterwards, we walked about seven blocks to stand in a reserved area to watch the parade. We saw many dignitaries, including Mr. Carl Albert from McAlester, Oklahoma, the Speaker of the House. The patriotic band music and the marching men from the four services made us proud. Many Vietnam protesters made their presence known, horribly cursing and badmouthing the war. It was difficult for me to restrain myself as the police contended with their rowdy and disrespectful behavior.

During the late sixties, several POW wives became very involved with the peace talks, vigorously working to get the men returned. Previously, they had been advised by our government to stay in the background and not "make waves." Impatient, they organized and demonstrated a loud voice and big influence in Washington and the Paris peace talks. I admire them for their courage to buck the system and their tenacity to make themselves heard! They started a petition-signing all over the U.S., and a big demonstration was held in D.C. on the acreage around the Reflecting Pool. Tables were set up on the grounds, and Dave and I joined other volunteers to solicit signatures. A scruffy young man approached me, snarling, "They ought to bring all those pilots home and re-educate them because they are stupid to be fighting." I restrained myself but called big Dave to my side and said, "Here is my husband, one of those pilots you slander. Say that to his face, and ask him about his compatriots and friends who died or have been in prison in North Vietnam for over seven years who fought for your freedom and right to stand here and scream obscenities and stupid remarks." He took one look at Dave, mumbled something, and sauntered off. An anti-war demonstration occurred that same day in the same area, which kept the police very busy. I don't know which smell was stronger: marijuana or tear gas.

Because we didn't live on or near a military installation, my "military wife responsibilities" were nil. My days and some evenings were filled with the boys' activities. Bruce played tee-ball, Little League baseball, softball, football, and much time was spent at the community swimming pool. Todd played two years of tee-ball. We kept them in the realm of sports that we believed taught them teamwork, sportsmanship, and a desire to win.

Bruce joined Cub Scouts, and I later became a den mother for two years. It was a lot of work for both of us. For one project, each Scout received a "Genius Kit" and was directed to create something from the items inside: pipe cleaners, toothpicks, corks, and other paraphernalia. It was amazing what those little "geniuses" came up with! Bruce won first prize for his Iwo Jima Memorial display. I assume the memorial had made a big impression on him when we visited the site in DC.

One summer vacation we joined Frances and Jim LaVigne and family at Myrtle Beach, South Carolina, for the first of many reunions. By then, they had Karen, one year older than Bruce, and Leanne, one year younger than Todd. No need to worry about our boys being too rambunctious for the girls. They could hold their own. In fact, the girls instigated many of the tricks played on each other. Bruce and Karen loved to play in the ocean while Todd and Leanne preferred the safety of the pool.

The LaVignes had been going to the same motel in Myrtle Beach for several summers and knew the owners. We had suites on the beachside next door to each other and immediately broke the first rule: Do not remove or mix kitchen utensils or dinnerware between suites. Big Dave projected himself headfirst down the kiddy slide into the pool, prompting a new sign to be posted the next day: "No one over twelve years old allowed to use the slide." When Dave jumped from the second floor balcony into the pool, splashing everyone and displacing a lot of pool water, the owners almost had a nervous breakdown.

Frances and I rented two Honda motor scooters, which she wrecked before ever leaving the rental parking lot, necessitating a visit to the hospital emergency room to stitch up her lip. Next, we tried riding horses—a more successful venture.

We had a wonderful time, but the motel owners never encouraged their Canadian guests or their friends to return to the motel.

The four grades Bruce completed in Fairfax County Schools provided a good educational foundation. Not academically oriented, he was fortunate to have good teachers. Bruce's third grade class was taught by a traditional teacher I liked. However, in spite of her experience, she misjudged Bruce. One day when he misbehaved, the teacher sent him to a corner desk and chair until he was willing to behave and ask to return to his regular seat. I told the teacher Bruce was stubborn and would never surrender, but she seemed to think he would eventually cave. Knowing my son, I just smiled when she finally relented and let him out of the corner.

Bruce attended summer school twice for remedial reading to increase his reading level. The second summer, he attended a wonderful private school where he made substantial progress. After reading a short story in the English workbook, Bruce answered the questions and drew a picture about it. His artistic talent was discovered! His teacher praised his drawings, saying he had natural talent.

Todd, on the other hand, had some teachers who really rubbed me the wrong way. Thank goodness for his carefree personality and ability to shrug off aggravations. He became the class clown much to the irritation of his second grade teacher, who continuously sent me bad reports on Todd's behavior. One day in anger, she accidentally slammed a door on his hand, cutting his finger. I unhappily dealt with the situation and was delighted to see the end of that school year. Todd continued to procrastinate and charm his way through the rest of his school years.

We had a real scare when Todd caught a "little wet creature" out of the creek. It bit him, actually penetrating his fingernail. I took Todd to the Fort Belvoir Army Post pediatric clinic where the doctor recommended the anti-rabies injections because we had not seen the guilty critter that bit Todd—he suggested that it could have been a rabid rat. I shook with fear. Fortunately, Todd wasn't aware of what he was facing. They immediately began the injections—one a day for fourteen days—all in the stomach. He never shed a tear until the second week when his stomach was getting very sore. What a trouper! We discovered the guilty critter was probably a runaway hamster, but the doc insisted that if we didn't see the particular animal bite Todd that I was risking his life. After two weeks, that terrible ordeal was finally over.

We had many visitors in northern Virginia and provided free room and board with lots of sightseeing in the Washington D.C. area—so much history, so many monuments, and so much hallowed ground. Both sets of grandparents visited, and the Forgans descended upon us for their annual Christmas visits.

Our most interesting guest was Roxie from Thailand, the Venereal Disease Control Officer at Korat Air Base when Dave was stationed there. She came to the United States to do an extensive study on venereal diseases and would be in the D.C. area for several weeks. I didn't know what to expect and was a little nervous about meeting this female who had been in charge of prostitutes. Dave said she was the Wing mascot—hung out at the bar and drank with the pilots—but was treated with all due respect. We invited her to spend a weekend with us shortly after her arrival in D.C., and I was pleasantly surprised by the tiny lady, about fifty years old, dark skinned, and always smiling. The boys asked us if she was a Negro, so I explained that other people in the world are dark skinned too.

Roxie adored our boys, and they loved teasing her—especially at the swimming pool. They pushed her into the pool, and she splashed and chased them. She never married nor had children. She had a special fondness for the American pilots at Korat, and we still correspond every Christmas.

One of our summer vacations during this assignment included a trip to the mountains around Asheville, North Carolina. Dave's parents escaped Florida's hot summer weather for a couple months by heading to the cool mountains. We drove down there for a week's stay, and the boys played with a "real mountain farm boy." They chased chickens, collected eggs, wallowed in the mud with pigs, and were exposed to farm life.

Without Dave, we went on a relaxing vacation to Lake Carmi, Vermont, staying in a cabin next door to one of Bruce's classmates and his mother. Other vacationing families there were very friendly, and all the children had fun fishing, swimming, and boating.

I made the return trip to Springfield stopping only for lunch, gas, and potty breaks. Focusing on my driving, I left the boys pretty much on their own. They entertained themselves by flipping each other over the front passenger seat into the backseat. They weren't fighting, so I didn't care; however, as I drove through Newark, New Jersey's heavy traffic, I demanded they curtail all gymnastics and remain absolutely quiet. With a few pulls of their hair, I reinforced my yells and demands! I drove into our driveway eleven hours later, so stiff I could hardly get out of the car.

With the boys back in school in the fall, I had a little daytime freedom. I went skiing for the first time across the border from Maryland into Pennsylvania to Charnita, a little three-slope ski resort. Like an idiot, I went to the top of that little hill, which, from my perspective, looked like Mt. Everest. At the first turn, I went straight and headed for the trees. Fortunately, I had the good sense to sit down to stop. I returned to Charnita several times while we were in Virginia and eventually learned the snowplow technique to make my way downhill.

Dave pinned on his major's rank when he was stationed in Thailand, and he was promoted to lieutenant colonel while in this assignment at the Pentagon. No big deal. He put on his new rank and went to work without fanfare. With the new rank, he was eligible to attend the third military school for professional leadership education. In the spring of 1971, he was notified of his next assignment to the Army War College in Carlisle, Pennsylvania. We would have preferred the National War College in the D.C. area, allowing us to stay in our house another year. However, I looked forward to experiencing another part of the United States. The boys had been in a stable environment for three and a half years—our second longest residence.

We sold our house for a small profit—never seemed to make much money on our real estate investments. The packers and movers arrived, but this time it took them a little longer because we had accumulated more furniture, including an old upright piano that I antique-painted an ugly yellow.

We said good-bye to the neighbors, new and old friends, and drove the two cars to our new residence in Pennsylvania. Ugly, skinny Hazel made her first and easiest move. A new adventure was around the corner in Pennsylvania Dutch country. We never gave the boys the time or a reason to be sad about leaving a place, always convincing them of exciting things awaiting us at our new residence. They had been with us when we visited Carlisle and saw the house we selected to rent. They were excited about it, especially the creek running along the edge of the backyard. Visions of water adventures danced through their heads.

Good-bye, George Washington
and to our nation's home of history and government.

Yellow Britches Creek

Mount Holly Springs, Pennsylvania
Carlisle Barracks/The Army War College
July 1971-July 1972

We rented an antiquated, two-hundred-year old house in Mt. Holly Springs, a little town outside of Carlisle. Another air force couple had leased it the previous year while attending the Army War College, and we moved in after they departed. It was situated on an acre with the Yellow Britches Creek running along the back edge of the yard. The creek's name was traced to a Revolutionary War story about the British soldiers' white pants that turned yellow when washed in the creek. Trout were released into the creek every spring, and fishing entertained the locals, including our boys. They fished, swam, and floated in little plastic boats all summer. This new country lifestyle was so different from the Washington D.C. city living.

Right on schedule, Todd claimed the first injury prize. Kids were chasing each other, and Todd went head first into the creek to make his getaway and unfortunately crashed on a big rock. The kids brought him home. Watery blood covered him head to toe, but he had only a small cut on his forehead that required no stitches. I, on the other hand, sat a spell to regain my composure.

The large house was really interesting. It had two stories and was painted white with green wooden shutters that, when closed and latched, covered the old, wavy-glass windows. A white picket fence bordered three sides of the house, making a very picturesque scene. Allegedly, a secret tunnel existed from the house to a small, stone building on the edge of the creek where runaway slaves hid until escaping via the creek. The boys tried to find the tunnel, but my fear they might find rats or snakes deterred their efforts.

The kitchen's wooden floor slanted, making walking on it somewhat awkward. I felt like one of my legs was shorter than the other. An upstairs bathroom had a toilet mounted on a wooden platform. Naturally, we called it "the throne." The bathtub had the old four-legged claw feet. The closets in two of the bedrooms were only about four feet high, which readily accommodated our shorter ancestors and Bruce and Todd. Our master bedroom and bathroom were newer, more updated additions. That house had a lot of history. I wished the walls could talk.

We unpacked a majority of the moving boxes and ten days later left for the best three-week vacation we ever had. We visited Philadelphia, absorbing its history, then drove to New York City. Crossing one of the bridges, I saw the Statue of Liberty for the first time and choked up—such an awesome sight to behold. How excited and frightened our immigrants must have been arriving in this great land of opportunity. My maternal grandmother arrived from Italy at the young age of fifteen, not speaking a word of English. (I remember how scared and nervous I was at twenty-three traveling alone to Japan.) We continued to Hauppauge, Long Island, to visit friends.

A couple days later, we drove the length of Long Island, and took the ferry to the nautical towns of New London, Groton, and Mystic Seaport, Connecticut. Submarines, sailboats, and tall ships were everywhere. We visited Newport, Rhode Island, renowned for its ostentatious mansions lining the coastline where a daughter's playhouse was bigger than my family's house in Oklahoma.

Boston was our next stop, and I insisted the boys listen to my historical narration, which probably went in one ear and out the other. Those were the hippie days, and unfortunately, we had some unexpected, negative impressions. We were having lunch in McDonald's when police chased some hippies into the restaurant. The girls were *topless*. I quickly put my hands over the boys' eyes while Dave stared. Drunken, homeless men were lying all over the place, and we actually saw one getting beat up. I do not have fond memories of Boston.

We drove up the eastern shore and took a ferry to Woods Hole near Martha's Vineyard where we rode rented bicycles, did some sightseeing, and played on the beach—a very relaxing day.

Continuing up the coast of Maine, we came upon a lovely, big, white-framed inn in Kennebunkport. Dave understood them to say accommodations were $50 a night. What a deal. We stayed two nights, sightseeing during the day, and devoured delicious seafood while Bruce insisted on hamburgers. When Dave checked out, the bill was $400. It was *$50 a person* a night. He was mortified, but we enjoyed a beautiful place on the rocky coast.

In shock from the expensive bill, we left Maine with less money in our trip budget and drove across picturesque New Hampshire and Vermont and headed north to Lake Carmi, the second visit to the lake for the boys and me. We had a wonderful time, relaxing, swimming, and enjoying the company of other families. Dave and the boys fished, and Bruce learned to water ski. Todd kept trying but never quite made it, swallowing a lot of lake water in his attempts. After a week, we reluctantly packed and headed out again. Having blown our budget on the lovely Maine inn, we canceled our visit to Montreal and went directly to Toronto to see the LaVignes.

Our two sons and their two daughters enjoyed each other's company, as usual. We visited a safari park where the animals roamed freely. Posted rules stated "Do not feed the animals," but we ignored the rules. Frances rolled down her window to give bites of banana to a monkey; then he tried to get inside the car, grabbing for more. We screamed and laughed as he grabbed what was left of the banana. Then he sat in front of the windshield, showing Frances his appreciation and amorous feelings with his male organ.

On the circuitous route back to Pennsylvania, we stopped by Niagara Falls. Beautiful. The railing where we stood overlooking the falls wasn't high enough for me to feel comfortable. I don't like heights. I wished we'd taken the boat ride on the lake that went beneath the falls, but as usual, Dave was sticking to his schedule. "Time to go."

We arrived back at our historical old house, finished unpacking, and attempted to settle for the one-year assignment. Nancy and Irv, from New York, happened to visit when we hosted a party for the air force student officers and wives assigned to the Army War College. Nancy helped me hang three pictures of old-fashioned people in large, oval frames I'd purchased in an antique shop in Vermont. We eyed their arrangement, measured, nailed the pictures in place, and then stood back to admire our work. Inadvertently, we'd hung one of the ladies upside down. We left her that way, curious to see if anyone at the party noticed. Late in the evening, one of the men looked at the picture and asked, "Is that picture upside down?" We answered, "No," and with that, he rose from his chair and said to his wife, "It's time to go home. I've had too much to drink." That old lady stayed upside down on the wall the entire year and was a popular conversation piece.

Bruce and Todd entered the fifth and third grades. Bruce had a male teacher, which I thought might be good for him. Todd's teacher was a Mennonite lady with a Pennsylvania Dutch accent, and after a year, Todd spoke with the same accent. The boys continued their sports activities and Cub Scout activities. When the commandant of the Army War College observed some young boys misbehaving on the army post golf course, he ordered the golf pro to provide lessons so youngsters could learn the game and the etiquette associated with it. Bruce and Todd took advantage of those lessons and can still play a nice round of golf.

When Bruce was almost ten years old, we decided it was time to talk about "the birds and the bees." I bought a special book on the subject, we curled up on the sofa, and I read it to him. I occasionally stopped and asked if he had questions, but none came forth. When I finished, I asked him once again, and he replied, "One." *Uh oh, here comes the big question all parents fear: How does the baby get in there, and how does it get out?* Well, Mr. Logical Bruce asked, "When the newborn baby is measured, do they measure him with toes pointed out or straight up?" I almost fell off the sofa, answering, "I don't know. It's never come up, and it's not in the book. Now get ready for bed." Whew.

In the fall, both sets of grandparents made their usual treks to our newest location. In December, we flew to Sarasota, Florida, to have Christmas with the paternal grandparents—the only Christmas we ever spent away from home. We celebrated again back in Pennsylvania because Santa Claus had left his gifts from the North Pole at our house. The boys had been concerned Santa wouldn't find them in Florida.

We became good friends with June and Neil Eddins. A former member of the Thunderbirds, the air force acrobatic flying demonstration team, Neil had the required looks, charisma, and very talented flying ability. June and I, innocently, always managed to get into trouble. An army friend called us the "double-trouble twins." Our "trick of the year" was ingenious.

June and I were playing bridge with the wives' club one afternoon—a tough day in the life of the air force wife—and I planned to go to the commissary afterwards. June needed a few things too, so she suggested we go in her car. We loaded her trunk—mostly with my groceries—and returned to the officers' club. June suggested taking her few things home in my car and exchanging cars that evening when we returned to the club with our husbands. "Good idea." I drove thirty minutes to my house then discovered I didn't have the separate trunk key. With perishables, I couldn't wait until later to exchange cars.

I drove thirty minutes to June's house, unlocked her car trunk, and transferred my groceries to my car trunk; then June couldn't find my keys. We gave Craigie, her two-and-a-half-year-old, the third degree. "Where are Aunt Dobbie's keys?" "Let's play 'Find Aunt Dobbie's keys'." "You can have some ice cream if you find Aunt Dobbie's keys." "If you don't find Aunt Dobbie's keys, you will get a spanking." Nothing worked. He giggled and ran around the house.

I finally called home and said to Dave, "Don't ask questions. Don't get mad. Just come get me at the Eddins' house, and bring a spare car key." He drove to the Eddins' house, and we headed home in both cars with barely enough time to put away the groceries, feed the boys, change clothes, and return to the club. By the time we arrived, our story was already circulating with the general consensus of "They've done it again." So much for saving time. The next day Craigie turned up with the keys he had hidden in the garage—too cute to get mad at.

Members of each service branch attending the Army War College were responsible for planning formal functions in honor of its branch—the Infantry Ball and Artillery Ball (army), the Marine Corps Ball, a Ship Wreck party (navy), and the Air Force Ball. A few members of various small units hosted the "Odd Ball." Since it was the air force's twenty-fifth anniversary, our beautiful decorations were blue and silver. June and I were in charge and made it through the whole affair without a glitch! Surprise! The Forgans and the Eddins became friends with "Gene, the Marine" and his wife, Ginny. Gene, exhibiting Marine Corps pride, always wanted to be the last officer departing the club after a party. He had a lot of competition from Dave and Neil, and many times, we wives dragged them home before the break of dawn. On one formal occasion, in jest, Dave exchanged mess jackets (formal military attire) with "Gene, the Marine" but immediately traded back. He has such admiration and respect for the Marines that he couldn't keep the jacket on; he felt it was disrespectful.

The Army War College invited various personalities to speak to the student officers, and Dave and I were privileged to host Bill Mauldin and his lady friend, who eventually became his wife. Mr. Mauldin was the famous World War II cartoonist who depicted what life down in the trenches was like for the soldiers—wet, cold, muddy, dirty, hungry, hot, and sweaty, following orders and doing their duty.

In the spring, Dave received notice of his new assignment: *Spain.* Wow, what a surprise. The boys completed school, and we prepared to move overseas. Dave's rank of lieutenant colonel restricted the weight of our household goods to 13,500 pounds. That's not much—living and dining room furniture, three bedroom suites, washer, dryer, freezer, clothes, kitchen table, chairs, and decorative accessories. The packers loaded the moving truck in a rainstorm and went to Harrisburg, Pennsylvania, where their warehouse began to flood. We were informed that the truck with all our belongings had been driven to higher ground; all we could do was cross our fingers.

Dave sold the Corvair, and we piled into our Caprice with one bag each—Dave's restricted allowance. We had to live for a couple months with what we took with us, so I purchased the largest bag I could find. We shipped some things via air to get us by until our regular household shipment arrived. We took Hazel with us for her second move. We said good-bye to our new air force, army, and Marine friends and headed for McAlester to visit my parents and friends.

From McAlester, we drove to Sarasota, Florida, to visit the Forgan grandparents. The "guys" golfed and fished, and we frolicked on the beach. Dave had difficulty selling the Caprice though it was attractive, well maintained, and only four and a half years old. He practically gave it away, which almost made me sick to my stomach. Dave's rationale for not taking it to Spain: he wanted something smaller for maneuvering narrow Spanish streets, and he feared a lack of local maintenance for an American car.

We left Hazel with the grandparents to ship commercially after we arrived in Spain. Poor Hazel—destined for trauma in the years ahead, and I seemed to be the only one upset over her terrible ordeals. From Florida, we flew to Charleston, South Carolina, and spent the night. This was "bag drag" number ten, and Dave got grumpier each time he loaded and unloaded the bags. We left Charleston AFB the next day on a military C-141, sitting in rear-facing seats surrounded by cargo, eating boxed meals, and worrying about poor little Hazel. I preferred the commercial airlines with comfortable seats, good food, and alcoholic beverages. The boys thought it was "cool" to be flying in a military plane.

Good-bye, Yankee Doodle Dandy.
Hola, amigos (Hello, Friends).

Olé

Madrid, Spain
Torrejon Air Base
16th Air Force Headquarters
401st Tactical Fighter Wing
July 1972-July 1974

After a long, eight-hour, uncomfortable flight, we arrived at Torrejon Air Base (TAB) near Madrid and stayed in temporary quarters on base while searching for housing. We immediately bought a small Peugeot station wagon for our family and a used Fiat sports car for Dave's use. We were on a waiting list for base housing, and in the meantime, we rented an eighth-floor apartment in downtown Madrid, moving in with the small shipment of household goods shipped earlier. The shipment was a disaster. Anything that was breakable was broken, and the clothes had mildewed from getting wet in the Pennsylvania storm. We salvaged what we could and spent hours completing the paperwork for the damage and replacement. We bought new dishes and borrowed necessary household items from Family Services until our regular household shipment arrived. (Family Services on air force bases provides needed essentials until a family's household shipment arrives. The air force takes care of its people.)

We called Grandma and Grandpa Forgan to dispatch Hazel

to her new home in España. We drove to Barajas Airport to retrieve her, but no one could find our dog. I was frantic—yelling in English, stomping past baggage and freight employees—and found our pet all by myself. She was one scared doggie, curled up in a corner of her huge crate. Recognizing me set her tail in motion, and a longing whine rose from her throat. She was glad to see us, and the feeling was mutual. That day Hazel "Ugly Dog" became Hazel "Super Dog" because we were proud she'd survived the ordeal.

Our lovely, spacious apartment consisted of two bedrooms, a combination living/dining room, and a maid's room behind the kitchen, which Dave used for his den. The base supplied us with a few basic pieces of furniture temporarily. A small *terrazza* (balcony) was off the dining room, and the living/dining room's outside wall was floor to ceiling glass with large panes that opened outwards. The windows in the kitchen also opened outwards. *No screens!* I had a knot in my stomach the next four months, petrified the boys would roughhouse right over the edge. Our strict rules made the terrazza off limits without an adult and prohibited climbing on kitchen counters to hang out the windows (to throw food scraps to doggies on other balconies).

Our young Spanish maid occasionally babysat the boys, and she soon informed us that our little *diablos* (devils) were dropping paper cups of water out the living room window onto pedestrians below. *Malo, malo* (bad, bad). Bruce tied his G.I. Joe to a fishing line and reeled it down to dangle above the heads of people on the sidewalk. Someone finally grabbed it and took off. Bruce yelled, and I yelled at Dave, but from the eighth floor, what could we do? One soldier MIA (missing in action).

Each floor had two apartments accessed by a small freight elevator and a small passenger elevator (maximum four occupants unless one was big Dave; then only three could ride). Spanish law prohibited children under twelve from riding elevators alone—a law we Americans ignored. When the kids played on the concrete area behind the building, they routinely rode the elevator up to use the bathroom or get something from their apartment, leaving the door open for their return descent. This brought the *portero* (apartment building manager) up the freight elevator, ranting at the kids in Spanish; they learned Spanish curse words quickly. I pacified him with "*Lo siento, Lo siento*" (I'm sorry, I'm sorry") while shooing the kids back downstairs or into our apartment.

The concrete play area was less than desirable—and full of dog poop, a big adjustment for Bruce and Todd after having an acre of grass and a creek in the country. I did not care for city living with rambunctious boys and a dog. The first week, Bruce kicked a football, breaking a neighbor's second-floor window. Good punt. Luckily, the occupants were understanding Americans. I apologized in English and paid in dollars.

Dave and I developed a doggie-potty routine. After dressing for work, he took Hazel to the concrete "dog-potty" playground. After five minutes, I hung out the window to check her progress. When she'd finished her business, Dave put her in the elevator and pushed the eighth-floor button. I opened the elevator doors and brought her into our apartment. Dave was the only early bird in our building, so our routine was never interrupted. We joked about teaching Hazel to push the button herself.

The boys entered sixth and fourth grades at Royal Oaks Elementary School in an American residential area outside Madrid (where we preferred to live but there was a waiting list). Since many Americans lived in our downtown Madrid neighborhood, the school bus collected students in front of our building. I watched out the window until the bus came. Once, to my dismay, I saw Todd standing in the street, playing traffic cop. I screamed at him loud enough to be heard in Portugal. Another time, when Todd misbehaved on the bus, the Spanish driver deposited him on a street in Madrid. At Bruce's insistence, the driver finally let Todd back on. Had I known at the time, that driver would have been looking for another job.

Dave was frustrated with his new job, which was special assistant to the commanding general. He called himself "the assistant hall monitor." He started bugging Colonel Chuck Donnelly, the Deputy Commander for Operations with the 401st Tactical Fighter Wing at TAB, about possibly commanding a squadron flying the F-4. Chuck made excuses while awaiting the release of the colonel's promotion list. It kept getting delayed, and week after week, Dave's frustration grew. Eventually, a friend at the Pentagon saw the promotion list and called Dave in the middle of the night to congratulate him on his promotion to colonel—five years ahead of his contemporaries. Surprise. This promoted Dave out of a squadron commander's job, a position for lieutenant colonels. Now Dave had to reconsider.

Our regular shipment of household goods finally arrived. In the middle of unpacking, I received a phone call from air force friends Joan and Bill Thurman. They were in Madrid. Terrible timing. I couldn't invite them to stay with us—we were up to our eyeballs in wrapping paper and boxes—but I dropped everything and went sightseeing with them. Bill had bought the book *How to See Europe on Five to Ten Dollars a Day* and was inclined to follow its advice. In Madrid, we went to the cheapest shoe store and cheapest restaurant. The little restaurant was owned and run by the *señor* and *señora*, with the assistance of *los niños* (the children). We were served a three-course meal for 75 pesetas (about a dollar). After a small green salad, we gnawed on tough, thin pieces of beef accompanied by a few potatoes and green beans then welcomed rice pudding for dessert. A big kitty-cat rubbed against our legs under the table, and when I offered a piece of meat, it stuck up its nose and sauntered off. The three of us looked at each other in alarm, wondering if we had just eaten one of the cat's relatives. Gross.

I attended Spanish language classes on base four afternoons a week and was exhausted at the end of the day, saturated with nouns, verbs, pronouns, and pronunciation. While in class, I lent my car to Joan and Bill so they could continue sightseeing. I learned the Spanish word for cheap, *borrato*, and we nicknamed Bill "El Borrato." Later, I learned in translation that "things" are cheap, not people. However, we thought the name applied and continued our tirade. I also discovered the Spanish word for drunk, *borracho*, and I frequently confused the two words. It didn't matter because sometimes the situation called for either or both. "We were *borracho* from drinking vino *borrato*."

We introduced the Thurmans to our city of fountains, which Americans personalized with their own descriptive names. In a huge roundabout, the one with a lady sitting on a chariot pulled by two lions was aptly called "Dotty on the Potty." Astride a horse, a military man pointed toward the Castellana Hotel—popular with Americans. We said he was giving directions. Another fountain lit at night by orange lights was nicknamed "Orange Juice Fountain."

We soon learned to take our own toilet paper along wherever we went because Spanish toilet paper was like sandpaper. Paper products were expensive, and if anything better than cheap paper was put in public restrooms, it was stolen.

Joan and Bill departed Spain, and I returned to unpacking boxes, but the knot in my stomach got bigger every day. The boys and I found it difficult to adjust to city and apartment living, but when Dave pinned on his new colonel's rank in November, Chuck Donnelly got him transferred into the 401st Wing as the Assistant Deputy Commander of Operations (ADO). Dave didn't care what he was the assistant of as long as he was flying again. This position put him on the way up the ladder to wing commander—the ultimate for a flyboy. His new job required us to live on base. Thank you, Lord.

I was fascinated, watching the Spanish workmen move all our belongings over the eighth-floor balcony on ropes and in baskets. It made me nervous. I occasionally had to close my eyes. The house on base was a three-bedroom duplex—small but adequate. Once again, Dave's den was the maid's room behind the kitchen in the rear. Bruce and Todd each had his own bedroom for the first time, which they liked. Carolyn and Chuck Donnelly lived in the adjoining duplex; our bedrooms were back to back. Occasionally, we knocked on the wall, calling, "Good night, Carolyn; good night, Chuck," and they responded in kind.

The boys transferred from the Royal Oaks Elementary School to the base elementary school within walking distance from our house. Hazel was extremely happy heading out the back door to potty on *grass!* The Spanish gardener cautioned me to be watchful of Hazel because sheepherders might steal her. "A very intelligent breed, she would make a good sheepdog." In the future, when frequently asked, "What kind of dog is she?" we proudly answered, "A Spanish sheepdog." Hazel finally got a title. In my eyes, she was already beautiful but now also reputed to be smart.

Speaking of sheep, they roamed the base, "mowing and fertilizing." Dave took a great picture from the cockpit of his F-4 while waiting at the end of the runway for a herd of sheep to cross before he could take off—a reminder of how modern technology is stymied by ageless traditions.

Dave and I formed new friendships in the neighborhood and in the fighter wing, and the boys also had many new friends who lived in the base housing area—nice for after-school playtime. Since there was no active Cub Scout pack on base, I knocked on doors to find ten-year-old boys and started a Cub Scout den. Ricky, one of Todd's little friends, was bilingual, his mother was Spanish, and I often used him as my translator. When we left Torrejon two years later, he gave me a Spanish ceramic tile that I still treasure today. Sometimes, it's the small things that become significant and special.

When the mountains north of Madrid opened for skiing, Bruce went on a day ski trip with friends. Dave and I were hosting a cocktail party when Bruce sheepishly walked in from the trip, holding a bloody towel to his face. He kept saying, "It's all right; it's all right," but after one look at his face, I directed Dave to take him to the emergency room. He had been hit in the nose by an errant ski lift. The result was a deep cut, a slightly cracked nose, and a black eye. The accident curse that always hit us at a new assignment had just been delayed several months. Shortly after the ski incident, Bruce got into a fight on the school playground. When a teacher yelled, "Stop it," Bruce turned to look at her and *wham*, the other kid socked him in the nose, a setback for the healing of his broken nose.

After Christmas, the boys and I joined the base ski club for a ski trip to Andorra, a small independent country between Spain and France. We rented ski equipment in town, and at the ski area, I gave Todd *pesetas* to purchase tickets for the bunny hill rope tow. Bruce and I took off in different directions. About the third day, a Spanish lady found me on a slope and said, "Your son has been injured and taken to the emergency clinic." I wondered how she found me in this country where everyone spoke Spanish, Catalan, or French. Later Bruce explained that he told her to look for a woman in a ski suit that looked like a red and white checked tablecloth. Bless her, she found me and spoke enough English to tell me all I needed to know.

I sped to the clinic—a very austere place, cold and damp. Bruce was lying on an examining table in his underwear, turtleneck, and sweater. He was shivering from the cold, so I covered him with our ski jackets. The doctor said Bruce had fractured the growth plate in his ankle, and they put a flimsy cast on his lower leg and handed me a prescription for pain pills. I don't remember how I got Bruce back to the hotel. That night as I dressed for dinner, sitting on the end of the bed with one leg in my pantyhose and the other leg about to go in, there was a knock on the door, and the doctor and his assistant just walked right in. I almost broke *my* leg trying to cover up, but the doctor waved away my modest behavior, ignored me, and checked Bruce. He gave me suppositories to combat swelling, and although I'd never heard of suppositories for swelling before or since, they worked. Unfortunately, I misunderstood the Catalan doctor's poor English directions and gave Bruce too many! It's a wonder Bruce didn't shrivel up like a prune.

Bruce awoke the next morning in pain, so I reluctantly left the boys alone to search for a *farmacia* (pharmacy) to fill the pain prescription. I walked and walked and walked with no luck. It was New Year's Day, and nothing was open. With my sparse Spanish vocabulary, I asked a man standing in front of a *farmacia* if he knew when it would open. He answered me with his sparse Spanish, and then we laughed, realizing we both spoke English. He needed medicine for his wife and had been told since it was New Year's Day the locals would show up "whenever"—or not at all. Glad we weren't dying. We sat on the curb for a while, waiting for someone to show, but I guess they were too hung over from New Year's Eve festivities. I went back to the hotel and started plying Bruce with aspirin.

My next challenge was to return all our ski equipment: three pairs of skis, six poles, and three pairs of ski boots. Leaving the boys alone again, I trudged to the ski shop, dropping items, picking them up, and cursing all the way. I finally found an open *farmacia*, and the pills worked wonders for Bruce's pain and my sanity. He rather enjoyed all the attention and everyone signing his cast. One of the men in our group carried him to and from the dining room, and he was placed on the wide backseat of the bus for the eleven-hour ride back to Torrejon. He slept all the way.

The day after we arrived home, the base medical clinic replaced the flimsy cast and gave Bruce some crutches. He recalls throwing one of the crutches at Todd like a spear, and I remember him playing soccer in the street, using the crutches for balance and leverage. The accident didn't slow down Bruce.

During our first winter in Spain, President Nixon restarted the bombing of North Vietnam with B-52s, bringing the North Vietnamese back to the peace talks in Paris. The "war" finally ended, and the first POWs were returned in February 1973. What an emotional time. The men had suffered terrible torture and horrible living conditions; however, nothing deterred their smiles as they exited the planes returning them to the American military base in the Philippines. What they'd endured was momentarily forgotten in their enthusiasm to be free again. Brave men who had survived the unthinkable—some fully recovered, but others had residual symptoms that affected them mentally and physically. We had no TV at TAB so our news and pictures were limited to what we saw in the military's Stars & Stripes newspaper.

Dave knew several POWs who had flown with him at Korat, and we were shocked at their pale skin and white hair. Many had been in prison over seven years. The families of all the prisoners also experienced extreme hardships, not knowing if their loved ones were dead or alive, wondering what condition they were in, and trying to raise a family without a husband or a father. It's said that 80 percent of the marriages ended in divorce—the separation too long and adjustments too difficult.

The spring of 1973, both boys played Little League baseball. Bruce played with the Knights, a team coached by a nineteen-year-old GI, Mike Yeberneski. In twelve years, I had never seen Bruce respond to authority and management as he did with this young man. He would have walked into the ocean and not stopped until Mike gave the word. Bruce never argued with him and didn't quit when things got tough. Mike had been dumped with the youngest and smallest guys for his team, except for Bruce and his friend Gary Reese, two stalwart players.

The Torrejon All Star Team for the two previous years had been selected and coached by a cocky sergeant who got to choose those same players for his regular team. It wasn't fair to have all the good players on one team; however, young Mike used his ingenuity, teaching his little guys to bunt and steal and his big hitters, Bruce and Gary, to bring them home to score. Bruce was the starting pitcher for the Knights' first game against the former

All Star Team. We were all nervous wrecks, but Bruce was the hero, striking out thirteen batters. The Knights won, dethroning the "king" and his court. Pandemonium reigned. Bruce was mobbed. It was one of those moments of glory that athletes remember and treasure. The Knights won the regular season championship—to the chagrin of the former All Star coach. Bruce did most of the pitching, had several shutouts, and while helping his team win the pennant added a no-hitter to his record. And if that weren't enough, he blasted a grand slam home run.

Todd's team, the Caballos, also won their regular season championship. It was a victorious baseball season for the Forgan boys. This mother sat through thirty-six ballgames that summer. My butt was sore, my skin was sunburned, and my nerves were on edge from all the tension. Forgans hate to lose.

Naturally, Bruce made the All Star Team, coached by the older, more experienced, cocky sergeant. We parents thought Mike Yeberneski deserved to be the coach. Our guys beat the All Star teams from Zaragoza Air Base and Rota Navy Base in southern Spain, making them eligible to fly to Naples, Italy, for the Mediterranean championship against teams from Italy, Greece, and Turkey. The winner there advanced to the European championship tournament in the Netherlands. That winner then headed to Williamsport, Pennsylvania, for the Little League World Series. Wow, we were excited.

However, it was not to be. In their opening game at Naples, Bruce pitched his team to a five-to-zero victory, giving up only two hits. They lost their second game. Bruce came back to pitch in the third contest and was the loser in a ten-to-three game. Bruce did his best; his team's three runs resulted from his home run with two men on base, and he was presented the home run ball after the game ended. It was a wonderful experience and taught him a lot about leadership and teamwork. The boys continued to play sports while at Torrejon—football, basketball, and baseball, but no season was as exciting as that of summer '73.

Dave's Aunt Grace and Uncle Fred and Aunt May visited that

same summer. They stayed in a hotel near the base, and we did the typical tourist stuff. They were impressed with my new command of the Spanish language. Did I have them fooled! At a restaurant, I ordered dinner for the *mujeres*. The waiter told me "*mujeres*" was not a polite term for "women" and that I should say "*las señoras,*" the "ladies." Lesson learned. It was neither the first nor the last time I was corrected.

In the winters, we skied in the Navacerrada Mountains north of Madrid. On weekday mornings, Sharil Caffery, Celia McCauley, and I shoved our kids out the door to school, drove two hours to the ski slopes, and got home by six o'clock to quickly prepare dinner. On weekends, we allowed the kids to join us. Celia was Spanish, and she and I exchanged verbal expressions that made no sense. For example, in English, we called someone a "dirty old man" if he was sexually obnoxious or flirtatious. Celia taught me to say "*Viejo verde hombre,*" meaning "old green man." Also, in English, when we tease someone, we say, "I'm pulling your leg." In Spanish, they say, "I'm pulling the cat's tail." This is one way we entertained ourselves on the long chair-lift rides. There were others—but not for print.

It was obvious when Prince Juan Carlos arrived to ski at Navacerrada via helicopter. One day when skiing down a slope, we spied the prince and his wife. They each followed a personal instructor, and bodyguards trailed behind trying to keep up. My friend got so excited she fell over. Ever so gallant, Prince Juan Carlos skied over, offering his hand to assist her to her feet. She declared she'd never again wash that hand. I just stood there with my mouth agape. (I did not mention this incident when we had the good fortune to meet the prince a couple years later at the Spanish Military Academy in Zaragoza. I stood there with my mouth open again while he and Dave exchanged a few words about the military. His English was excellent; therefore, Dave didn't need me to translate—thank goodness—no telling what I would have mumbled.)

From 1972-1974, I did my best to see most of Spain (except the northwest) and took tours with the wives' club to Germany, Morocco, and Greece. When I went to the Oktoberfest in Munich, we drove by McDonald's on the way to the hotel. It had been several years for some of us without a McDonald's burger. We threw our luggage in the hotel rooms and raced back to the golden arches to devour and savor delicious burgers and fries. Brats and wiener schnitzels are fine, but we missed our All-American fast food. Dave and several other husbands went with us to Greece, and it was mind-boggling trying to absorb all the history. Dave was fascinated with a group of prostitutes in a bar; they thought he was so cute. Instead of leaving my purse in a restaurant (my usual trick), I left my raincoat in the bar. Dave faced those "ladies" again the next day to recover my coat—they thought he returned to see *them*. Wrong.

Morocco is one of the most interesting places I have ever visited. Surreal. "Ready, set, action." I thought I'd see Bob Hope, Bing Crosby, and Dorothy Lamour come around the corner any minute. The locals were frantically begging and bartering. When I refused one little girl trying to sell me a knit cap, she swatted me on the arm with it. I rode a camel and ate food with my hands (and don't care to do either again). A beggar tried to pinch one of the wives on the bottom and had to deal with her angry husband. The beggar just grinned stupidly and walked away. Many times when we wouldn't buy something being pushed on us solicitously, the local sneered and said, "You American, you rich." It was an interesting place to visit, but I wouldn't want to spend much time there. From Marrakech, we were bussed to a village in the Atlas Mountains about two hours south. It was market day, and I actually saw a donkey parking lot. Fortunately, there were no airline carry-on restrictions in those days because we wives were loaded with purchases—brassware, birdcages, caftans, and a Moroccan broom (a bunch of twigs tied onto a stick). We did our best to contribute to their economy.

After returning to Torrejon, I invited two couples to go with us to a Moroccan restaurant in Madrid, where I could demonstrate my knowledge of Moroccan-style eating. I made the reservations in my "Spanglish" and told the man we wanted lamb *por todos* (for all). One couple canceled, and when I called the restaurant, I was asked repeatedly what I thought was "Do you still want lamb *por todos?*" "*Si,*" I kept insisting. We arrived at the restaurant, sat on the floor as was the custom, and were brought a tray with a *whole* lamb on it! "*Todos*" also means "whole." I ordered lamb for *all* and was served *whole* lamb for all. More Spanish lessons for me! Knowing a little Spanish sometimes got me in trouble!

In a taxi in Seville, the driver kept repeating, "*Chucalor, chucalor.*" I had no idea what he was saying. Back in Torrejon, I asked my Spanish friend, Celia, what it meant. She laughed and explained that down south (just like in the States), people cut the beginnings or endings off their words. The driver meant to say, "*Mucho calor,*" which translates to "It's really hot." Of course, I couldn't understand the southerners in Alabama either. I enjoyed trying to speak Spanish because the people smiled hearing my attempts and corrected me or helped me find the right word. I was never embarrassed to try, and my efforts were appreciated. Once in a taxi in Madrid, I gave the driver directions in my "Spanglish," and he responded in perfect English. Joke was on me. He was from London attending the University of Madrid and driving taxis for extra money.

Fighter pilots have been known to do almost anything. At a pool party for junior officers at the officers' club, Dave and his boss, Sandy, decided things were a little too dull. Dave walked to our house and brought Todd's bicycle back to the pool. He and Sandy climbed onto the high diving board with the bicycle.

Dave straddled the bike, Sandy sat on Dave's shoulders, and Dave pedaled the two of them off the end of the board. I shut my eyes, and most of the young officers and wives could hardly believe what they were seeing. This was no easy feat, as there was no seat on the bike! Then the two swam to the side, retrieved the bike, climbed out, and rode around in the same stacked position, riding off the edge of the pool. Sandy went one way; Dave, gripping the detached handlebars, flew the other way; the bicycle remains took a nosedive. And we trusted those men to fly million dollar airplanes? The young officers and their wives probably still remember the two crazy colonels.

Our third summer, 1974, after the boys' baseball season was over, Dave's parents and another couple came for a three-week visit. After local sightseeing, we borrowed a car and traveled in two vehicles to western Spain, to the southern coast, and on to Grenada. Wonderful sights—Roman ruins in the west, very Mediterranean in the south, and Moorish in the Grenada area. As I drove our Peugeot toward Ubeda, the entire windshield suddenly shattered. Bruce, sitting next to me in the front seat, and I were sprayed with tiny glass particles, which embedded in our hair and clothes. We could do nothing about our dilemma, so I drove with my head stuck out the driver's open window to the next town where we had hotel reservations. Dave took the car to a repair shop, and they knocked out the remaining glass. We were surprised when they told us to drive with all the side windows rolled up so an "over-pressure" was created inside the car; then no wind would blow through the open windshield. Dave, Bruce, Todd, and Mr. Copeland rode in the Peugeot, and I drove the borrowed car with Dave's father and the two women. The downside of the open windshield was incoming bugs. Everyone wore sunglasses for protection, but of course, Bruce was stung by a bee. He was always an accident waiting to happen.

"Doc," Dave's father, became ill and was coughing. He had emphysema, and I was afraid he was getting pneumonia. The hotel called a Spanish doctor, who came to his room to examine him. Between my Spanish and the doctor's English, a diagnosis was made and an antibiotic was prescribed. We eliminated a day from our travel plans and headed for home.

We had wonderful sightseeing, interesting experiences, and a great trip. The boys were bored most of the time—not the greatest tourists—but I must give them some credit for putting up with us old folks. Dave took few vacations, and this was a good one.

Dave was notified that he was getting his *third* new boss, the DO from Zaragoza Air Base, commonly called ZAB. Dave had been the ADO for two years and now was passed over again for DO. He was frustrated, but he never let it deter him from doing a good job. A few months later, the air force suddenly assigned Dave to the 406th Tactical Fighter Training Wing at ZAB, naming him the wing vice commander, a complete skip of the DO's job at either air base—a complex and strange decision. Why didn't they make the DO at ZAB the vice commander and promote Dave to DO at Torrejon? I think personnel threw darts at a target filled with names and assignments.

This would be an easy move—no house hunting, no long plane or car ride, no *big* suitcases or bag drags, no traumatic travel for our Spanish sheepdog. We said our good-byes, were honored at several farewell functions, packed overnight bags, and drove two hours north to Zaragoza to meet the moving truck the next day. It was hard to leave Madrid—my favorite European city—and exchange a large air force base for a small base and small city; however, we would return to Torrejon several times in the next three years, so it wasn't a complete loss.

Adios, Madrileños (Good-bye, Madrid folks).

La Casa Numero Uno

Zaragoza, Spain
Zaragoza Air Base
406th Tactical Fighter Training Wing
July 1974-July 1977

We arrived at ZAB and moved into the three-bedroom vice commander's house, next door to the wing commander. Our fourteenth residence in sixteen years, it was bigger than the little three-bedroom duplex we had at Torrejon. In fact, I liked its Spanish look with white stucco walls and a red-tiled roof. Dick Skelton, the commander, and his wife, Pat, became our very good friends. My job was to support and assist Pat in her endeavors: entertaining, wives' club projects, and being a friend.

Shortly after our arrival, the Torrejon Wives' Club tour bus stopped at ZAB for lunch and collected me to go to the San Fermin festival in Pamplona, celebrating the running of the bulls. Dave was busy getting acquainted with his new job (as usual) and missed one of the most fun excursions ever. Major General Felices, commander of 16th Air Force Headquarters at Torrejon, and his wife were along for the trip, which was advantageous as Spanish was his first language. Using his rank and influence, he got us onto an official city building's second-floor balcony to watch the bulls and runners race up the street, the runners scattering from those menacing bulls' horns. Spectators packed the sidewalks behind barricades, and at times, there was no space for a runner to reach safety—ouch.

Every year someone is killed or injured in the run. This festival is held on the seventh day of the seventh month for seven days, and the bull run begins at seven each morning. These bulls are used for the daily bullfights. They run to the bullring and are put in holding pens until their turn to entertain and die. (This reminds me of the Romans being entertained by Christians and lions.)

We Americans dressed according to festival custom: white pants and shirt with a red sash and a red scarf around the neck. Parades and band music were prevalent throughout the day in addition to the daily bullfights and jota dancing, a Spanish folk dance. Never had I seen so much wine and beer consumed, and we did our best to keep up. All were happy drunks. When making our way back to our hotel at 3:00 a.m., we saw the central park shrouded with sleeping bodies. I'm certain they were up at seven o'clock the next morning, regardless of hangovers, ready to repeat their daily celebrations. The police were evident but always in the background, discreet, and obviously lenient toward the celebrants. We survived another Spanish festival, hung over and sleepy, but had a great time.

Early on, Dave and I and several other American colonels and their wives were invited to a Spanish party to welcome the new Spanish two-star general. The typical Spanish workday concluded at 2:00 p.m., when everyone went home for their main meal and a siesta. In contrast, our American-military work hours lasted until at least 6:00 p.m. This particular party started at 9:00 p.m. with dinner served at 10:00 and dessert at midnight—at which time we Americans thought we'd depart for home. *Wrong.* We adjourned to the tennis courts for music and dancing. The Spanish adhered to the tradition that *no one* leaves a function until the senior officer has left.

The new Spanish general was having a delightful time, and all the Americans were yawning. Sneaking a peek at our watches about 3:00 a.m., we thought for sure that the general would leave any time. *Wrong.* The waiters appeared with hot chocolate and *churros* (Spanish donuts). In a stupor, we all went home about 5:00 a.m. While our husbands had to go to work that morning, the Spaniards had the day off. They always criticized Americans for working too hard. We went to many Spanish functions during the three years we were there, but none lasted as long as that first party. Thank goodness, or we wouldn't have survived.

I tried to utilize my small Spanish vocabulary, and our Spanish acquaintances refused to speak English to me (even if they knew how), forcing me, in all good humor, to speak their language. I did a lot of translating for Dave. If they said something to me in Spanish and I didn't understand, they would tell Dave in English, but not me. (Later, at one of our farewell parties, a Spanish officer sat next to an American wife, and I told her I would help translate. To my amazement, he spoke English to her the entire evening. In three years, I had never heard him utter a word of English. *Que un diablo.* What a devil.)

As usual, the boys made the move to ZAB with ease. Most military kids seem to adjust to the constant moving as they're all in the same boat. Bruce's athletic reputation had preceded his arrival, and all the base kids were eager to meet the All Star baseball player from Torrejon who had been their staunch opponent. Bruce entered eighth grade and Todd sixth grade. Because ZAB had a small population, there were only five colonel assignments, which meant the younger ranking officers had younger families. This left few choices for friends for our sons, and I wasn't too enthused with the choices. I watched our boys and their activities like a hawk.

Our first startling experience was Bruce's new girlfriend—a sophomore in high school. Our thirteen-year-old son was five feet and ten inches tall, weighed about 150 pounds, shaved, and looked older than his biological years. Debbie caught the eye of the good-looking, new kid on the block.

The school counselor mentioned to me one day that Bruce and Debbie were "smooching" in the school halls. I asked, "Where are the teachers?" "Sorry, they don't pull hall duty, lunch room duty, or recess duty in Department of Defense (DoD) schools." I confronted the young couple and told Debbie that if she wanted to date Bruce, she would abide by our rules because Bruce was only thirteen, and I told them that "smooching" in the halls would cease. Bruce, of course, was embarrassed and tried to resist my orders. I threatened to drive him to school every morning, make a round trip for lunch, and pick him up again after school.

I guess I scared them enough because we had no more reports—or perhaps the teachers just turned their heads, not wanting to be confronted by the vice commander's wife. Debbie's mother called me (her husband was a sergeant; she was pretty brave to call a colonel's wife under the circumstances), offering to forbid Debbie from seeing Bruce if I so desired. I told her I didn't want to forbid them but that Debbie had to understand our position. I must say, Debbie was always very polite and respectful. Thankfully, her father was reassigned to the U.S. the next summer. I would be grateful more than once for a new assignment to break up a teenage romance.

Todd took up bowling, continued playing baseball and football, and still enjoyed Scouting. Bruce played soccer, basketball, and football. He had outgrown Little League, therefore, played baseball one year for a school team that played Spanish teams downtown. He dislocated his shoulder when he fell in a ditch chasing someone, and that ended his baseball career.

The base had a wonderful youth center for the kids, and that's where Bruce and Todd spent a great deal of time. It provided a snack bar, games, and weekend chaperoned dances. In Europe, teens cannot get a driver's license until they are eighteen, so our kids needed a place to recreate. Once "stamped in" at the youth center, you couldn't re-enter if you left; however, some kids got "stamped in" then caught the recreation center bus, which took enlisted men into town for the evening. There was no age limit for drinking in Spain—very tempting for some youth. These kids would later return to the youth center, wait outside for their parents to pick them up, the parents unaware they had been to town. Bruce and Todd denied ever doing this.

When my parents visited, we made the usual rounds of sightseeing, and one weekend, we drove to Biarritz, France, just over the northern Spanish border. For some reason, Daddy really wanted to go to France, and we granted him his wish. We were thankful for Dave's two years of high school French; otherwise, we might have slept in the car and eaten snails. He depended on my Spanish, but I certainly appreciated his limited French. The grandparents sadly returned to the U.S., depending on letters and photos to keep abreast of our activities. I was dedicated to the task of corresponding with all the relatives.

Dave and I signed up for the Swiss Ski School, held annually the first two weeks of December, alternating among ski resorts in Switzerland. Our school was located at Wengen, in the shadow of the famous Eiger Mountain featured in the James Bond movie *On His Majesty's Secret Service.* Dave was placed in a low-intermediate class, and I was stuck in a more advanced group that was difficult for me. The instructor refused my request to go to a lower level. I was nauseated every morning, thinking about striking out into that cold, cruel, white world. One day a heavy fog rolled in as we headed for lunch. Bringing up the rear of the class, as usual, I couldn't see a thing and had to ski toward my instructor's voice as he calmly guided me to him. It was like skiing blind. When he came into view, I gratefully hugged him.

In the evenings, we played bridge in the lodge lounge, and two Spanish men showed interest. Dave and I invited them to play some games with us, and we learned how to play bridge in Spanish. A spade is *pico*; a diamond is *diamante*; a heart is *corazon*; a club is—funny, funny—*tres boles* (three balls); no trump is *sin triumfo* (without trump). Playing bridge knowing only a few critical Spanish words was amusing.

I didn't learn a lot of skiing technique at the Swiss Ski School but felt fortunate just to have survived. I discovered I was capable of facing a challenge with sheer guts and determination. I didn't know whether to hate the instructor for putting me through such torture on the slopes or to love him for getting me through the week.

We prepared for our first Christmas at ZAB. One of the wives created a special Christmas card, which I copied to send to our friends.

'Tis the night before Christmas and all through la casa,
Not a creature is stirring. Caramba! Que pasa?
The stockings are hanging con mucho cuidado
In the hopes that Saint Nicholas will feel obligado.
Los niños are snuggled all safe in their camas,
It is frio outside, but they're warm in las pajamas.
Their little cabezas dreaming of things buenas
And hoping that Santa is not off playing tennis.
Madre in her nightie and padre muy contento
Are just settling down for a glass of vino.
When, what to our ojos should appear
But viejo Saint Nick and his ocho reindeer.
His cheeks are like rosas, his nariz like a cherry!
His ojos—how they twinkle! His dimple, que merry!
We all join together on this holiday
To our muchos amigos we cheerfully say
We wish you many Blessings from Heaven's Holy Light,
Merry Christmas a todos, y a todos good night
The Forgans

Clever, eh?

I had lots of issues with the Department of Defense (DoD) Schools in Spain and their liberal attitude toward students. This was in the seventies when children were "allowed to do their own thing," their rights considered more important than their responsibilities. I sometimes wondered who was in charge of the school: the students or the faculty. For example, the Parent-Teachers Association (PTA) was reorganized and renamed the (PTSA), the Parent-Teacher-Student Association to include the students who expressed themselves vehemently without respect or consideration. It was the "me" generation.

Another example of the questionable capability of some of those DoD teachers was Todd's English teacher, also the assistant principal. I ran into him on a ski slope (not literally, unfortunately), and he informed me that Todd would get a C on his report card because he lacked a book report. He added that if Todd turned in his report the following week, it would raise his grade. On Sunday night, I reminded Todd of the book report, and he assured me he would get it done. He created a nonexistent book title and cleverly concocted a story for the oral report, which required the listeners to read the story to learn the ending. The teacher didn't realize the scam and gave Todd an A.

Of course, there were some good teachers on the staff, and the dedicated teachers could always be seen at school functions. Sadly, some teachers were barely there in time for class and were difficult to find after school.

Bruce's artistic talent continued to flourish. His art teacher said he had taught Bruce everything he knew and suggested he take a mechanical drawing class. The drawing instructor told Bruce to research and design a house on his own, which he did that semester. The final design was exquisite, but the teacher said, engineering-wise, it would collapse. "So what? That's what engineers are for," exclaimed Bruce. I still have a pen and ink drawing that won an award in a high school competition in Europe.

In 1975, after we had been at ZAB one year, Dick Skelton, the wing commander, was reassigned to Germany, and a colonel from another base was selected to take over instead of Dave moving up the ladder from vice to commander to commander. Here we go again—Dave was skipped. Although it was hard to swallow, he prepared himself to continue doing his vice commander's job (always a bridesmaid, never a bride, so to speak).

The new colonel took command, but because he was divorced, he was not allowed to live in the commander's designated number one quarters—a stupid decision. Even after all the negotiations on his behalf, it was a lost cause. Dave made arrangements to enlarge quarters at the BOQ (Bachelor Officers' Quarters) to accommodate the new commander. That left the big question, *Who would live in quarters number one?* It couldn't sit empty. Specific houses were designated for the commander, the vice commander, the base support group commander, and the deputy commander of operations, house numbers one, two, three, and four. This complicated situation put the whole sequence out of order, requiring everyone to "move up" to the next house.

I really didn't look forward to moving again so soon, especially since Dave had been passed over for the commander's job, but I acquiesced, and we began transplanting from quarters number two to quarters number one. Our Spanish maid, Nati, and I loaded two grocery carts from the commissary and traipsed next door with our kitchenwares. When I emptied one cart, she returned for another load, and with this assembly line operation, we had the kitchen organized in about two hours. What we couldn't load in the car, the moving truck transferred next door. Quarters number one was a little bigger but didn't have the pretty Spanish architecture of quarters number two.

Two months later, we spent the day at the base Fourth of July festivities and dragged home about 10:00 p.m. An hour later, the general from 16th Air Force at Torrejon AB called Dave, trying to contact our new commander, who happened to be out of town. The general told Dave to inform the commander that he was being transferred to command the wing at Torrejon. Toward the end of the brief conversation, after absorbing the shock, Dave meekly asked, "Who will be the wing commander here?" The general replied, "Oh, you." And that's how Dave found out. The first thing he did Monday morning was cancel the cement pour for a new patio at the BOQ! No one ever believed that we didn't already know these arrangements when we moved into quarters number one, and it was a mystery why the colonel was assigned to ZAB for a couple months before he was reassigned to Torrejon. The vice commander's wife at Torrejon was not too happy with the situation—since the colonel was divorced, she was stuck with the commander's wife's responsibilities. I'm glad the responsibility was changed from me to her.

Dave was finally in the number one position, and we could set policies and standards and do our own thing! I went nuts! I reorganized the thrift shop to include the officers' wives, cutting the expenses in half and increasing charity contributions. I started a scholarship fund-raiser fashioned after the one I worked on at Torrejon, and sat on the PTSA board and made changes (which a few teachers didn't like). People were scared to see me coming. What was I up to next? The officers' wives' club required that I sit on the board as an adviser, where I tried to keep my opinions to myself. As adviser to a floundering Red Cross program, I re-established a well-organized service for the only all-volunteer office in Europe. For the Family Services office, I established a program sending baked goods to remote air force personnel and developed a tourist guide for Spain. I hosted coffees, teas, cocktail parties, dinner parties, and on one occasion, prepared appetizers for one hundred guests at our quarters. I had the daily help of Nati, who inherited all my domestic chores, allowing me time to pursue my other interests.

ZAB was officially a Spanish military base with the U.S. Air Force occupying half the installation. In addition to the numerous

American activities, we were invited to all the official Spanish functions, which included many fiestas. The Spanish were always celebrating something. We sat through ceremonies, Catholic masses, lunches, and dinners observing the patron saints of artillery and the air force. The Spanish Army Military Academy was in Zaragoza, and we attended their graduation ceremonies, which included a "kissing of the flag" by each graduate, symbolizing their allegiance to God and country. These affairs lasted for several hours, and we were always exhausted when finally dragging home our tired bodies and mentally challenged minds trying to communicate in Spanish. Because the base was Spanish, we were not allowed to fly an American flag. We were thrilled when Dave received special permission to fly our flag on the Fourth of July 1976 to celebrate our bicentennial. A special flag pole was installed, and the Scouts performed a patriotic ceremony. This was a special moment of pride in our country.

When our social life interfered with our dinner hour, I frequently sent the boys next door to the Officers' Club where they were served at the commander's reserved table. The Spanish waiters, Jesus and David, quickly learned what the boys liked—red meat, French fries, salad without tomatoes—and they lined up four eight-ounce cartons of milk at the top of each plate. The friendly waiters liked to tease Bruce and Todd about girlfriends and sports.

In February 1976, Daddy passed away from heart failure. He had been ailing with ventricular fibrillation but was feeling better and was supposed to go home from the hospital. They called Mother in the middle of the night, and she raced to the hospital, but he was gone. She notified the Red Cross, who contacted Dave at his office, and he came home to share the sad news. Losing a close family member was a new and traumatic experience for all of us.

Downtrodden, we four flew to Tulsa, where a friend of my parents met us and drove us the hour-and-a-half trip to McAlester.

I suggested the boys buy something in an airport shop to take to their grandpa, a "memory item" to put in his casket to be buried with him. Todd selected a small ceramic angel, and Bruce purchased a little plastic baseball player, bringing tears to my eyes, then and now. I had not shown my father much respect in the past due to the tough times resulting from his occasional alcohol abuse, but I know he loved us all very much and was so proud of Dave and his grandsons. Still, he was my father, and I mourned his death.

While in Spain, Bruce discovered a new hobby: building remote-controlled airplanes. He spent months building the first one, and on its initial flight, it crashed shortly after takeoff. What a disaster after all that work, but he continued to build others and kept crashing. He continued playing sports, and at the end of his sophomore year at the sports banquet, Bruce was recognized for his participation in football, soccer, and basketball.

Todd played football and baseball but was heartbroken when he didn't make the baseball All Star Team the first two years at ZAB. The third year he was finally selected. The All Star team traveled to Rota Naval Base on the southern coast of Spain to compete in the All-Mediterranean Tournament, and I listened to the game broadcast on the Armed Forces radio network. By the end of the third inning, Todd's team was getting slaughtered 27-3. How painful for those little guys; I was a nervous wreck listening to the agony of defeat. Then the coach put Todd in to pitch. I cringed, thinking of what poor Todd had to face—*they'll kill him.* He rose to the occasion, allowing the opposition *only* three more runs in the final three innings. Todd's team was humiliated, but he'd saved them from any further embarrassment. The coach told us he'd discovered how to get Todd to run faster: he'd put a Coke on each base. Todd was always first to arrive at the refreshment stand after a game.

In the winters, we spent most weekends at Formigal, a little ski area three hours from ZAB. Some of us mothers drove up on Friday, and the kids came on the base recreation center bus for the weekend. We stayed at The Nievesol (snow-sun), a small hotel where dinner was served on Spanish time at 9:00 p.m. My hungry boys couldn't wait that long to eat, so I always brought along a loaf of bread and peanut butter and jelly to pacify them until dinnertime. Since they didn't like the taste of Spanish milk, I tied a half-gallon of regular American milk to the ski rack on the car when I drove up on Friday then placed it outside the hotel window to keep it cold. Next to the hotel was a small, family-run bar where we passed the time drinking Gluhwein (hot-spiced wine) until dinner. The owner (the father) had never seen peanut butter, so Bruce made him a sandwich. Tasting it and passing it around to his family created quite a stir and gave us all a good laugh. They didn't like the texture of the peanut butter because it stuck to the roofs of their mouths. On our last ski visit, before we returned to the States, I took the family a jar of peanut butter and a good bottle of Scotch. Scotch was a highly regarded gift as it was quite expensive in Spain. Bourbon was the most expensive and hard to find in a bar. I resorted to drinking cheap (*borrato*) Spanish wine.

Other than wine, a Spanish after-dinner drink I found to be quite tasty was called a "*Sol y Sombra*," translated "sun and shade." Half cheap brandy and half anise, not mixed up, it represented the light of sun and the dark of shade. A couple of these can put you on your butt. When we attended Spanish dinners, and there were many, the Spanish wives always had a little anise after dinner (good for the digestion), and the men had brandy. Mary Gibson and I loved the *Sol y Sombra* combination. Cocktails before dinner, wine with dinner, and *Sol y Sombras* after dinner—it's a wonder we didn't all become alcoholics.

Two consecutive winters, Dave took off a few days from work—a rare event—and we took the boys skiing at Baquiera Beret on the border of France in the Pyrenees Mountains. The apartment kitchen was pretty austere, we had trouble using the cook stove, and we ate a lot of soup and sandwiches. We went to a hotel dining room for dinner one evening after a family "fight" about the boys' attire. Dave insisted they wear nice pants instead of blue jeans. We looked around the dining room and observed most of the Spaniards wearing blue jeans. Obviously, these were "well-to-do" Spaniards because blue jeans were a hot item at that time and very expensive in Europe.

The ski conditions weren't great the first time we went to Baquiera Beret; however, Bruce and I decided to ski to the base of the slopes while everyone else sensibly rode the chair lift down. I followed Bruce through some trees into some deep drifts and discovered him crawling around in the snow. I asked, "What in the world are you doing?" He had sneezed and accidentally spit out his retainer from his teeth. Unbelievable—he found it. Bruce could find a needle in a haystack. (I used to offer him five dollars to find a frequently lost earring in the house, and he always came up with it.)

One year, Dave decided our family would go to Majorca for New Year's Eve. We drove to Barcelona and spent the rest of the day sightseeing, eating greasy hamburgers and waiting for the overnight ferry.

We boarded our ferry and found our cabin—more like a closet. It had a tiny bathroom and four beds, two upper and two lower, with a one-person aisle in between. We crawled into the uncomfortable beds, and from the bunk above me, Todd announced, "I think I'm going to be sick." *Uh oh, here comes the greasy hamburger.* With that, he leaned over the bunk and hurled. I tried to catch "it" in my hands while screaming at Dave to get the bathroom wastebasket—of no use since it was wire mesh. My shoes caught some of the regurgitation; unfortunately, they were the only pair I had with me. We cleaned up the best we could with towels, and I sloshed around in wet shoes until we reached our hotel the next day.

At the hotel, we were assigned to a dinner table with all Spanish guests, so I translated for the family and went to bed every night with a "Spanish headache." Mentally exhausting! We got along okay with my Spanglish and "*muchas gracias*" to the Spaniards for their patience and graciousness with my communication struggle. We did a lot of sightseeing on the island and made it back to ZAB a few days later with no other mishaps.

I kept my bags packed for many trips in and out of the country. The fiestas in Spain are fantastic, and one of the best is Las Fallas in Valencia, held for the past two hundred years and a bit like Mardi Gras. A year is spent planning and building enormous Disney-like figures and scenes—sometimes a bit bawdy but usually having a biting political theme. The wacky part is, during the two-week fiesta, one scene is set on fire each night. Fireworks, bull fights, parades, paella cook-offs, and women and girls dressed in elaborate, expensive eighteenth-century costumes add to the daily festivities. A huge figure or scene with special meaning is built in the main plaza just for Las Fallas and is set on fire the last night of the festival. When we were there, the central figure was an enormous, beautiful Statue of Liberty. When she began to burn, I started to cry. Several Spaniards put their arms around me, consoling me with "It means *nada* (nothing)." This certainly made me feel better, but wish I'd known the reason she was the "main fire" event.

My trip to Italy with "the girls" was fun. We arrived late at the hotel, assuming the Italian dinner hour was also late like in Spain. However, searching for a restaurant around nine o'clock, we found the chairs stacked atop tables and the floors being swept. We finally found a nice little Italian restaurant where the staff kindly served us spaghetti while they cleaned.

I loved Italy. Because my mother was Italian, I decided I could easily adapt to the language, their lively spirit, and even their maddening driving habits. In Spanish, things are "*bueno*" (good), but in Italian, they are described with great gusto as "*bene, bene*" (especially good).

A highlight of the Italy trip was a tour of Pompeii. It is awesome and unbelievable that entire towns were obliterated, not by Mt. Vesuvius lava, but from gases produced by the explosion of the mountain. Casts were made of human and animal vacuums in death repose—a gruesome sight.

One summer, the baseball staff had difficulty recruiting volunteer coaches, and I said, "I can do this!" I had no idea what I was getting into, and two colonels' wives declared I was putting myself in a "conflict of interest" situation because of my husband's rank and position. Well, that made it only more of a challenge, so I became the coach of a six- and seven-year-olds' tee-ball team. What an experience. I drafted a teenage boy to help me with practices, and another mother became my manager.

One little boy threw the ball so hard the other players dodged it rather than try to catch it, so I put him on first base. We had the typical little right fielder who picked grass and filled his glove, totally unaware of the game. The first time this same boy hit the ball off the tee, he ran all over the infield, as I shouted, "Run to first!" Finally I asked him, "Where's first?" He shrugged his shoulders. He didn't know, so we had a drill, repeatedly naming first, second, third, and home plate, which solved the problem. Another little guy was so uncoordinated his parents hadn't bought him a ball glove not knowing if he was right-handed or left-handed. I felt sorry for him and gave him lots of encouragement. He never missed a practice. He *finally* hit the ball off the tee in one game. Per the rules, I stood by home plate. If the batter hit the ball, I (or another adult) was to remove the tee in case a player ran for home plate. In my excitement over this player hitting the ball, I grabbed his hand and ran with him to first base, his feet barely touching the ground. He was safe, but because I didn't "pull" the tee, he was ruled out. I felt badly, but no one cared. That little guy was one happy ballplayer in his moment of glory; he hit the ball. To him, it was as good as a home run.

To this day, Dave has never forgiven me for not accepting an invitation to the Paris Air Show. My team was undefeated with one remaining game—the same weekend as the air show. We won that last game, my players were the champions, and we celebrated with a picnic in our backyard. Those little guys will always have a special place in my heart, and I hope they fondly remember those first baseball days. I wondered why Bruce or Todd didn't assist me with the team. They probably didn't want to hear me "barking orders"—they heard enough of that at home.

Being the chapel youth choir director was another challenge I inflicted upon myself. When I took Todd to choir practice one afternoon after school, the pianist asked if I could help since she couldn't play the piano and lead the children in song at the same time. I stayed, helped, and found myself still "helping" the next two years. I could barely carry a tune, much less direct. A pencil was my baton, and I selected easy songs. I really didn't care how we sounded. What was important was the kids were in God's house, singing his songs.

Mother came for the holidays in December 1976, our last Christmas in Spain. It was her first Christmas since Daddy died, and I didn't want her to be alone. She had a badly broken arm in an immobilizer, an apparatus that kept her arm strapped to her body. We talked her into going with Bruce, Todd, and me to Formigal ski area. What were we thinking? How bored and lonesome she must have been in the hotel all day by herself, and to make matters worse, she was coming down with a cold. Unknown to us, the hotel shut off the heat in the rooms during the day, so she stayed in bed. Luckily, with her Italian language background, she communicated her needs to the Spanish maids who brought her extra blankets and orange juice. I'm sure she had a miserable time.

In 1977, we had been in Spain for five years, at ZAB for three of those years. Our relatives and friends in the U.S. thought we were never coming back! Since we had been to the U.S. only once, when Daddy died, *we were all ready to go home.* The boys had finished tenth and eighth grades, and I was eager to get them into good schools in the U.S. The two-star general from 16th Air Force Headquarters at Torrejon AB visited our base and confided to me that Dave was going to be asked to stay one more year. I told him, "Fine, but the rest of the family is going home." When asked about extending for another year, Dave answered, "Thanks, but no thanks." Thank goodness, "bucking the system" didn't seem to have any negative repercussions.

Dave received his new assignment to Langley AFB in Hampton, Virginia, on the southern peninsula of Chesapeake Bay. We were leaving the mountains and high plains for the beach and water.

We were honored with numerous farewell parties, including some hosted by the Spanish officers. The Spanish ladies presented me with a beautiful, hand-embroidered, linen tablecloth. While I graciously admired it, my scant knowledge of Spanish enabled me to understand a *señora* say under her breath, "Wait until you have to iron it." I have fond memories of *las señoras* who were so nice to me. They told me they understood my English *and* my Spanish because they "read" my eyes and animated facial expressions. In the days before we were packed, I frantically shopped for Spanish artifacts and souvenirs that, of course, I just couldn't live without.

Dave took his last flight in the F-4 fighter plane. It was traditional for the departing pilot to be met by the fire truck, sprayed with water from the fire hose, and presented a bottle of champagne. Gleefully, the boys and I joined some of the other pilots for this celebration, and Bruce and Todd had the dubious honor of spraying their dad with the hose. In the tussle for the hose, they got as wet as Dave. Before we left, the Spanish three-star general awarded Dave a huge medal—in importance and size—the *Cruz del Merito Aeronautico con Distintivo Blanco* (Cross of Aeronautical Merit with White Distinction), a prestigious award. Dave was honored.

Our Spanish adventures bring a smile to my face. I loved the cheap (*borrato*) vino, the happy (*feliz*) people, all the marvelous fiestas, the bloody bullfights, and the Spanish spirit. A young man in my Spanish language class asked the teacher if Spaniards ever slept, because it seemed there was always something happening or being celebrated, day and night. I can hardly believe how busy I was at ZAB. What a super woman, wife, and mother I tried to be. I hope all I accomplished benefited my family and the base. I certainly have wonderful memories.

We sold the Peugeot station wagon to Todd's English teacher. We packed our bags, Dave limiting us to one suitcase each as usual, put ten-year-old-ugly-but-smart, Spanish sheepdog Hazel in her shipping crate, and we were driven to the Zaragoza Airport for the flight to Madrid. Much to our surprise, several Spanish officers were at the airport to bid us *adios*. While Dave and I were busy checking in and conversing, I delegated Bruce and Todd to take care of Hazel outside the terminal. When boarding time was imminent, I called them inside to put Hazel in the crate, and in the middle of the lobby, she "dumped." The distinguished and honored colonel wiped up the dog poop with paper towels, looking somewhat chagrined and undistinguished.

We flew to Madrid's Barajas Airport for our flight across the big pond to New York City's J.F. Kennedy Airport. The Torrejon Air Base protocol office had upgraded us to first class, so we wined and dined our way across the ocean in the lap of luxury, relaxing comfortably in plush, reclining seats. First class is the only way to go on long flights, but unfortunately, we've done it only once since. Poor Hazel was stuck in cargo.

Back to the land of round doorknobs, fast food, and teenage drivers, inches instead of meters, pounds instead of kilos, miles instead of kilometers, and quarts instead of liters. Lacking mathematical skills, I never quite figured out those measurements. I knew a meter was thirty-nine inches, a kilo was a little over two pounds, one hundred kph was about sixty-two miles per hour, and a liter was slightly more than a quart. Shopping was going to be a lot easier.

Adios, mis amigos español (Good-bye, my Spanish friends).
Muchos recuerdos (A lot of memories).

Garbage Can Command

Hampton, Virginia
Langley Air Force Base
Tactical Air Command Headquarters
July 1977-July 1979
(Dave reassigned to The Pentagon, January 1979)

After a deluxe flight across the big pond, we landed at New York City's J. F. Kennedy Airport, where everyone spoke English! Wrong! We heard so many foreign languages spoken in the terminal it was easy to forget where we were. We collected our luggage and looked for Hazel, shipped as "excess baggage." She became a no-show, and we began to panic! Airline Customer Service made some calls, but she still wasn't found, and we feared she'd been left in Spain. We had only two hours to spare before catching our next flight to Detroit (where we were to pick up our new, 1977 gold Pontiac sedan), so Dave called his father in Sarasota to help find Hazel. The four of us, sad and distraught, boarded our flight sans Hazel. I was in tears and just knew we'd never see our Spanish sheepdog again. Embarrassed as the boys were to be seen with Hazel, she was family, and they were quiet the entire flight—no complaining, no arguing, no laughing.

We landed again, plodded through bag drag number four, and called Dave's dad. Good news. He found Hazel at the SPCA.

Since no one had claimed her at the airport—yeah, right, like we didn't try?—she was shipped off to the SPCA. They fed and bathed her and put her on a plane to Sarasota. We all cheered and headed for Sarasota in our new car. After driving small cars in Spain for five years, the Pontiac felt spacious and luxurious. The Forgan grandparents retrieved Hazel at the Sarasota airport and put her in a kennel because dogs were not allowed in their retirement community. More trauma for the poor animal.

We drove into Sarasota several days later and reunited with all the relatives. Dave's Aunt Grace and Uncle Fred and Aunt May, all from California, and Mother from Oklahoma flew to Florida to welcome us home. Dave's dad rented condos for all of us. It was relaxing after the previous hectic weeks of farewell socials and move preparations. The boys enjoyed the beach and American TV. For the next several years, we watched reruns of shows we had missed in their original airing.

After a week, the relatives reluctantly returned home; we packed for bag drag number five, collected Hazel at the kennel, and marveled how she had survived ten days without her family. We were mutually overjoyed to see each other. Her little fifteen-pound body curled up in my lap, and she slept peacefully on the drive to Virginia. I was so happy to have her back that I vowed never to call her ugly again. She was now labeled "Super Survivor Dog."

We drove to Hampton, Virginia, and entered Langley AFB, a beautiful base with tree-lined streets and large, stately brick homes. Dave checked us into temporary two-bedroom family quarters, and we struggled with bag drag number six.

The housing office assigned us to colonel's quarters; however, we had a three-week wait before we could take occupancy. Packing again (bag drag number seven), we moved into a motel with a kitchenette. I started looking for Hazel—no one could find her—and we realized, to our horror, that we'd left her in the bedroom at the base. Todd and I raced in the car to retrieve her and found her still under our bed, asleep. Was she beginning to think we wanted to get rid of her?

Shortly before school began, we had bag drag number eight into our new quarters—a large, two-story, Tudor-style brick home with a full basement, living room, sunroom, large dining room, small kitchen, and maid's quarters, which we used for a TV room since *no maid* was included. The upstairs had three bedrooms and another sunroom, which Dave used for his office. After our small houses in Spain, this looked like a mansion. Rank was finally generating its privileges.

Dave's new job as Director of Programs at Tactical Air Command Headquarters meant he and his staff determined the type of fighter airplanes needed in the future and where to place them. He was disappointed to be "flying a desk" again, but he wasn't alone; several other newly-assigned colonels were "flying desks" too. I wondered if Langley AFB was the garbage can for all ex-wing commanders.

The school situation was disappointing. Because of desegregation, the all-black Pembroke High School student enrollment was divided, and half the students were distributed and bused to the other four area schools, making all the schools integrated. Langley AFB was rezoned, requiring all high school students living on base to attend Pembroke. We investigated a private school, Hampton Roads Academy (HRA), for both boys; however, Bruce was determined to go to Pembroke because he had already met several students. Todd's academic test results didn't qualify him for HRA's ninth grade program, so he had to repeat eighth grade; however, since he didn't know anyone at the school and we didn't tell Bruce, no stigma was attached to him repeating the grade.

We enrolled Bruce in the eleventh grade at Pembroke and were pleased with their system. The courses were numbered one to five with numbers four and five designated college preparatory, grouping students by ability levels. Bruce attended football practice, but his previous shoulder injury flared up. The doctor said Bruce would need surgery if he wanted to play football, to which Bruce replied, "No, thank you," and skipped sports his junior year. He joined the golf team his senior year and did well for not having played consistently through the years. His lowest score in a tournament was seventy-four.

Todd had a difficult time adjusting to HRA. Most of the students had been schooled together since kindergarten, and it was tough for a new kid to break in. (Years later, he told me he felt sick at his stomach every school day morning.) The academics were difficult, and he was under a lot of pressure, but he never complained. The headmaster wasn't pleased with Todd's low grades because it lowered their school grade point average, which was very high in national rankings. One classmate befriended him, and I occasionally drove Todd to his house for weekend get-togethers or sleepovers.

Todd missed the ZAB youth center activities, and with little to do on weekends, he started getting into mischef. Bruce had given me gray hair on half my head; now Todd was "coloring" the other half. He and some other boys moved a Volkswagen from a residential driveway onto the street. Another night they removed several fire extinguishers from boats at the Yacht Club and had a grand ole' time spraying each other. Catching sight of the base security police driving nearby, they threw the extinguishers into some bushes and sat on the curb looking like innocent little angels when the police asked what they were doing.

I had a difficult time deciding appropriate punishment for these "criminal acts." Grounding him only exacerbated the problem—nothing to do but watch TV. He needed a hobby. Sports helped occupy Todd's time—playing football, baseball, and soccer at HRA—keeping *me* busy driving one hour round trip to all the practices and games.

Todd's next fiasco almost got us kicked out of base housing. Dave and I had gone to a picnic with his office personnel and their spouses. In our absence, Todd and two friends got caught by the base security police shooting Dave's 22 rifle out the window of our house. I was devastated. What was happening to the sweet little boy who had never given me any trouble? The three boys were put on probation and sentenced to weekly meetings with a social worker for one year. Those meetings lasted about ten minutes and consisted of, "How is school?" "Fine." "Are you getting along with your parents?" "Yes." "Anything you want to tell me?" "No." Ludicrous. Dave sold the gun, and Todd was grounded! He walked on eggshells the rest of our time at Langley.

Another downer was the notification that our good friend and Dave's former commander at ZAB, Dick Skelton, had died of a heart attack in Germany. When landing the two-seater F-4 at Spangdahlem Air Base, the plane began to yaw; the navigator in the backseat grabbed the stick, brought the plane to a stop on the runway, and radioed the tower that something had happened to Colonel Skelton. They tried to revive him, but Dick had died instantly. His wife, Pat, was on a wives' club bus trip to Belgium when she was notified of her husband's demise. Poor Pat, and the rest of the wives, spent several agonizing hours on the bus, returning to Spangdahlem. I'm sure the silence on the bus was interrupted only by the sounds of weeping. Per the family's request, Dave flew to Germany to escort them to Roanoke, Virginia. Bruce and Todd, friends with Julie and Clay Skelton at ZAB, accompanied me to the funeral service—a sad time.

I thought the "move-have-an-injury curse" had dissipated, but Bruce provoked the first trip to the ER. He and Jennifer, his new girlfriend, were horsing around with glasses of water at her home. She started to throw some water on Bruce, and he stuck his hand out to stop her. The glass broke, cutting a four-inch slash up his arm. Jennifer called me, and when I unwrapped the blood-soaked towel, I saw the wound was bad and raced him to the hospital. In the exam room, the doctor instructed Bruce to move each finger to see if any tendons were cut. A lower arm muscle was visible, and I watched it move up and down with each finger movement. Fascinated, I remarked, "Wow, look at that." The doc abruptly asked, "Who are you?" When I told him, "Bruce's mother," he couldn't believe I had the stomach to watch. However, when they began stitching the cut, I departed. Bruce was lucky no damage was done to any nerves, tendons, muscles, or arteries.

After a rough beginning, our holidays were brightened by Mother coming for Thanksgiving and Christmas. The boys enjoyed her visits, and Todd especially liked to tease her. The Forgans made their usual trek to join us for Christmas. We were one happy family, together again for the holidays and back on U.S. soil. Todd was on his good behavior, charming the grandparents as usual, who thought he could do no wrong. Had they known the truth, they would have been shocked, but I was not about to disillusion them.

That first winter, Frances and Jim LaVigne, from Toronto, invited us to join them for a ski week at Snowmass, Colorado. As usual, Dave canceled because of work, and I went solo. Flying into the Denver airport, I took a numbered ticket for a flight to Aspen and waited for my number to be called. Waited and waited and read and read and then fell asleep. When I awoke, the waiting area was empty. I dashed to the counter and showed my ticket— number eighty-nine—which hadn't been called. The attendant took the ticket, turned it right side up, and said sixty-eight had been called and that plane was long gone. One last flight to Aspen was about to depart, luckily with an available seat.

I had a difficult time locating the LaVignes in Snowmass Village, lugging my suitcase, ski boot bag, and skis up and down ice-packed stairs with the help of a taxi driver. I was tired, hungry, and frustrated. From a restaurant, I finally called a telephone number they had given me, and with the help of a stranger, trudged my way to the condo.

We were up early every morning, first in line at the ski lift. My eyes were barely open. They wasted no time—first ones up and last ones down. Frances and Jim were vacationing with other Canadians friends, who were all avid skiers. I did my best to keep up, but most of the time, I was on the edge of disaster, kissing the snowy ground every afternoon, thankful to have survived another day. Struggling, I followed the extremely enthusiastic group of Canadians and managed to successfully ski my first double-black diamond run. That was one of the most difficult runs I ever attempted in my thirty-four years of skiing. Maybe the wine packed with our lunches gave me such courage and false sense of security. I made it back to Langley AFB, happy to be alive.

My passion for skiing did not diminish after the harrowing days at Snowmass. I continued to ski at Wintergreen, a small resort in Virginia four hours away. I became a trip leader on chartered buses to Wintergreen. I met the bus at a shopping mall at 5:00 a.m., arrived at Wintergreen at 9:00 a.m., skied the day, boarded the bus at 5:00 p.m., arrived back at the mall by 9:00 p.m., and got home about 9:30 p.m. All that to get a free day of skiing.

Dave joined us for a two-family ski weekend at Wintergreen. I had previously broken my thumb while skiing and had a cast up to my elbow, but I was able to gradually twist my arm to hold a ski pole in that hand. For warmth, I wore one of Dave's ski gloves, large enough to fit over the cast. As the plaster cast got cold, it conducted the cold to my arm, and the pain was terrible—like having my arm in a bucket of ice, unable to remove it. I was in tears until Todd had the ingenious idea of using my hair dryer to blow warm air into the cast. Ah, what a relief! He saved the day! Thereafter, I skied until the cast grew cold then headed to the rental house to warm both arm and cast and returned to the slopes. Thankfully, the ski area was small, and the house was easily accessible for my "emergency" trips.

To provide more quality family time and keep Todd occupied on weekends, Dave purchased a twenty-five-foot boat in the summer of 1978. We envisioned the boys water skiing, fishing, relaxing, and swimming. Wrong. Two weeks after purchasing the boat and ski supplies, hordes of jellyfish filled the bay, ending thoughts of getting in the water. Bruce decided to make a final effort, wearing socks, gloves, and nylon pants and a jacket with elastic around the ankles and wrists. He slid into the water, and we quickly threw him the ski rope. He thought he'd evaded the jellyfish, but as he grabbed the rope, his wrist was exposed, and a jellyfish stung him. Thereafter, we just fished or cruised.

The crabs liked to latch on to our fishing bait, making the boys think they had a fish. They'd reel in, but the crab let go of the bait just as it surfaced. It became a game to see if the boys could hurl the crabs into our boat before they let go. Succeeding several times, they roared with laughter as I screamed, "If one of those crabs lands on top my head, you'll see me walk on water!" Dave was very particular about *his* boat, getting grumpy if we weren't neat and hollering at us for minor infractions. We started calling him Captain Queeg and renamed the vessel "the D--- Boat." Weekend excursions became less inviting or enjoyable.

The LaVignes visited in the summer of '78 with their daughters, Karen and Leanne. We enjoyed the boat outings, and Bruce—no longer without a driver's license— "was volunteered" to take everyone to the movie. On the way home, Leanne decided to teach Todd how to play "Chinese Fire Drill." When Bruce stopped at a traffic light, Todd and Leanne exited the backseat, ran around the rear of the car, and got back in on the other side. Bruce yelled at them, ordering them to quit or he would leave them. *They didn't and he did.* When Bruce and Karen arrived home without Todd and Leanne, I ordered Bruce to retrieve them. He found them sitting on the curb where he left them, not the least bit concerned. The LaVigne daughters and our sons kept our lives interesting.

The summer vacation was too short, but I was happy to get the boys back in school where their daily lives—and mine—were more organized. The HRA headmaster had sent us a letter, stating he didn't think it was a good idea for Todd to return for ninth grade. Angry, I had a little tête-à-tête with the school guru, reminding him of his statement that Todd, as a newcomer, would probably need a year to adjust to their high academic standards and requirements and become socially comfortable. I pleaded with him to give Todd a chance to improve during his second year, knowing we probably would be transferred the third year. He relented but required Todd to write him a letter, stating the reasons he wanted to return. Todd's grades improved slightly that year, and as I predicted, we were reassigned. I'm sure the headmaster was glad to be rid of us.

Autumn was peaceful until the day I lost June Eddins's son's suit at the mall, where it was being altered at the department store. I had to buy him another suit, race back to the base, and while her son showered, June hemmed one pants leg as I hemmed the other. We tied the last knot, and he was only thirty minutes late for his date. My own son didn't attend the homecoming dance, but it cost *me* $80. Dave was not too kind when he saw the checkbook, but June graciously continued our friendship. She and I chuckle every time we recall some of our own "war stories."

Early fall I had received a call from the wife of Dave's boss. She asked me to chair the officers' club decoration committee for the Christmas holidays. How do you tell a general's wife that you don't want to do it? I reluctantly and fearfully accepted the challenge. The club was large with lots of rooms—a big responsibility! I selected a "Joy to the World" theme and researched various countries' Christmas traditions, discovering the longest way to say Merry Christmas in any language is Hungarian: *Kellemeskaracsonyi Unnepeket Kivanok.*

I met with my committee, the officers' wives representing each military unit on base, and they each chose a room for their unit wives to decorate. The result was spectacular. The Japanese tree was decorated with origami birds, fans, and tinsel. The Swiss tree had straw ornaments. We strung the German tree with artificial candle lights and placed an Advent wreath on the door and a cornucopia on a table. With their husbands' help, one group built a large English Yule log, decorated the walls with Della Robbia garland, and painted a wall scene depicting the "Twelve Days of Christmas." Mexico was represented by a piñata, pots of poinsettias, scattered luminaries, and a *Feliz Navidad* greeting sign. Another oriental tree was hung with bread dough figures and Chinese lanterns, and a children's tree was decorated with youthful ornaments and toys from Santa Claus. A "Festival of Lights" wall hanging represented Hanukkah. A huge papier-mâché globe painted with continents and countries hung from the foyer ceiling, and a large Joy to the World sign was tacked over the club's entrance.

Only one problem occurred. When the base four-star general, Tactical Air Command commander, commented how much he liked a tree in one of the rooms, his aide exchanged trees, placing the general's favorite in the general's private dining room. It didn't belong there and disrupted the rooms' themes. I called the aide and told him to put the trees back where they belonged but discovered you can't argue with a general or his aide. The trees stayed in their misplaced locations.

Personnel informed a surprised Dave that he was being considered for the wing commander at George AFB in Victorville, California—a very desirous job—commanding a large flying wing comprised of five squadrons of F-4 fighter planes and one squadron of F-105 fighters. *He would fly again.* They called back, asking if he would rather command the wing or be assigned to the Pentagon. He shouted, "Are you kidding? Definitely the wing." He was notified he passed all the interviews and would take command of the wing in January 1979.

Poor Bruce, this move would be in the middle of his senior year, and he wasn't happy about it. We couldn't blame him; it was a rotten situation for him to accept. We considered letting him stay at Langley with another family until graduation, but we couldn't come to grips with that decision. We raved about George AFB—the Pacific Ocean only one and a half hours west and Las Vegas about two and a half hours northeast. We did not tell them it was out in the middle of a desert with frequent, nasty sandstorms. With Dave as the commander, we'd probably get to meet Roy Rogers, whose ranch was in nearby Apple Valley. Bruce wasn't the least bit thrilled. Todd was happy to escape HRA. We sold the "D--- Boat" and prepared for our western adventure. "Happy

Trails to You," "Whoopi ti yi yo," and off we go. We had been at Langley only one and a half years.

On Friday before the packers were to come on Monday, Dave called and said, "Sit down. I have news." My first thought was *Who died?* I wasn't far from wrong because the news was deadly. We weren't going to California after all. Someone decided Dave should go to the Pentagon again—so much for asking him what *he* wanted. The process of making assignments was a puzzle. I had been looking forward to a new adventure in the west—no rush hour traffic, no expensive house payments because we would live on base. I also looked forward to being "the first lady" of George AFB. On the other hand, in a Virginia suburb, I would be free of military spouse responsibilities, and Todd would be in Fairfax County's good school system. I kept reminding myself that military families should remain flexible with a sense of humor. I was being tested!

Dave had to report right away in January 1979, and the boys and I were left up the creek without a paddle. Since Dave was making a permanent change of station, we were *persona non gratis* for base housing, and they refused my request to live on base for the next six months until Bruce graduated from high school.

The good ole' air force support system failed us this time. We finished our packing, with a different destination, and had everything put in storage except what we needed to survive in a townhouse outside the base. We had not needed a second car at Langley because Dave walked to work, so he bought a cheap, little Chevy Monza to take with him. He rented a furnished apartment near the Pentagon, and we parted ways. In 1967, when he was a major, his parking area was about a half-mile from the building. As a colonel, he could park a couple hundred yards from the entrance. Things were looking up. *For him.*

For the next six months, we survived in the townhouse without Dave. Actually, mealtimes were easier for the three of us, and life was more relaxed. For extra spending money, Bruce worked as a part-time cook/dishwasher at a small Mexican restaurant located outside the base entrance. Without any military spouse responsibilities, I stayed busy with the boys' activities, skied the rest of the winter, and played a lot of bridge.

Bruce turned eighteen in May 1979 and wanted to have a birthday dinner party at our townhouse with no adult supervision. I didn't approve of one of his friends—didn't know him, just didn't like his looks. I told Bruce he could have the party if I approved the guest list, and the fellow I didn't like would not be included. He stubbornly stated, "In that case, I won't have a party." His choice. Bruce's stubborn streak grew stronger his senior year, and I became just as unbendable. The old adage "the irresistible force meets the immovable object" was in play many times.

June arrived with seniors excited about their final school activities at Pembroke High School. The white students lacked school spirit, complaining the blacks dominated the music and activities, but several capable student leaders in Bruce's class decided they wanted a memorable senior year. They organized, planned, and attended all the activities, creating good senior memories.

Baccalaureate and graduation concluded the senior events. Dave broke away from his Pentagon duties in time for the celebration. The Forgan grandparents didn't come because Doc wasn't feeling well, and for some strange reason, my mother declined to attend or explain why. I never dreamed she would miss her grandson's graduation. Dave's Aunt Peg and Uncle Glen Forgan and cousin Mac came from Houston, so a few Forgans attended, and we ended up with a memorable photo of six Forgan men together. Doc wasn't there, but I copied the photo with another picture of Doc superimposed.

We hosted a party at the townhouse, and I composed and sent the following invitation to several other graduates' parents:

TGIO!
(Thank God, it's over.)
The kids have grown up.
It brings tears to our eyes.

After twelve years of suffering,
We *all* can breathe sighs.
When the speeches are over
And the grads have run,
It is time for the parents
To have some fun!
We shall pop a few corks
On June 7, the date.
Please come to the Forgans
To help celebrate!

School mementos, golf clubs, yearbooks, a furry bedspread, wood and brick bookshelves, model airplanes he had built and crashed, his stereo, large speakers, and earphones—they all bring back wonderful memories as I dust Bruce's room. That all-male aura in the room—is it shaving lotion or sweaty sneakers? I move a sports team picture, and underneath it is a college brochure. I stare at it in dismay. He'll soon leave us, and what will I clean from his room then? Just dust. I ached to turn back the clock and see a little blonde head in the crib. Those days were gone.

When school dismissed at HRA, we thumbed our noses at the headmaster, and Todd and I visited the northern Virginia suburbs of Washington D.C. to search for a Forgan family house. It boggled my mind to face a $100,000 purchase price, heavy traffic, a long commute to the Pentagon, crowded commissaries, and about 2,400 students in each high school. Frightening. A good air force wife, I took three deep breaths and pressed on. The real estate agent said we looked at a record number of houses he had shown in one day. Having selected a couple of schools I preferred for Todd, I restricted my house search to those areas. I finally settled on a lovely house in Fairfax with a large, beautifully landscaped yard. Had I taken more time, I might have found something more appealing in a friendlier neighborhood; however, after seeing so many houses, my brain was saturated, and I made my decision by the process of elimination.

We returned to Hampton, the movers came again, and we

cleaned the townhouse before making the short drive to northern Virginia. The townhouse owner refused to refund our security deposit, stating we left the house a mess—fingerprints on the walls, not vacuumed, and the toilet full of cigarettes. After the movers left, the boys and I had wiped down all the walls with Miracle 409, I borrowed a vacuum cleaner to clean the carpet, and as for the cigarettes in the toilet, *none of us smoked.* I was livid. The principle mattered to me more than the money involved.

We didn't have any sad farewells from Langley; we had a good time but added only the Elys to our Christmas card list and continued our friendship with the Eddins. They were there when we arrived and were still there when we left two years later.

This was the first of three times we played catch up with Dave and his assignments—when he moved alone and we came later. This first separation had been six months long. Little did I know in 1979 what lay ahead. I was sure we'd spend the next three years in Fairfax, and I'd promised Todd he'd get his last three years of high school in one school.

"The best laid plans of mice and men…"

Mrs. General Forgan

Fairfax, Virginia
The Pentagon
July 1979-July 1981
(Dave reassigned to Fort Bragg, North Carolina, September 1980)

We moved into our new house and met the neighbors on one side. They had two teenagers and invited Todd to ride with them to W.T. Woodson High School in the fall. Our neighbors on the other side were very quiet and unsociable—a cemetery. Huge evergreen trees separated us. In all good humor, I claimed I took flowers from the graves for my dinner table centerpieces. Bruce attempted to fly his remote-controlled airplanes on the roadway through the cemetery because there were no power lines or traffic to interfere with the flight paths but was chased away by the caretaker who said it was a disturbance. Bruce couldn't understand how he could disturb the dead. I explained he wasn't disturbing the dead but the people visiting their deceased loved ones. He still huffed about it.

I never met any neighbors who lived down the street, and woods were across the street, so we were somewhat isolated. Our lot was on a very sharp curve in the road, and our curbside mailbox was demolished several times by errant cars. One car didn't make the curve and ended up on its side in our front yard, taking out a small tree and bush. Thankfully, our house was situated far back on the lot, out of potential danger. We became accustomed to cars screeching around the curve.

Bruce concentrated on college plans. He didn't know where he wanted to go, but he didn't want to stay at home and attend a local school. He wanted to spread his wings and get away from his parents. Our legal residence was in Florida where we qualified for in-state tuition, but, unfortunately, Bruce wasn't interested. He applied to the School of Architecture at the University of Colorado, his dad's alma mater, but they would accept him only in the School of Business—not to Bruce's liking. I suggested he call James Lane in McAlester, a friend from previous visits. James and several of his friends were going to Oklahoma State University, and James needed a roommate. Done deal. I was thrilled he was going to my alma mater, and on the short vacation breaks, he could go to Mother's house in McAlester. He also was accepted into the School of Architecture at OSU. Ha! That'll show you, CU.

Pulling a U-Haul loaded with Bruce's clothes, posters, pictures, towels, bed sheets, comforter, and stereo equipment, we drove to McAlester. James came to Mother's house and said he was going to an orientation for the First Baptist Church summer camp. Having read the camp brochure James sent him earlier—very strict dress code and separate swimming times for the boys and girls—Bruce had said, "No, thank you," but he went to the orientation anyway. Two hours later, he raced through Mother's back door, yelling, "I need a Bible and a pillow!" He'd met a cute girl at the meeting and suddenly decided to attend church camp. He returned to McAlester a week later, still not heavenly spirited.

After driving three hours to Stillwater, Oklahoma, we deposited Bruce into a dorm room with James. Leaving our firstborn on his own for the first time in his life, I was sure he couldn't survive without his mother. I thought about all the things I should have taught him. Did I show him how to do laundry so he wouldn't end up with pink underwear? Did I tell him about the dangers of driving if he'd been drinking? I mailed him a cartoon that read,

"Hello, Bruce Darling. This is Momma. I just called to see what you are doing and tell you to stop it."

The family, minus one son, returned to Fairfax, and I enrolled Todd in high school. Poor fellow, he'd attended small schools all his life, and as a sophomore, he now faced integrating into a swarm of 2,300 students, not knowing a single one. We were soon inundated with female phone calls, but Todd seemed to be "lost." He checked into playing football, which was big in the area, but so were the players. He told me, "There's no way I'm playing football here; they'll kill me."

School was out at two, and Todd came home with nothing to do. Most of the kids hung out at the mall after school, but I quickly squelched that idea. Determined to stop his idle time, I issued an ultimatum: find an after-school activity or get a part-time job. Time passed with no productivity on his part. When he strolled in from school one day, I ordered him to the car, saying, "We're looking for work and not coming home until we find something." We spent a lot of gas, energy, and time, enduring wear and tear on tires and my nerves, hearing negative responses from possible employers. The next-to-last opportunity was a nice restaurant three blocks from our house. Success. Todd was hired as a busboy. Across from the restaurant was a veterinarian's clinic, where we made a last ditch effort. Success again. Todd was hired to work at the vet's every day after school, all day Saturday, and every other Sunday and "bus" at the restaurant Friday nights. Todd received his driver's license that fall, but his work hours left only Saturday nights for socializing.

In November 1979, Dave informed me of his new assignment—still at the Pentagon but one he couldn't discuss, and I was not to question. The first three months he worked nights and came home to sleep during the day. He virtually disappeared from the air force for five months. Todd and I, holding down the fort at home, were kept in the dark. We certainly knew something was *Top Secret* but had no clue what it was until April 1980.

Thanksgiving-time rolled around with Bruce not at home

to celebrate the holiday for the first time in his life. He went to Mother's, and she prepared manicotti instead of turkey. Bruce loved Nonna's manicotti, and she loved cooking for someone besides herself.

Bruce returned to school and succumbed to the predictable Forgan boys' injury curse. Sitting on his bed with his right hand propped up on the door frame, someone closed the door, smashing three of his fingers. At the university medical clinic he received stitches and painkillers (later losing two fingernails). The injury handicapped his ability to complete architectural projects, but, thankfully, instructors gave him some extra time.

Bored at home while Todd was in school and working and Dave was spending long, strange hours at the Pentagon, I searched for a job. Answering a newspaper ad, I was hired for part-time work in a ski travel office, and I use *office* loosely. It was in an old building's basement with two crummy rooms equipped with desks, chairs, telephones, and typewriters. A bathroom and large room were at the end of the hall where the owner slept on a sofa. Ski trips to Killington, Vermont, were advertised around the northeast U.S., and I took phone reservations. It appeared legitimate, but the operation seemed a little shady, and the owner was definitely weird. I received several complaints by letter and phone regarding a few ski trips. I handed the complaints to the owner—his problems, not mine—but I think he ignored them.

In December, we were happy to have Bruce home again for Christmas, and the Forgan grandparents joined us. Grandpa Doc was not feeling well but never complained. Unfortunately, it was our last time to be with him.

After Christmas, I arranged for Bruce to wait tables in a hotel dining room in Rutland, Vermont, the hotel co-owned by my ski office employer. I volunteered as trip leader for a ski bus to Killington Ski Resort, staying in the nearby Rutland Hotel.

Todd came along, and the bus driver picked up skiers in Virginia, Washington, D.C., and Pittsburg, Pennsylvania, arriving at the hotel at 6:00 a.m. I was shocked; the place was a real dump. I finally aroused a very sleepy young girl to show me the room assignments—totally unacceptable. She had placed an older couple with a young couple and newlyweds with an unmarried twosome. I had a mutiny on my hands. Several passengers refused to stay, and while I helped them find other accommodations, the bus driver unloaded the luggage onto the sidewalk. People bailing out retrieved their luggage and left. Though unhappy, those who stayed were assigned to more appropriate rooms. The teenagers were assigned to a third floor dorm-style arrangement. That was asking for trouble.

When I found time to retrieve my luggage, both the bus and my suitcase were gone. Distraught, I asked one of the men on the trip to be responsible for the skiers on the return trip, and he agreed. I stayed the night and left for Virginia the next morning with the bus driver and a very reluctant Todd, who had one day of skiing. The bus made its scheduled return the next week to bring folks back to their respective locations. Bruce worked at the hotel and skied the rest of the week.

When I returned to the ski office, I found several letters of complaints with demands for refunds piled on my desk and irate phone messages. A few complaints would have been funny had it not been for the horrible conditions and the money paid. A guest's bathroom had a gaping hole in the ceiling with wet and rotting exposed wooden beams. One room had a filthy rug on the floor, stained linen on the bed, rusty tap water, and roaches in the dirty bathroom. Others complained of a "bed" consisting of a mattress and springs mounted onto four blocks of wood. Carpet holes were patched with duct tape, light fixtures were missing, and banisters and handrails on the stairs were broken. Some rooms had no lights, no chests of drawers for clothes, no heat, and no private bathrooms. What a nightmare.

Soon after this fiasco, the bookkeeper told me to pick up my paycheck at the office, advising me to cash it immediately. When I arrived at the "office," repossessed typewriters, phones, and other equipment were being loaded into trucks. The owner declared bankruptcy and went across the state line into Maryland to start another ski trip office. A real scam artist, he had nothing to show for it, living like a pauper. An eye-opening experience.

At breakfast one morning in April, Todd and I heard the TV news describing an attempted hostage rescue mission in Iran. "Now we know what Dad has been doing!" I let him skip school that day, as we stayed glued to the TV, watching military history being made.

An elite U.S. military force launched a bold but doomed attempt to rescue fifty-three American citizens from captivity in Tehran. In the early hours of April 25, the mission was aborted and ended in a fiery disaster at a remote spot in Iran. A helicopter repositioning itself slid sideways into a C-130, igniting a raging fire, resulting in the deaths of five U.S. Air Force men and three Marines. Dave had assisted with the rescue plans and then helped write the press release, delivering it to the Secretary of Defense at the White House to be read by President Carter. It was Dave's first and last visit to the White House, and he wished the circumstances had been better. The failure haunted the U.S. military for years. Twenty years later, an article appeared in the January 1999 issue of *Air Force Magazine,* which Dave says is accurate.

On May 2, 1980, the day before my birthday, Dave's mom called to say that Doc had passed away. I called Dave at his Pentagon office, and we immediately arranged to fly to Florida. Doc had suffered from emphysema for years, and his heart finally gave out. I recall thinking, *Was there something special I should have said to him the previous Christmas? Should I have been kinder and more thoughtful?*

Did he know how much we loved him? I regretted not being able to say, "Good-bye," and, "Thank you for being in our lives."

Bruce flew from Oklahoma, and Doc's brother, Glenn, came from Houston to join us for the memorial service. Doc was cremated, and his ashes were scattered over the Gulf of Mexico waters where he had spent many hours fishing. Dave spent a few extra days in Sarasota, taking care of family business and acquainting his mother with her inherited responsibilities. It wasn't an easy task, as Doc had handled everything—including the cooking. She was now on her own. Dave arranged for the bank to handle the finances, and her only responsibility was to write checks—after Dave instructed her how. (Advice to ladies: learn early how to take care of yourselves before widowhood is thrust upon you at an unexpected time.)

A few weeks later, Dave picked up Bruce at the Washington National Airport. Oldest son was home for the summer. I ran out to greet him and almost fainted. He sported a full-grown beard, mustache, and shoulder-length hair. Any female would crave his long, beautiful, wavy hair; however, it was unacceptable on my son. He looked like Barry Gibbs of the Bee Gees or Jesus Christ, Super Star. Long hair was popular in the seventies, and we'd fought the hair battle for several years. Bruce took advantage of his college freedom and let his hair grow. I immediately made an appointment for him at a beauty salon the next day. He went but was not a happy camper. The before and after pictures of him reveal that if looks could kill I'd be dead.

Bruce worked hard, hot hours at a townhouse building site that summer. One day, a friendly lady living in one of the townhouses invited him to sit down for a glass of cold lemonade. During their conversation, he learned she had also attended Oklahoma State. Lo and behold, she was a sorority sister I had not heard from in twenty-seven years. I paid her a visit, and we had a lot of catching up to do. Small world.

That summer, Frances and Jim LaVigne came from Toronto to Fairfax, bringing daughter Leanne and her friend Kathy. After a few days, we headed for the beach at Ocean City, Maryland.

Because he was working, Bruce stayed home with Hazel. Todd commandeered a friend to drive, and the two boys and two girls left early, planning to meet us at a restaurant parking lot. While they were waiting for us to arrive, a big, mean man came out of the restaurant and demanded they immediately move the car. They explained they were waiting for their parents and would move shortly. He left, returned with a menacing blackjack in hand, kicked a dent in the car door, and then disappeared. When we arrived, the kids were upset, and I became furious. After an unproductive enounter with the police (if we pressed charges, all four kids would have to return to testify), we despondently departed.

After a delicious seafood dinner, the kids went back to the hotel, while Jim, Frances, Dave, and I sat on a curb and slurped big, delicious ice cream cones. Our second crisis for the day occurred when we returned to the hotel, relaxed after the ordeals of the day. Todd ran to our car, exclaiming that his friend and Leanne had taken Kathy to the hospital. Kathy's face had started to swell, and she was having trouble breathing. Kathy had eaten shrimp for dinner even though she knew she was allergic to shellfish. The ER attendant gave her an injection, the swelling subsided, she could breathe, and we all sighed with relief. What a day. It was always an adventure with the LaVignes—never a dull moment.

We made it back to Fairfax—safe, but thanks to the traumas, not very "sound." Jim continued his usual antics by posing as a waiter at our dinner table—a sieve on his head, a towel tucked in the front of his shorts, and a basket in his hand. Not to be outdone by her father, Leanne climbed on a chair in the upstairs hallway and lit a cigarette lighter under the smoke detector. The alarm screamed, and that's how they got Bruce and Todd out of bed, as we all raced around the house trying to find the nonexistent fire. Our Canadian friends returned to Toronto, and we took a well-deserved rest.

One weekend, Dave, the boys, and I drove to Shannon Airport near Fredericksburg, Virginia, to see a superb air show and a static display of old and new airplanes. While we sat on the grass waiting for the air show to begin, Bruce told us about an OSU class in which, for $50, a student could receive instructions and make three jumps. Of course, Dave and I wouldn't agree to such a preposterous idea. The Army's Golden Knights, a demonstration parachute team, opened the show. Two Knights began their free falls. One pulled his cord releasing his parachute, but the other Knight kept free falling. We held our breaths, thinking it was part of the act. I whispered, "Come on, open, open…"

Seconds before he hit the ground, his chute opened, fortunately covering his body. I will never forget the sound, a loud *whumph*. Stony silence hung over the hundreds of spectators; you could have heard a pin drop. Bruce turned to Dave and meekly said, "I don't think I'm going to take that jump class at school after all." The air show continued, as the announcer said it was what the soldier would have wanted; however, many people departed after the accident, and those who remained were quiet and less enthusiastic.

That summer Bruce won the debate with Dave to purchase a car for college. We bought him a '79 Ford Mustang Pace Car, meaning it had a fancy paint job to replicate a race-track pace car. He made it back to school okay, but the car soon quit running. After much haggling by Bruce with the local Ford dealership, and my ineffective trip to Oklahoma baring my fangs, the lemon car was sold "as is." In the meantime, Mother bought a new car and gave Bruce her nine-year-old '71 Pontiac LeMans with only seven thousand miles on the odometer. He had wheels again, the car performed perfectly, and because of his grandmother's generosity, Bruce didn't complain about driving an "old-fashioned car."

Todd entered the eleventh grade in the fall of 1980 and continued working his two part-time jobs.

I became bored again; there was just so much cooking, dusting, vacuuming, washing, and ironing I could do. I scanned the classified ads for part-time employment, possibly four days a week. I reserved Wednesdays for skiing at Wintergreen, the same little place we had visited from Langley; now it was *only* three hours away instead of four.

I answered an ad for work at an architectural/engineering firm in Annandale only fifteen minutes from our house. When the young lady from Human Relations (personnel) asked what my "career goals" were, I nearly fell out of my chair laughing. I replied, "Honey, I'm too old for career goals, and I don't even have a 'career.' My husband works long hours at the Pentagon, my son is gone all day, and I don't have anything to do." She said, "I think I have just the position you are looking for," and directed me to a young secretary in the Planning and Zoning Department. This young woman was trying to take care of a very demanding boss and five other workers and couldn't keep up the pace. She told me she could handle the boss if I was responsible for everyone else. I could work from nine to three, the days I specified; she was desperate. I couldn't have created a better deal and readily accepted.

I typed, answered the phone, and filed (which was weeks behind and in utter chaos), and occasionally took letter dictation from the boss. That made me nervous as my shorthand skills were rusty. The boss was a real jerk, but everyone else was very nice, especially a young landscape architect who patiently taught me the Latin names and spellings of the plants and bushes I had to type in proposals. One day the young secretary and boss went out to lunch and didn't return to the office until three o'clock. Long dessert course? (I was shocked at the sexual overtones that prevailed in the workplace.)

In late September, Dave came home from work, promptly mixed me a bourbon and water, and said, "You'd better sit down as I have some news. I'm going to Fort Bragg, North Carolina." I exclaimed, "What? Why are you going to an army post, and when will you be back?" He meekly answered, "I've been assigned there, and I'm not coming back." I gulped that bourbon and water and demanded another. "Todd and I have been here only one year!" I cried. In addition, Mom Forgan had been in a car accident and planned to recuperate at our house after her surgery. "What about your mother?" Dave answered, "Good luck."

Dave left for Fort Bragg three weeks later in his little Chevy Monza. I collected his mother at the airport, mixed us both a bourbon and water, and then gave her the same news Dave had given me. She was clearly upset. Fortunately, Dave came home a few weekends to relieve me of my "duties." Even though my work hours were from nine to three, I started going to work earlier and staying later to escape her grumbles. The company didn't mind, and since I was paid by the hour, it was a financial boost for me.

She finally decided she wasn't getting enough attention and could take care of herself in Florida where she could watch her own TV. Relieved, I gratefully drove her to the airport for her return flight home. I tried to be nice, but the situation and her behavior had really gotten on my nerves.

Dave was assigned to Fort Bragg as the deputy commander of the newly-organized Joint Special Operations Command (JSOC), acting as the liaison between the Pentagon and the command. The army commander, Major General Scholtes, had never been assigned to "Fort Fumble" (as the Pentagon was frequently called), so he depended on Dave's knowledge of its bureaucracy and what "doors to open." Work days at the Pentagon resulted in his being home frequently.

One day Dave called me at my job and announced he was on the brigadier general's promotion list. Wow. I had a hard time restraining myself. During my lunch hour, I bought a bottle of champagne and brought it back to the office. I poured everyone a glass and told them our good news. They were somewhat intimidated. One minute I was little ole' part-time employee, a "gofer," and now I was a general's wife. I believe I gained a little more respect after that.

Dave wanted to pin on the stars and go to work as he had done with his other promotions, but we didn't let him get away with it this time. His secretary arranged a small ceremony at the Pentagon. General Scholtes came from Fort Bragg, and our friends from Kansas City, Judy and "Boomer" Roberts, flew in for the celebration. General Scholtes pinned one star on Dave's shoulder, and I pinned one on the other. Todd beamed with pride. We had coffee, snacks, and a receiving line so people could pay their respects and offer congratulations.

Jean, a friend whose husband had already made general, called to congratulate *me*. She told me about the wonderful perks and benefits Dave would receive with the new rank and then asked, "Do you know what *you* get?" I eagerly anticipated something wonderful, only to hear Jean say, "You get a new mop." I cracked up laughing, later using her same line when I congratulated a new general's wife. It certainly brings one down to reality.

We planned a great promotion party at our house, and joining Judy and Boomer were guests from our first assignment in Japan, who lived nearby. Also included were our former Springfield neighbors from the sixties, military friends from former assignments, and new friends with whom Dave currently worked. Pat Skelton drove all the way from Roanoke, Virginia, to join our celebration.

I wrote the following poem and read it aloud at our party:

> There once was a pilot named Dave—
> Every weekend, good-bye, he'd wave—
> From coast to coast
> Two thousand hours he *must* post,
> While his wife would rant and rave!
> From Florida to Canada, he flew near and far.
> He spent more time in a plane than a car.
> Let's hope he stays home—
> No more to roam,
> Now he's been awarded his star!

Judy and Boomer gave Dave a T-shirt imprinted with one star and "General Forgan." They presented me with a T-shirt imprinted with "Mrs. General Forgan" and *four* stars. Knowing Jean's humorous remark, Dave followed through and gave me a new mop.

My new mop   *Dave's new star*

Boomer read the following poem:

"In General"
It's a "Forgane" conclusion,
Dobbie a four-star general
Was always meant to be.
And under her careful tutelage,
Dave, a Brigadier General
We could possibly see.
So we're not surprised
To hear the news
Of our friend who wears
The Air Force blues.
Who will give the orders?
Is the question we ask,
And who'll be the one
Brought to task?
Who will pull rank
And be the boss?
And will there be one

To gather moss?
These complexities we'll leave
At the foot of your bed
Where many a problem
Has been shed.
If Dave has a "headache"
Or is not in the mood—
And you can't even bribe him
With a backrub or food—
Dobbie, yank him to "*Attention*"
And on this you can bank
Your four-star authority
Is enough to pull rank.
So congratulations to
A beautiful pair.
May God be with you
Is our prayer.

I think Boomer really scratched deep for words that rhymed, but it was a sweet poem, and his efforts were appreciated. We had a great party and enjoyed the felicitations—some sincere, some jealous, and some "I told you so" friends who said they'd always predicted Dave would someday be a general. Glad they thought so because Dave was ready to give up on the idea. We were all proud of him. Dave and I only wished his father had lived long enough to relish his son's success.

Christmas came and went—and so did Dave's mother. It was our first Christmas without Doc, and we missed him and the traditional fudge he always brought us. Bruce was home and spent most of the holidays trying to finish an overdue architectural project. It was a quiet holiday. Sometimes uneventful is good. Bruce returned to OSU, Todd returned to W.T. Woodson High School, Dave returned to Fort Bragg, and I returned to my part-time job and Wednesday ski trips to Wintergreen.

I went with Joan Thurman on a weekend ski trip to Snowshoe in Slaty Fork, West Virginia, with a busload of skiers. Dave was home for the weekend and stayed with Todd. Joan and I shared a ski chairlift with another lady who, in conversation with Joan, said she and her air force husband had just returned from Spain. Joan responded, "My friend here recently returned from Spain." We lifted our goggles to look at each other. She said, "Shirley?" I said, "Ann?" Her husband had worked for Dave in Spain. Small world. It became even more bizarre when she said, "You won't believe this, but we are here with my cousin and his wife and their friends, the Killefers from Knoxville, Tennessee. The Forgan name came up last night in conversation, and Bob Killefer told us he had known Dave in college and both of you in Dallas when he went through pilot training at Perrin AFB." At lunch, I saw Bob for the first time in twenty-four years and met his wife. Our encounter on the chairlift was an incredible coincidence. What are the odds of running into old friends in Slaty Fork, West Virginia?

In the spring, Todd went to his first prom with a new girlfriend I was apprehensive about. His jobs kept him occupied, so I had only an occasional worry when he was out with her. Bruce sprung his bad news for the spring semester. He'd flunked calculus and physics and was notified he couldn't return to the School of Architecture. He'd have to skip a year and reapply or switch his major to Fine Arts, which he did.

Dave put me on notice that he was tired of living in the BOQ (Bachelor Officers Quarters), threatening to get an apartment and a mistress if Todd and I didn't move to Fort Bragg in Fayetteville. We went for a weekend visit, and he tried to wine and dine us. It was the worst dinner and the most horrible wine I had ever tasted, made from a North Carolina grape which tasted like Pine Sol. We checked out Fayetteville Academy (a private school) and the public high school, and I was not impressed with either. We talked to Todd, who was my main concern regarding another move. He had to make the decision since I'd promised him his final three years at the same high school. He said he'd move if he could have a car and attend the private school. Dave promised me another new mop, so the die was cast.

Bruce worked in Stillwater that summer. Todd bought a cool '80 Camaro Z-28, white with red and black trim, paying for half with money earned working his two jobs. I was actually pleased to move Todd from the large school where he'd been unable to find his niche and to release him from his girlfriend's clutches. Another permanent change of station "killing" a teenage romance. After only two years at Fairfax, we rented our house to another military family. The movers did their thing, and Todd and I drove to North Carolina for a new military adventure. Our second assignment to an army installation would prove to be very different from anything we had previously experienced.

Good-bye, Virginia,
for the third and last time.

Purple Suiters

Fayetteville, North Carolina
Fort Bragg
Joint Special Operations Command
July 1981-November 1982

Todd in his "cool" car and I in my Chevy sedan followed Dave's directions to our new army quarters. The post is open, meaning there are no fences or guarded gates. The place is huge! Including all its training areas and drop zones for the 82nd Airborne Division, it is second in size only to Fort Hood in Texas. Pope Air Force Base is next door, a secured base with fences and guarded gates.

The new headquarters command was the result of the hostage rescue tragedy in Iran. The joint chiefs of staff created a ninety-five-man headquarters composed of army, air force, navy, and marines called the Joint Special Operations Command (JSOC), tasked with combating terrorism. The organization was secret, causing others on post to wonder who the new people were, where they belonged, where they came from, and what they were doing at Fort Bragg. JSOC headquarters occupied two newly-constructed buildings, fenced and guarded. Calling themselves "The Purple Suiters," the men made battle fatigues the uniform of the day, so there was no uniform distinction between services.

General Scholtes was the commander; air force one-star Dave was the deputy commander; and Navy Captain Norm Olson was the chief of staff. Norm had an impressive background. A career navy seal, he jumped out of airplanes, swam great distances, cleared mines, and performed other dangerous assignments—tough man! He also participated in "sport jumping"—free falling and creating various formations in the sky—calling it fun! He had accumulated approximately 3,500 jumps. Dave nicknamed him "Sky Fossil."

We settled into the new quarters in our usual quick manner. The floor plan was the same as we had at Langley AFB in Virginia, but this house was stucco with a red-tiled roof. The only crisis occurred after Dave hung our wrought iron chandelier in the dining room. I came home one day and found it sitting in the middle of the table, my alabaster centerpiece in pieces on the floor. The table was refinished but still has a noticeable dent in the center.

The first day of classes at Fayetteville Academy, Todd drove into the school's parking lot looking "cool," ready to impress everyone with his white-with-red-stripes Camaro Z-28. A good-looking girl in a white-with-blue-stripes Camaro Z-28 pulled up beside him. Instant magnetism connected cars and drivers. Todd and Michelle became boyfriend/girlfriend.

September 28, Todd and Dave celebrated their eighteenth and forty-eighth birthdays, respectively. The thirty-year difference made it easy to figure their ages. I usually made a chocolate cake, Dave's favorite, but I was not a very good baker. My cakes were normally ugly and messy; baking was low on my priority list.

One day I was playing bridge at Jane Doe's (ficticious name to protect her identity) house when her husband, John, (also a ficticious name) came home. He was assigned to the noteworthy and very secret Army Delta Force. Highly trained in hostage rescue and antiterrorism, they were experts in their field—tough and intimidating! Jane introduced me to her husband who was rather curt. He asked if it was my son in the Camaro who drove from the alley every morning, spinning tires and throwing gravel. I admitted that it probably was, and he said, "You tell him that if he doesn't slow down, I am going to shoot that car full of holes."

I think I dropped my playing cards all over the floor and shakily responded that I would relay the message. When I told Todd what the soldier around the corner said, he "pooh-poohed" the whole thing—until I told him the officer was with Delta Force and meant what he said. Todd never went around that corner again, wisely choosing to head in the opposite direction.

Another story regarding John Doe happened before we were assigned to Fort Bragg. Jane came home one afternoon, and the cleaning lady told her, "Mistuh Doe done cum home and tuk all the tootpaste in the house wit him when he done left." Jane didn't know where he had gone but assumed he would be gone for a while. John had been deployed with Delta Force to Egypt, Oman, and Iran, preparing for the hostage rescue mission in Iran. I was told that when hearing about the fiasco, reporters flocked to the Does' and Joneses' (also a ficticious name) homes at Fort Bragg and camped out on their lawns. When a reporter rang the Joneses' doorbell, Mrs. Jones answered but said she was the maid. Jane and Mrs. Jones were secretly flown to safety to escape the media and avoid the possibility of repercussion from anti-Americans. It was interesting to meet and hear the personal stories of some of the key players whom I had heard so much about.

The JSOC commander's wife already had the wives organized by the time I got there. She was like a mother hen, making everyone feel welcome in her new surroundings; therefore, my responsibilities were few. Three ladies became my best friends when we signed up to play tennis with the officers' wives' club. We called ourselves the "Fearsome Foursome." After our weekly tennis matches, we adjourned for lunch at each other's houses or at the golf club restaurant, a good excuse to replace burned-up calories. Occasional movie nights with the Fearsome Foursome, bridge games, monthly officers' wives' club luncheons, JSOC socials, and hosting social functions at our quarters kept me busy. Of particular note were the monthly "street meets" with the generals' wives to socialize and discuss various issues. I never felt comfortable at those "street meet coffees," as I was the only air force wife, and they discussed army issues. I mostly sipped my coffee and listened.

I thought the army wives were very rank conscious—and more so if their husbands were one of the elite West Point graduates (commonly known as "ring knockers"). While I was jogging with several generals' wives one morning, West Point was mentioned. I turned and asked Sally if her husband had gone to West Point. She replied, "No, he only went to the Citadel." *Only?* She was almost apologetic about her husband's attendance at another outstanding military school. The Air Force Academy didn't exist when *my* husband went to college, so I had nothing to apologize for.

In November, Frances and Jim LaVigne arrived with daughter Leanne. We always expected them to visit wherever we went, and they were always welcome. We drove to the beach for the weekend, Leanne and Todd in his Camaro with her feet sticking out the window most of the way and the parents in our car with feet on the floor. It was a little cool to go in the water, but Jim skimmed down to his skivvies and got wet, saying, "It's unthinkable to go to the beach and not get in the ocean." Leanne and Todd cavorted in the water like a couple otters. The two always had such a good time together, but nothing romantic ever seemed to develop. We returned to Fort Bragg; Frances talked me into jogging with her, and the fellows played golf at the beautiful Pinehurst Resort.

The only time I ever saw Jim mad was when Todd and Leanne raked leaves from the yard into a bed sheet, which Todd then hauled onto the front porch roof. Leanne called her father to come outside, and as Jim descended the steps, Todd dropped the sheet and leaves rained down on him. Jim did not think it was funny. I don't know why Jim got mad. We had learned to expect the extraordinary from the kids.

Todd was supposed to be studying for the Scholastic Aptitude Test (SAT); however, the night before the exam, he and Leanne stayed up until about three in the morning. Todd, in no shape to take the exam the next morning, made an average score. I believe he would have done better had he been well-rested. He had received an Air Force Academy application his junior year but gave up completing it after realizing he didn't have the credentials required for consideration. His basic high school grades were average; he worked part time, and played a little football, baseball, and soccer. The application required numerous and impressive school activities, and I understood why only top-notch students were accepted. It is tough to get in and tough to stay in.

We seemed to have houseguests coming in the front door as others were leaving out the back door. Shortly after the LaVignes left, Mother came for Thanksgiving. At six o'clock every morning, an army unit shot a cannon permanently stationed in the parade field, a half block from our house. It was reveille (military wake-up call), but if the wind blew in the right direction, it was also our neighborhood *loud* wake-up call. Mother claimed it shot her right out of the bed! The second attention-getter was a large group of soldiers, jogging in combat boots through the housing area, counting cadence and singing, "I wanna be an Airborne Ranger, live a life of sex and danger, right, left, forward, march." Various and risqué musical phrases kept them in cadence and good spirits. Life was different on an army post.

Mother went home with the sound of cannons blasting in her ears, and Christmas quickly descended upon us. Bruce came home from college—the only time he was at our Fort Bragg house since he stayed at OSU to work during the summers. Dave's mother flew in from Sarasota, and we traditionally hung the personalized stockings and arranged the tree skirt she'd made for us. (The stockings and skirt are still displayed annually as well as the Advent wreath centerpiece she created and filled with tiny porcelain nursery rhyme figurines, a nativity set, and a Santa Claus. Its center contains a red "May Pole" with red streamers to four candle holders on the edge of the wreath. I hope future Forgan families will treasure these special works of art.) Santa Claus brought Hazel a red sweater to cover her skinny body on cold Carolina mornings and a red bow for her hair, which she did not like. We dressed her up, but her looks didn't improve.

As soon as Grandma Forgan returned to Florida after Christmas, we headed for Snowshoe Ski Resort in Slaty Fork, West Virginia. Driving from Ohio, Joan and Bill Thurman and son, Chris, met us there. Unthinkable, Frances, Jim, and Leanne also decided to join us. When they pulled into a Slaty Fork gas station, an elderly, female attendant noticed their Canadian license plate and asked what brought them to West Virginia to ski. Jim said, "We're meeting friends here." She shook her head. "You sure must value that friendship a great deal."

For an isolated and unfamiliar place, it certainly was popular over the holidays—so crowded that lift lines sometimes had an hour wait. Leanne and Todd solved that problem by asking people to save their place in line while they waited on a picnic bench. They continuously played "chicken" over who would turn around first to sit in the ski chairlift. Another time, we saw Todd skiing downhill with Leanne riding him piggyback. What those two thought up for entertainment! Bruce pretended he didn't know them! The three families had a grand time, celebrated New Year's Eve, and played hysterical games of charades. It didn't take much to entertain the adults either, especially after sipping champagne.

The Thurmans went back to Ohio, the LaVignes left, vowing never to ski Snowshoe again, Bruce returned to OSU after the holidays, Todd remained at Fayetteville Academy, Dave continued "flying his desk," and I resumed wife and mother duties and kept a busy social schedule. Tough life.

Disaster hit Fort Bragg when, during an 82nd Airborne Division exercise in California, a sudden wind swirled nine paratroopers to their deaths. After the accident, one of the widows discovered her checks were bouncing at the bank. She was unaware that her husband's pay stopped the day of his death and his paycheck to the bank had been recalled. Since JSOC was composed of men from four branches of service and each branch handled crises and deaths differently, it was decided the wives needed an orientation. I took on the responsibility for air force wives. (I still hadn't learned to say no.)

A panel consisting of a banker, a military representative from each service branch, a lawyer, and the commander, General Scholtes, spoke to us with revealing, beneficial results. The air force has a Casualty Assistance Office on every base, with assigned men and women trained for the job. The army has a Casualty Assistance Office also, but men and women from various units are assigned to the office for temporary extra duty. The navy has a Casualty Assistance Office, but one office may cover a five-state area. We air force wives preferred our system with assistance coming from trained personnel. Our husbands frequently put their lives on the line, and now we felt prepared in case of an emergency. Dave had told me appropriate personnel would personally notify me if he were killed. Wives lived in fear of seeing the blue military staff car curbside, a chaplain and commander approaching the house. If he were shot down, wounded, or taken prisoner, I would get a phone call. Ignorance is not bliss. Military wives need to be informed even though talk of losing husbands is a distasteful subject.

Sometime after the orientation, several wives were sitting around, chatting and drinking wine, which probably prompted someone to create poetic "one liners" regarding a husband's demise. It got us on a roll, and with what we thought was perfectly good humor, we produced the following:

Nothing but the best when he's laid to rest.
You don't have to save when he's in his grave.
You can spend, spend, spend when he's met his end.
Turn on the charm when he's bought the farm.
Be a fox when he's in the box.
You'll have a full purse when he's in the hearse.
Who to hold when he's cold?
How to behave when he's in the grave.
Get ahead after he's dead.
How to spend his cash when he busts his ash.

Don't be broke if he should croak.
Don't let some honey get his money.

As I recall, several wives—including the commander's wife—didn't appreciate this "sick humor." Perhaps it was distasteful and insensitive, but it demonstrated one way we faced danger: with laughter. Dave thought it was funny. Whew.

I had reluctantly agreed to cochair the officers' wives' club's annual fund-raiser, and then the date changed to the same weekend as my previously scheduled Colorado ski trip. I told the JSOC commander's wife, who sucked air through her teeth and asked if I'd notified Mrs. "Army Three-Star"—the first lady of the post. When I told her I hadn't, she sucked more air through her teeth, suggesting I should. So I explained to Mrs. "Army Three-Star" that everything would be accomplished before I left and another wife would substitute for me the night of the function. She wasn't too happy, but I told her there was nothing I could do about it; my plans had already been made. In twenty-four years in the air force with my husband, this was only the second time I felt pressure from a higher-ranking officer's wife. She ordered wives around as if *she* wore the three stars on her shoulders. She insisted I write the "After Action Report," summarizing my part of the function and making suggestions for the next chairman. I did. The fund-raiser was successful without a hitch.

Todd was doing well, happy to be a big fish in a little pond. He thrived in a smaller, private school and enjoyed playing soccer and baseball. He played the role of the sinister nephew in the play "Arsenic and Old Lace." I was glad he took more interest in school activities, including a trip with his senior class to New York City. Michelle, his girlfriend, was a steady force in his life, but when spring arrived, Todd was invited to escort Mary Ann and Scotty Morgan's daughter to the public high school's senior prom. She was adorable, and I didn't understand why she didn't have a date, but she told her mother she wanted Todd Forgan to take her to the prom. Todd later said they had a nice time, but he was uncomfortable since he didn't know anyone there. I don't know why Michelle allowed this date, but the Morgans' daughter got her dream date, and the Forgan son returned to his own girlfriend. He took Michelle to the Fayetteville Academy prom, but oops, I failed to get a picture. Bummer.

A distinguished visitor made an appearance at Fort Bragg: Joe Namath. Fearsome Foursome friend Betty heard he was going to greet the troops when they returned from their early morning run, and with her photography hobby, she wanted to record the moment. Conning me into carrying her camera bag and extra lens, she and I were waiting on the parade field at 6:30 a.m. when the troops arrived. The commanding general and Joe greeted the troops, while General Forgan's wife (me) tried to keep up with Major Baumgartner's wife (Betty) as she took pictures. Recognizing me, the commanding general asked, "What are you doing out here?" I replied, "I don't know, sir, but I wouldn't do this for anyone but a good friend." Very gracious, Joe Namath stayed until the last soldier shook his hand or got his autograph. I got his autograph for Todd (who couldn't have cared less), and my farewell scrapbook from the officers' wives includes pictures of me with Joe. A memorable day.

Another distinguished, but not so welcome, visitor that year was Thomas Fleming, author of *The Officers' Wives*, a novel about the army wives of four West Point graduates. Fleming's characters tended to represent all that is tragic, romantic, and sordid in army life: concomitant sex lives, nervous breakdowns, and alcoholism. The story was fictional, but it left a bad impression of army wives. Mr. Fleming was invited to a Fort Bragg Officers' Wives' Club luncheon to speak about this book that raised eyebrows and more than a few hackles. Several ladies wanted to take him to court, send him to jail, or at least take him to task. A few wanted to roast *him* alive and serve *him* for lunch.

Fleming had already done "combat" with the West Point Officers' Wives Club; therefore, he was well armed for the conflict he faced at Fort Bragg. He skillfully defused the situation, taking the first twenty minutes to acquaint the ladies with the overriding theme of most of his books and the broad scope of his work as historian and writer. The initial reception was cool and polite with the listeners attentive, if not exactly enthralled. They seemed to conscientiously struggle to like this man and simultaneously fight to hold on to their bruised feelings. They reluctantly gave him a standing ovation and a T-shirt that read, "Army Wives Are Special." We all know some military wives with the same traits as the book's four dysfunctional women, but I believe it was unfair of Mr. Fleming to create a bad impression of military wives, who, for the most part, are exceptional women.

In the meantime, Todd was trying to decide where to go to college. Dave again pushed for a Florida school with in-state tuition, especially since we were already paying out-of-state tuition for Bruce in Oklahoma. Dave and Todd visited the University of Florida and stayed in nice VIP quarters on Patrick Air Force Base where they received a tour of the military missile launch area. Unfortunately, Todd wasn't excited about the university, so a disappointed Dave drove back to Fort Bragg. Todd called his best friend in Fairfax, Virginia, David, who said he was going to the University of Arizona. Todd decided to join David in Arizona. Michelle begged Todd to go with her to the University of North Carolina, but he resisted.

Todd's high school graduation came (too soon for me) on May 8, 1982, with forty-seven graduates in the class. A few relatives arrived for this special event. Dave's Aunt May, Aunt Grace, and her husband, Uncle Fred, flew in from California, and Grandma Forgan came from Florida. Once again, Mother inexplicably refused to come for the graduation. We all had a good time, and Todd and Michelle were quite jovial and amiable, making everyone's visit worthwhile.

After graduation, Todd worked on new building construction at the JSOC site until he left for his college adventure. It scared me to think about my "baby" leaving the nest. In August, he and I left Fort Bragg in his Camaro, pulling a little trailer with all his worldly goods. We drove to McAlester to stay a few days with Mother then on to Stillwater to visit Bruce. He stayed to work for the summer and had moved into a house with some other fellows. His bed was a mattress on the floor, and he was living out of suitcases and boxes. His art supplies were scattered around the room, some stacked on wood and brick shelves he had built. Bicycles and motorcycles were inside and outside the house, which was also cluttered with beer cans. Neither amused nor impressed, I was concerned about Bruce's new "friends." I knew nothing about girlfriends, and he volunteered no information about his social life. Out of sight, he had declared *freedom* from his mother's nosiness and his dad's control. Todd and I returned to McAlester, leaving my firstborn once again, a knot in my stomach, trying to convince myself that Bruce had to make it on his own.

Nonna, squeezing into the tiny backseat of Todd's car, joined us on the drive to Odessa, Texas. Mother had been "dating" a widower, a former next-door neighbor in McAlester who had moved to Odessa years earlier. We spent two days at his house, and Dave flew into nearby Big Springs for military business at Webb AFB and joined us. I squeezed into the backseat of the Camaro as Dave, Todd, and I headed west to Tucson, while Mother remained with her friend for a few days.

During the entire trip, I teased Todd, suggesting he look at the many trees along the way because they'd be the last trees he'd see for a while. Except for Spain, every place we'd lived had an abundance of trees, and we were now leaving the beautiful pine trees of North Carolina. Todd had never been west of Oklahoma, and as we drove across barren west Texas and the Arizona desert, his face took on the look of "What have I gotten myself into?"

He got quieter by the mile; however, as we drove into Tucson, an oasis with lovely palm trees, green grass, and mountains in the background, he finally smiled—a bit nervously.

We carried Todd's things into the dorm room he shared with David, who had already moved in. Space was sparse even though the beds were bunked. We registered Todd for school, and Dave forked over the out-of-state tuition. Touring the city and campus, Todd got excited about being on his own for the first time in his life. Mother and friend arrived in his car, Dave flew back to Fort Bragg from Tucson, and I tried to leave my "baby" without getting emotional, but I couldn't stop the flow of tears.

I was not ready for an empty nest or to give another son his wings. The umbilical cord was cut. I just prayed we had given both sons the values and guidance they needed to survive. A cartoon in my photo album says, "I have the feeling that if I could just get over this next hump in life, it'll be smooth sailing the rest of the way. Unfortunately, I've been saying that for years. Someone keeps moving the hump."

After this big hump, we left Todd in Tucson with spending money and a Visa charge card for emergencies. Mother, her friend, and I drove to California to visit relatives living in the high desert near Hemet. I thought Arizona was barren. As far as my eye could see in the high desert was sand, tumbleweed, fruit trees, and lots of trailer parks! The relatives had left Los Angeles congestion for these quieter, smaller towns developed for senior citizens. A few days later, Mother and friend left for Reno and I visited Dave's relatives in Sun City and air force friends on Coronado Beach in San Diego.

I finally flew back to North Carolina, happy for peace and quiet after August's strenuous activities. Labor Day weekend, sitting in the sunroom reading a good book and enjoying my newfound freedom, I nearly fell off the sofa when Todd and Michelle unexpectedly walked into the house. "I just left you in Tucson two weeks ago. What are you doing here?" I exclaimed. Lonesome for her "Toddy," Michelle had her daddy pay for Todd's flight back to Fayetteville. I think she still hoped to sweet-talk him into transferring to UNC, but no such luck for her. He returned to Tucson. My hair got grayer every day.

A month later, Todd's roommate called to inform me that Todd was in a terrible state of mind. Michelle was calling him several times a day, crying, missing him terribly, and pressuring him to return to North Carolina. Todd met with a counselor, who advised him not to return to North Carolina unless it was on *his* terms. I recommended to Todd that he wait until Christmas to see Michelle, to give each other some breathing room. He agreed to stay in Arizona, and I breathed a sigh of relief.

What I didn't tell Todd was that Dave had already received a new assignment—to Brunssum, the Netherlands, Allied Forces Central Europe (AFCENT). I knew Todd wouldn't see Michelle at Christmas since he would join us overseas. That settled that, and the next time Todd saw her was at their tenth high school class reunion.

After researching AFCENT and locating Brussum on the map, Dave left for the Netherlands. This was his fourth consecutive "fly a desk" assignment, and he wasn't thrilled about it. He would be gone for three weeks then return for our farewells from JSOC and concurrent travel with the dog and me. While he was gone, I prepared for our seventeenth move. It's a wonder poor Hazel didn't hide when she saw the packing boxes. I said, "Get prepared, 'Super Survivor Dog,' here we go again across that big pond where you got lost. You are a real trouper." Had she known, she'd have run away rather than experience another plane ride in her cargo "kennel-prison." She was thirteen years old and not very active. I called Mother about our leaving the U.S. again, and she could only cry and mutter, "Oh no, oh no." I also called Grandma Forgan, who wasn't happy about the move but expressed her disappointment with little emotion.

Dave flew back to Fort Bragg in time for final packing and paper signing. Once again opting for a smaller car to drive in Europe, we sold our American cars. The Chevy Monza sold easily, but the nice, four-year-old Pontiac was left with a young officer who finally sold it after our departure.

The JSOC wives honored me with a lovely farewell tea. I felt a little guilty because I had been there only one year. The generals' wives bid me farewell at my final "street-meet coffee." Mrs. "Army Three-Star" snidely inquired if I would have any responsibilities where I was going, obviously referring to my "irresponsible behavior" as the cochair of the wives' club fund-raiser. Unabashed, I replied, "I assume so," and turned my attention elsewhere. I would not let her intimidate me! My tennis friends and their husbands had a farewell dinner for us, and the commander of JSOC, Dick Scholtes, and his wife hosted a casual dinner at their house with several couples.

From wood and metal, Dick constructed a miniature hangar. When the hangar door was unlatched, the airplane (attached to a metal rod) flew around the hangar while a music box played "Off We Go into the Wild Blue Yonder." Adorable—a truly memorable keepsake. JSOC held a farewell reception where everyone, including the enlisted, came through a receiving line to say good-bye. We stayed at the VIP Officers' Quarters at nearby Pope Air Force Base, and the morning we were to leave, the other three in the Fearsome Foursome showed up with roses and a bottle of champagne. They made me feel as if they were really going to miss me. "Poet laureate" Patti wrote the following poem:

'Twas just a year ago today,
The four of us began to play.
A day we will not forget
Of hitting balls into the net.
In fact, some went o'er the fence,
Even the score didn't make much sense.
Was it love-forty or thirty-all?
And why did we have just one ball?
That great big gate, 'twas hard to latch it!
And Shirley didn't even own a racquet.
Our tennis game…well…it was folly,

Patti didn't hit one volley.
Betty's balls were nice and slow,
If o'er the net they did go.
Judy couldn't hold her tongue,
Out it slipped—that first pun!
Running around, out in the sun,
This tennis game was becoming fun!
That seventeenth day in the month of September,
It was a day we'll long remember.
But, to nothing else can be compared,
The wine, the talks, the lunches shared...
As Tennis Friends.

Two army wives and one navy wife (three of the Fearsome Foursome) were my best friends at Fort Bragg. We shed tears and waved good-bye as a driver in a military staff car took us to the local airport, where we flew to New York City's JFK Airport. Poor Hazel, curled up in her crate, looked forlorn.

We arrived at JFK, fetched Hazel in her crate, and grabbed our other baggage. No problem so far, but were we in for a surprise! Checking in for our overseas flight, we were informed our flight had been canceled. Dave went ballistic. *General Forgan* let them know, in no uncertain terms, that was unacceptable. Whatever argument he put forth worked because they sent us to Sabena Airlines who rescheduled us for the next flight to Brussels, only one hour from our Brunssum destination in the Netherlands. I don't know whom Dave notified of our new flight schedule or how he contacted them. Did he call Fort Bragg to notify AFCENT? Did he call someone in the air force? Did he call AFCENT? Did he call God? I think I heard him refer to God several times, but it wasn't in good terms.

Good-bye to the mountains, beaches, and "Pine Sol wine."
Hello to the land of Dutch cheese, tulips, and wooden shoes.

Cheese and Tulips

Nieuwenhagen, the Netherlands
NATO, Allied Forces Central Europe (AFCENT)
Brunssum, the Netherlands
November 1982-August 1985

We arrived in Brussels and immediately retrieved our luggage and poor little Hazel, who had survived another trip across the big pond with no problems this time. An AFCENT driver in a staff Mercedes met us, and the trip to Brunssum was breathtaking, occasionally reaching 120 miles per hour. We were in the Province of Limberg at the southernmost tip of the Netherlands, situated between Belgium and Germany. The locals' language is a blend of Dutch and German. Brunssum is one hour east of Brussels, one hour west of Bonn, and four hours north of Paris. Nice location. The Netherlands is mistakenly called Holland, but Holland is actually one of twelve provinces.

The visiting officers' quarters connected to the officers' club was to be our "bed and breakfast, lunch and dinner" for several days. We picked up our new Mazda 626 and drove ten minutes to Nieuwenhagen village to see our quarters. All military families leased houses in Dutch neighborhoods—no base, no base housing. Several houses were designated "generals' quarters," contracted and leased by the army or air force. When one general left, another moved in. Nieuwenhagen, Brunssum, Heerlen—knowing what village you were in was determined by street signs, due to the close-knit neighborhoods.

Located in a heavily wooded neighborhood, our large, unique house was two stories, brick and wood inside and outside, very contemporary with a mansard roof. Not having enough furniture, we were supplied additional pieces by the military housing authority. The main living/entertainment room, including the dining area and kitchen, was about sixty feet long by thirty feet wide. The open kitchen was most unusual. It had a three-sided brick counter with a wood top and a beautiful, four-sided huge copper hood overhead. A small room between the kitchen and the garage housed the washer and dryer, an American kitchen stove (with oven), refrigerator, and cabinet that I used for a pantry and kitchenware storage. To the side of the entertainment area was another open room where we hung out—Dave's desk, our own living room furniture, and a newly purchased twelve-piece wall unit.

Open wooden stairs led to the second floor to three bedrooms and two bathrooms. The guest bathroom had a six-foot square shower. The bedrooms had armoires in lieu of closets because in the Netherlands, as elsewhere in Europe, closets were considered "rooms" and therefore were taxed. So, no closets, fewer rooms, less tax. Fortunately, all window treatments were provided.

The military was under high alert for terrorism, and measures were taken for our protection. We had two alarm systems in the house: a motion detector for night and a panic button in each room to alert the local police. Mistaken for a light switch, one button on a wall near the powder room was occasionally pressed. The police would call and ask if everything was all right. You bet I'm going to say everything is all right if a terrorist was holding a pistol to my head. I learned later that we should have been given a password that indicated "fine" or "not fine." To avoid more accidental "emergencies," I covered the confusing panic button with tape.

AFCENT's mission was to respond to a Russian attack, and Dave's division was responsible for planning the operations. Headquarters was located in the nearby village of Brunssum. Heading the command was a German four-star general, his deputy a British four-star, and a three-star from the Netherlands or Belgium, alternately. Following were nine more generals, ranging from one to two stars, including Dave. France maintained a three-star general liaison as they were no longer a part of NATO. We were running in high-rank cotton. Men and women from Germany, Belgium, the Netherlands, Canada, England, and the U.S. worked in Dave's Ops Division.

I was involved with three groups of AFCENT ladies: the main ladies' club, the Operations Division that Dave commanded, and the U.S. Air Force wives. All three groups welcomed me at a tea and coffees. At the Operation Division welcome coffee (attended by wives from all six countries), Ilse Marie Munch from Germany mentioned that I had on one navy shoe and one brown shoe. I looked down at my feet, looked back at her, confirmed her observation, and said, "You know, I have another pair at home just like them." It brought lots of laughter, and Ilse Marie loved to tell the story.

We shopped mostly at a U.S. Army facility about a half-hour from our house for groceries, items we American wives just couldn't do without, and a few clothes. For variety, we tapped into the local markets and shops. Since we were located near the borders of Belgium and Germany, I soon learned to carry four wallets of money—American dollars, Dutch guilders, German marks, and Belgium francs. Always prepared.

Our American neighbor's two little boys played with the Dutch kids and had played tricks on Dave's predecessor, ringing the doorbell and running away when the general answered. The more irritated he became, the more the boys misbehaved. They decided they were going to pull the same stunts on the new residents: us. After several doorbell-ringing incidents followed by them running around the corner of the house, I surprised them one day. Leaning out the powder room window (no window screens, probably another taxable item), I squirted them with a water pistol and shouted, "Gotcha!" Shocked, their eyes widened and heels dug in the ground. We beat them at their own game. When they realized their antics weren't disturbing us, they diverted their attention elsewhere. Dave was driven to and from work in an unmarked Mercedes by a driver trained to take evasive action in case of a terrorist kidnapping attempt. These same mischievous little boys stopped what they were doing, came to attention, and saluted as the car passed them on the street. Smiling, Dave returned their salute.

I took Dutch language lessons but found the guttural pronunciation difficult. Even the Dutch say their language is a throat disease. Most speak English with little accent, and except for an occasional "Please," "Good morning," "Thank you," and "Good-bye," I gave up trying to speak Dutch.

Every year the Dutch and Americans pay tribute to the eight thousand Americans buried at Margraten Cemetery. The Dutch are extremely grateful to the Americans, British, and Canadians for liberating their country in World War II. Continuing to show their appreciation, they created an organization called NAIL— Netherlands-American Institute of Limberg— comprised of local people who had been active in the Dutch resistance or who had worked with the U.S. forces. Annual social events promoted friendly relations between our two countries. One of the leading participants, Mimi Corbey, was the young woman photographed riding on an American tank as the liberators entered her town. Printed in newspapers and magazines, the picture became famous. Mimi fought with the Dutch Resistance, delivering secret messages on her bicycle. Had she been caught, the Germans would have shot her. It's rumored she fell in love with an American soldier who was later killed. Mimi never married. She was a delightful lady who spent years keeping alive the spirit of the liberation. We were honored to be her friends.

Frances and I schussing the slopes of Switzerland

Fighter pilots' wives with "The Right Stuff"

Bruce and Todd arrived from college for our first Christmas holiday in the land of cheese and wooden shoes, once again experiencing life in Europe. Hazel was happy to see them and frequently stayed curled up in Todd's lap. After a nice, quiet Christmas with only our immediate family for a change, we drove to Munich, had a typical German dinner, and drank beer at the famous Hofbrauhaus beer hall. It was crowded, hot, and loud with music and singing. Germans love to sing almost as much as they love to drink their liters of beer. The second day we skied the Zugspitze glacier. Bad weather prevented skiing the next day, so we toured one of crazy King Ludwig's castles and played Hearts card games at our accommodation in the beautiful, old town of Oberhammergau.

We visited Dachau, the former German concentration camp. To see this site, view vivid pictures, and read about the atrocities is almost unbelievable. How could humans behave like animals, subjecting others to such inhumane treatment? One man described the camp as "a world without God." Near the crematorium, a bronze statue of an emaciated "internee" is inscribed with "Forgive, but do not forget."

Rather subdued, we left Germany for our home in the Netherlands. The boys returned to college, and Todd was friendless when he discovered his roommate had transferred to Auburn. He participated in fraternity rush week for prospective members and pledged Sigma Phi Epsilon, finding himself a home away from home with young men he liked, giving him a sense of belonging.

The social scene at AFCENT was a high priority, and we were introduced to the more formal European way of protocol and culture—no "pig pickin's" here! We always took flowers to the hostess but soon learned never to take *red* flowers, the symbol of love. Hmm…to how many hostesses did Dave declare his love before we learned our lesson?

At the British four-star's house, port wine was always offered after dessert. Then the ladies departed to the powder room to freshen up while the men had cigars. We rejoined the men in the living room for coffee. It amazed me how the waiters knew when to come and go in the dining room; I discovered the hostess pressed a signal button on the floor with her foot.

The German four-star dinners were always black tie, and after dinner, we were provided with musical entertainment, for example, a cellist or a vocalist. I reckoned the best I could do was parade Hazel through our living room for our guests' entertainment. After all, she was a "classical" conversation piece, a work of art.

One of the most formal evenings we experienced was at a British three-star general's home. We were driven there in a staff Mercedes by a trained driver who soon displayed his expertise. Approaching a stopped car angled across the road with two men next to it, our driver slammed on the brakes and walked to check out the situation. The car had only a flat tire, so we drove around it and continued on our way. Scared me to death. Fourteen guests were at the dinner with a waiter for every two guests. Entrees were served with silver-domed lids. With typical British pomp and ceremony, each waiter removed the lids with precision and flair. I felt like we were in a movie.

Jeanine Bardon, the French general's wife at AFCENT, deserved the "dinners extraordinaire" award. This is an example of one of her menus:

Coquilles Saint Jacques Au gratin
Filet d'autruche au poivre vert
Salade de saison
Peches caramel
Champagne Renard Barnier cuvee speciale brut

Loosely translated: Shrimp in a cheese sauce, ostrich with vegetables, seasonal salad, carameled peaches, and champagne. Sounds better in French.

During another dinner at the Bardons' home, I struggled to cut into a small fowl of questionable species, and it scooted off my plate onto the table. General Schild, a Berlin native sitting next to me, retrieved my fowl, saying, "Your bird took flight!" Everyone laughed, and my embarrassing moment was diffused. Typical of a German's good sense of humor, General Schild told us that Berlin's statue of a naked man on horseback depicts the last taxpayer leaving the city.

The supreme allied commander for Europe (a U.S. Army four-star) had a U.S. Air Force four-star as his chief of staff. We were invited to the chief's house in Mons, Belgium, just south of Brussels, honoring the Secretary of the Air Force Verne Orr. Driven in the usual official manner in a staff Mercedes, we arrived at a mansion on a hill. Standing on the front porch, Dave, with non-red flowers in hand for the hostess, rang the bell, and the aide informed us we were at the supreme commander's quarters— the chief's house was at the bottom of the hill. Embarassed, we returned to the car and reversed directions.

I was Mr. Orr's dinner partner. Me nervous? Nah. Just had another glass of wine! During dinner, I shared with Mr. Orr how Dave and I had exchanged pleasantries with two young Japanese men seated next to us in a crowded Paris bar, telling them about our assignment in Japan. When they asked where we were from in the U.S., Dave answered, "Chicago," and I said, "Oklahoma." One of the men said, "Oklahoma? Oklahoma? You have battleship by that name?" I responded, "Yes, and you sunk it." Mr. Orr looked across the table and said, "Dave, don't ever go into the diplomatic corps." Thank goodness everyone thought it was funny. I behaved myself the rest of the evening.

Each country represented at AFCENT hosted an annual reception, ball, or celebration to commemorate a special occasion. The Dutch celebrated their queen's birthday (Koninginnedag); the Germans held a subdued reception; the French, with one representative, hosted a small reception; and, of course, the Brits celebrated Her Royal Majesty, Queen Elizabeth's birthday. They imported the Royal Green Jackets Band, and the "flypast" by the British Air Force Flying Team was spectacular. No one can top the

British pomp and ceremony. However, no other country could top the decorations by our creative and tenacious American wives. We celebrated three different themes while we were there: "Discovery of America," "Heritage of America," and the 209th birthday of our nation. The wives quilted an American flag that was sixteen feet wide, and I hope it is still used and appreciated.

Dave's Operations Division planned a "Native Dress" party at the officers' club. The costumes were interesting. An English couple wore dapper black suits and black derbies and carried an umbrella over one arm and a newspaper under the other—"veddy, veddy" British. Several German men wore lederhosen (short suede pants with suspenders), and the ladies wore dirndls (jumper dress with laced-up bodice). Dave dressed like a Chicago gangster, and I was a cowgirl.

Dave's mother missed the first Christmas with us but came for Easter and spring, a beautiful time to be in the Netherlands. Flowers were blooming profusely with the ever-present rain. The Dutch paid no attention to rainy weather. They walked, rode their bicycles, and carried on their daily routines. Initially, we Americans tended to say, "I can't go out today; it's raining," but soon learned, with that attitude, we might never get out of the house. We took Grandma Forgan sightseeing, and she loved the flowers. Even though she was eighty-three years old, she tolerated the trip well. Strong lady.

Summer of 1983, I flew to Oklahoma for my thirtieth high school reunion, winning the award for having traveled the farthest. This being my first reunion, I saw distinct changes in my classmates—fatter, balder, grayer, older. Generally, the women looked better than the men. I had a wonderful time. I stayed up all night with thirteen classmates, sitting and talking near the motel's indoor pool. Mother, extremely worried about me, called five of my friends in the middle of the night, desperately asking about my whereabouts. The next day, I apologized to everyone, explaining where I'd been, preserving my good reputation.

Todd joined us for the summer, and Frances, Jim, and Leanne LaVigne made their usual trek from Toronto to visit. Dave rented a van to accommodate the six of us, and we spent three weeks sightseeing in the Netherlands, Luxembourg, Belgium, Germany, and France. On a German autobahn, the van went *putt, putt, whoosh, sizzle* and died. Dave raised the hood, and each male expressed his specific diagnosis of the problem. The required red triangle to be placed on the shoulder of the highway to indicate a disabled car was broken, so Jim put it around his neck and stood on the shoulder. Traffic zoomed by, one hundred miles per hour or more, no one stopping to assist. Incensed, Jim dropped his slacks around his ankles as Germans whizzed by, jerking their heads around for a second look. Todd and Leanne retreated to the van, saying, "We don't know him." I used a nearby emergency phone box and said to the male who answered, "*Sprechen sie* English?" (Do you speak English?) "*Nein.*" (No.) I shifted into my foreign language mode. In four languages, I read the numbers listed on the emergency phone, indicating our location on a map. Finishing my multi-lingual dialogue of numbers, I asked, "*Komen?*" uncertain if that was German for "coming?" He replied, "*Ya.*" Whew. I responded in French, "*Merci.*" (Having visited several countries on this trip, my mind was boggled with too many languages.) The German mechanic arrived, and our three macho males incorrectly diagnosed the problem. Without a word, the German reached in, filed the contact points on the distributor, motioned to Dave to start the van, and *vroom, vroom*, we were ready to roll. After three weeks in western Europe, touring and eating, touring and eating, touring and eating, we put the LaVignes on a plane in Frankfurt, and Todd, Dave, and I went home for a well-deserved rest.

Before Todd returned to college, he, Dave, and I visited Berlin, a real eye-opener. We drove to Braunschweig, Germany, where we boarded a British military transport train. As we traveled along the West/East German border, we saw watch towers, electrified fences, guard dogs, and Soviet military guards. It was scary. At Helmstedt, the last station in West Germany, the train engine and guards were replaced with ones from East Germany. This "changing of the guard" was a staged performance on the station platform. The British soldiers' pomp and ceremony hugely contrasted to the lackadaisical and disrespectful Russian soldiers' attitude. A Russian officer took all the travel documents inside a small office, where they took their good ole' sweet time reviewing them, leaving the British soldiers waiting at attention. We were instructed to remain in our seats on the train and avoid looking out the window and taking any pictures. Todd became nervous when I tried to peer around him. Dave was required to wear his uniform on the entire trip. When the Russian officer returned our passports, he looked solemnly at Dave and said, "The general looks like a jolly fellow," and proceeded nonchalantly down the train aisle. Todd was holding his breath.

At the station, all train doors were locked and chained and remained so until we entered West Berlin. This wasn't to keep us *in* but prevented anyone in East Germany from sneaking aboard the train to escape to the West. As we continued our journey through East Germany, the countryside changed. Wheat and corn fields were scruffy and unkempt. Towns appeared old and drab with blackened and forsaken cathedrals, empty trains, buildings in disrepair, and few cars. We saw apartment complexes but not many people.

West Berlin was a much more modern environment—colorful flowers, better cars, and happier people. We were told that after the war, old men, women, and children had cleaned the city brick by brick. A driver met us at the station and drove us to our American Air Force lovely VIP apartment, formerly a hotel. A stereo, two TVs, nuts, fruit, and champagne were provided for our pleasure. There was even an ice machine. (Ice was difficult to get in Europe; you were lucky to get one ice cube per glass.) All this for $12 a night.

The driver returned the next day to take Todd and me on a city tour while Dave handled military business. The Kurfurstendamm Street is comparable to Paris's Avenue des Champs-Élysées. It is the heart of the city and the center of activity. The "Ku'damm," as the Berliners call it, is two miles of international restaurants, art galleries, boutiques, antique shops, nightclubs, cafes, cinemas, and luxury hotels. It has been said that "If it's not on the 'Ku'damm,' you didn't need it anyway." Next to a new church and bell tower is a bombed-out church, kept as a reminder of war's destruction. Berliners named the old tower the "Hollow Tooth" and the new buildings the "Compact and Lipstick." The "Ku'damm" was crowded and lively with couples showing rare displays of affection, hand in hand or arms around each other. We laughed at the movie advertisement *Der Rosarote Panther Wird Grejagt* (*The Pink Panther Strikes Again*). Another example of Berlin humor is a Russian soldier statue which Germans call the "Unknown Looter." At the train station, a memorial is erected over an underground area where five thousand bodies were found. People had taken refuge there from the attacks on Berlin, and Hitler ordered it flooded.

From a constructed platform along The Wall in West Berlin, we peered into East Berlin—fortifications, guard shacks, antitank barriers, and a mound of dirt marking the site of Hitler's reinforced concrete bunker where he committed suicide April 30, 1945.

The Brandenburg Gate stood in the eastern sector. Victorious Prussian troops used to parade through the triumphant arch on their return from successful campaigns. The last troops to march through it were not on parade. Red Army infantrymen stormed through it in May 1945. The famous quadriga, a two-wheeled chariot drawn by four stallions, sat on top of the gate and was shattered beyond repair. For twelve years, the sole adornment of the shell-pocked gate was a red flag. In 1957, East Berliners began repairing the Brandenburg Gate when West Berliners discovered the moulds in which the original quadriga was cast. A new one was poured, gilded, and hoisted to the top of the refurbished gate in rare, remarkable cooperation between East and West.

A Soviet War memorial stands in West Berlin in the British

Sector because it was built in 1945 before the city was divided into the four occupation sectors controlled respectively by the French, British, Americans, and Russians. It is dedicated to the forty thousand Russians who died occupying Berlin. Two Russian sentries stand guard, and they are protected by British soldiers because an angry German had previously shot one of the Russian sentries.

The airport's flight control center was manned by Russian, American, and British officers, a Russian major the ranking officer. A story is told about an American lieutenant colonel substituting one day for the American captain. When the Russian major saw the American's rank, he disappeared momentarily then returned with colonel insignia on his shoulders.

We entered the east side of Berlin at Checkpoint Charlie, a maze of barriers half a block long through which visitors had to either walk or drive, the only entry for foreigners into East Berlin from the American Sector. Next to Checkpoint Charlie was The Wall Museum with displays of political events and tragedies that occurred during and after The Wall's construction—photos, a mini-submarine, escape cars, and other escape objects. We cautiously crossed over into East Berlin through the maze, and Dave, required to wear his uniform with his general's insignia, received subtle "looks."

Beyond the phony facades of the buildings, we saw fewer cars and people. (We were told that it was about a five-year wait to get a tiny car that cost the equivalant of $12,000.) Because of a chronic food shortage and population decrease, the Soviets provided financial incentives to families to produce more children. We had lunch at a hotel's top floor restaurant with a spectacular view of nothing. Everything was dreary and in disrepair. Our lunch bill was about $10. The hotel restaurant was nice, but it was to impress visitors—like we couldn't see past the pretense? Spectacular memorials and statues surrounded the area; one a huge statue of a soldier's mother, head bowed over her fallen son. When it rained, it appeared she was crying; the raindrops from her eyes fell onto the soldier. The trees lining the walkway were wired to grow bent over, symbolizing sadness. Five thousand soldiers are buried there in a mass grave. The memorial inscription reads, "The Homeland will not forget its heroes."

Shop windows displayed a few items, but inside, sparse merchandise was available. Possibly a shopper could find a cup here or a jacket there, certainly no souvenirs to buy.

After a day in East Berlin, we crossed back over into West Berlin, breathed sighs of relief, and relaxed. We hadn't realized how much we felt on edge in East Berlin. We could actually *feel* freedom in West Berlin. Americans are so blessed, even spoiled, and we should be thankful for all that we have.

We returned to our American sanctuary in the Netherlands; Todd flew back to Tucson. In September 1983, we celebrated Dave's fiftieth birthday. In the Netherlands, this birthday is called "seeing Abraham," based on Jesus' talk to the Jews. I had a surprise "wake" party for Dave at our house, and everyone dressed in black. I bought an Abraham mask, stuffed clothes to create a body, topped it with a hat, and seated the dummy in a rocking chair on the front porch to greet everyone. Dave received lots of funny gifts, but his favorite was an iridescent, bright purple, ugly tie, which he *still has*. He received a birthday greeting from President and Mrs. Reagan and an eighteen-inch figure-of-Abraham cookie from his Dutch secretary.

In October, Dave and I celebrated our twenty-fifth wedding anniversary with a weekend in Scheveningen on the coast of the North Sea. The first night at the hotel, a bellboy, holding a bottle of champagne and a bowl of fresh strawberries, knocked on our door. When I opened the door, he looked at me quizzically, peered around me, and said, "I have a gift from the hotel for the married couple." I said, "That's us." I guess he expected a young bride and groom, not two old folks! Todd sent us Rachmaninoff's taped concerto of "Somewhere in Time" with a note saying, "This music is the epitimy [epitome] of beauty, for it evokes quietness and stillness. I hope that you may sit down and listen to it and remember the happy and romantic times you and Dad have shared the last twenty-five years. I love you, Todd." I cried, of course. He has a way with words.

Todd returned for our second Christmas in Dutchland, but Bruce stayed in Oklahoma and went to his girlfriend's parents' house. I was disappointed that Bruce wasn't with his family. He mailed us a Christmas card of Snoopy sitting in a tree that said, "I'm the world-famous Christmas vulture in a pear tree here to wish you a Merry Christmas." Inside the message read: "The partridge couldn't make it this year." At least his humor cushioned my disappointment.

After Christmas, one of Todd's fraternity brothers, Chuck, came for a visit. We met him at the Frankfurt airport on Friday and spent the weekend in Paris celebrating New Year's Eve with other AFCENT couples and their children also home for the holidays. When we drove home, Chuck couldn't believe he'd been in four countries in four hours. We went sightseeing the rest of the week and took him back to Frankfurt on Saturday for his flight home. He and Todd entertained their fraternity brothers back at school with their stories.

Sometime after the new year, we lost our precious, ugly, super, smart, survivor, Spanish sheepdog Hazel. I came home from a shopping day in Belgium and let Hazel outside to go potty. She was blind, hard of hearing, and never ventured far from the house. Dave came in from work, and I asked him to let Hazel indoors. An hour passed, and when Dave came downstairs, I asked him where Hazel was. He said, "I don't know. I haven't seen her." He hadn't heard me ask him to let her in. Frantic, I started searching the neighborhood. The Belgian officer across the street and I looked for several hours until it began to snow. The next day I called the police, the fire department, the dog pound, and the newspaper. The neighborhood kids hopped on their bicycles and looked for her—without success.

Two weeks prior to this, Dutch police had knocked on my door and informed me that the Province of Limberg was having a rabies epidemic, and I needed to keep my dog on a leash. I said okay but let her out leashless as usual because she stayed nearby. I think the Dutch police saw her, assumed she was a stray because she looked so bedraggled, shot her, and disposed of her. I was distraught that I couldn't find her little body. She had lived a good life of sixteen years, survived our many travels, and ignored the many critical comments regarding her looks. Many of our dog-loving friends told us she wasn't ugly; she just had "character." It makes me sad that I didn't get to say good-bye and, "Thanks for being a good pet and part of our family."

While in the Netherlands, I went on several great ski trips. I joined an American ski club from nearby Geilenkirchen Air Base in Germany for a week-long Austrian ski school. The last day, our instructor led our class round trip across three mountains, up and down, through fields, across creeks, over fences, and across a road. On our return, I fell over exhausted, lying in the snow, groaning. We were awarded a small "Three Mountain" pin for the accomplishment, but I wanted a gold medal.

Another ski trip I took with a group of AFCENT families, traveling by buses and trains to and from France's Les Arcs Ski Resort. As usual, Dave was working. During our return trip, I commented that Dave wouldn't care if I got hurt; he was interested only in dinner. So we planned a little ruse. Dave was there to pick me up, and two husbands helped me off the bus, telling Dave that I'd hurt my leg. He gave me some assistance then asked, "Who's going to cook dinner?" Everyone laughed, and I rolled my eyes and said, "What did I tell you?"

I went by train with the Geilenkirchen Ski Club again to Bled, Yugoslavia. I did my own bag drags with a suitcase, boot bag, and ski bag—a real challenge every time we changed trains. A few passengers' heads got smacked by my ski bag, which was strapped diagonally across my back. Arriving in Munich, we took taxis to the American military hotel. The next day, we boarded a bus to Bled, more bag drags. Our once-beautiful old hotel on the lake now catered to ski groups. The skiing wasn't enjoyable—bad weather, icy conditions, and primitive, wooden chair lifts.

We had planned to fly to Sarajevo for a day at the Olympics; however, the weather deteriorated, and our flight was canceled. Our bus took us to Ljubljana where we caught an all-night train to Sarajevo. Damage from the blizzard was evident, downed trees everywhere. We took a bus to the women's slalom race and trudged up a slope just above the finish line and waited...and waited and waited. Fog had us "socked in," and I saw only two skiers of the fourteen racers who were able to complete the run. I had told Mother and friends to look for me on TV in my yellow ski suit; however, since all Olympic workers wore yellow jackets, I was indistinguishable! We strolled around town in the afternoon, sightseeing and shopping for souvenirs (which were scarce). I finally bought a little towel, a tiny metal plate, and swiped an Olympic poster off the train station wall.

We watched an outdoor awards ceremony in town that evening, ate dinner, and then strolled over to the ice arena. Talk about being in the right place at the right time! The women figure skaters were in their final rehearsal, and we watched their entire routines from rink side. The American girls—Tiffany Chen, Elaine Zayak, and Rosalyn Summers—were having difficulty, but one skater took our breaths away—beautiful, smooth, and elegant. I was not the least bit surprised to learn later that Katrina Witt from East Germany had won the gold medal in women's figure skating. That evening made the whole trip worthwhile.

Very tired, we rode the all-night train to Ljubljana, bused to the Bled Hotel, ate breakfast, packed, bused to the Munich train station, and returned to the Netherlands. A long day. I'd survived another adventure but was exhausted and slept for three days.

Along with other officers and their wives, Dave and I made a cold and rainy official visit to Copenhagen, Denmark, where we met Her Majesty Queen Margrethe II. She is a pretty, stalwart lady, and when she was escorted into the reception by a small-in-stature British general, he was almost lost in the voluminous folds of her formal gown. He later took some ribbing about his escort duties. Queen Margrethe gave each of us wives a gold and white daisy charm, her name being the French botanical name for "daisy." She was very friendly and surprisingly informal.

We also met Queen Beatrix of the Netherlands when she visited AFCENT, also a pleasant lady. Her mother, Queen Juliana, had endeared herself to the Dutch citizens through tireless efforts, compassion, and concern after a storm devastated areas of their country. She relinquished her throne to Beatrix in 1980. These two queens and Spain's king comprised our royal repertory.

The newly appointed American ambassador to the Netherlands paid an official visit to AFCENT while we were there. He was quite charming, very handsome, and very young! A Kennedy lookalike. I added "ambassador" to my VIP list. His wife had cowritten the book *Coping With His Success*, personal anecdotes and experiences gleaned from a confidential questionnaire sent to hundreds of women across the country. She described her "difficult" life, but we knew she lived in a mansion complete with cooks, housekeepers, gardeners, chauffeurs, and nannies. We military wives had no sympathy for her since we often lived in 1,200 square feet duplexes or third-floor, walk-up apartments, cooked our own meals and cocktail fare for many events, and paid for gardeners, housecleaners (if we could afford them), and babysitters. We made do with less, while our husbands put their lives on the line every day.

Dave and I visited all twelve provinces of the Netherlands. The north, with its blustery winds and surrounding waters, was very different from the southern forests where we lived. We took many trips to Germany, Austria, Luxembourg, England, Scotland, Switzerland, and Belgium, going to "Brussels for mussels" on Sundays, and France, driving to Paris frequently. Dave always wanted to go to Paris on the weekends (he loved the city), and I'd whine, "But we go to Paris all the time. I'm tired of it." Dave wisely suggested, "For Pete's sake, don't make that comment when we return to the U.S.; they'll think you're a snob or crazy."

After a wonderful trip to the Paris Air Show with two American friends, we went to Normandy to tour towns, museums, cemeteries, and relics of the D-Day invasion. The cemeteries are immaculately maintained by the local people, financed with U.S. funds. We talked briefly to a groundskeeper, who told us he was ten years old when he watched the invasion from his farmhouse. The bunkers are now covered with grass, cows grazing. It was difficult to imagine a devastating invasion had taken place at this peaceful sight. Remnants of landing barges, tanks, and antitank obstacles were still on the beaches. The large memorials were breathtaking, and the rows and rows of grave markers brought tears to our eyes. We whispered to each other respectfully for those who had given their lives.

Dave's Uncle Glenn and Aunt Peg happened to be in France, and we planned to see them after our visit to the invasion sites. Our friend Ken was driving, and he stopped to see *everything*—significant or not—like a magnificent bull grazing in a field. Dave, anxious and impatient because we were running late, pressed Ken to keep his foot on the gas pedal. When we finally arrived, a straight-faced Uncle Glen walked out to meet us in the chateau courtyard, and before he said "Hello" or "Welcome," he said, "You're late." Ken almost fainted. "My god, a true Forgan; it's in the genes." We had dinner at the chateau, remained overnight, and returned home the next morning.

When we went to Scotland, we rented a car and toured the areas Dave's Scottish grandfather, Duncan Macmillan Forgan, described in his autobiography. We found the family home, his school, the castle ruins where he used to play, and the bank where he worked. Across from St. Andrews golf course, we located the building that formerly housed the Forgan Golf Club Manufacturing Company, owned by Duncan's cousin. Stopping at a roadside inn for lunch one day, we ordered spaghetti, the lunch special of the day. The waitress served us plates overflowing with spaghetti, corn, and potatoes. Obviously, the locals tolerate their chilly winters by eating all those starches. The Scots are the friendliest folks I have ever met.

Occasionally Dave hired a young, single sergeant to house and dog sit when we traveled. When we returned home the first time, we found a prepared dinner and a chilled bottle of white wine in the refrigerator. He had done our laundry and folded and placed everything on our bed. He went above and beyond the call of duty by polishing the large four-sided copper hood over the kitchen bar. Another time, along with the dinner, we also found Dave's bedside alarm clock in the refrigerator. Not wanting to embarrass the sergeant, we didn't ask about this mystery. (I didn't care what he placed in the refrigerator as long as that nice dinner was prepared.) However, the next time he house sat, a book Dave had been reading was missing. Poor fellow, he was at a loss as to its disappearance. The book was about Eisenhower, written by Stephen Ambrose. The sergeant wrote to Dr. Ambrose, explaining he had lost the general's book and requested a replacement. Dr. Ambrose mailed him two autographed books. He was scheduled to speak in Brussels and invited Dave and the sergeant to be his dinner guests. They were thrilled. The sergeant's girlfriend and I accompanied the men to Brussels, but she and I had dinner on our own. We met Dr. Ambrose during after-dinner drinks and were entertained by his good humor and lively stories—a real privilege. Add "prominent author" to my repertory of royalty and VIPs.

In May 1984, Dave and I flew from the Netherlands and Todd flew from Arizona to Oklahoma for Bruce's college graduation. I almost fainted when I saw him. His girlfriend had permed his beautiful, thick, wavy hair. His hair looked like curly spaghetti.

Swallowing my words of displeasure, I focused on how proud we were of his Bachelor of Fine Arts degree in graphic design and illustration. His impressive artwork was displayed in the Fine Arts Building. He had designed his own graduation announcement on a red card with a drawing of a Bruce lookalike with a beard, which portrayed a frustrated, frazzled, and confused artist and announced the following:

> Dear Mrs. Landers,
> Grief lies heavy upon my breast. I have been smitten
> By a rare flower called graduation.
> She is rich in beauty and has sworn of her love for me.
> But woe!
> Our employers have an ancient grudge for experience
> And have forbidden our love.
> We are helpless because,
> Although we are very mature for our ages,
> She is only five and I twenty-two.
> What do I do?
> Bruce D. Forgan
> Bachelor of Fine Arts
> Saturday, May 5th 11:00 a.m.
> Oklahoma State University

Hmm. It called for an explanation. Did it mean he had graduated and didn't have a job?

After Bruce's graduation, Todd returned to Tucson for summer school, and Dave and I visited Mother in McAlester (who, once again, declined to attend a graduation). Bruce and his best friend, Tom, met us at the Tulsa airport to accompany us back to the Netherlands. I was a nervous wreck as they barely made the boarding time. Two days later, I put them on a train in Aachen, Germany, to euro rail for two weeks. On the French Riviera, they took pictures of topless chicks, only to discover they had no film in the camera. (Did they make up that story?) The tired boys returned to the Netherlands, and we hauled them to the Brussels airport to return to Oklahoma. Bruce was moving to Tulsa to start a new job. Finally, he would be on someone else's payroll.

I returned to the U.S. in the late summer of 1984 after volunteering to move Dave's mother into a retirement condo in Sarasota, Florida. A "Discover America" package for a thirty-day trip was available, and I tackled my route plan according to Eastern Airlines' flight schedule. I flew from Brussels to Atlanta, to San Antonio, to Austin, to Houston, to Tulsa, drove to McAlester, flew to Tucson, and to Las Vegas, visiting friends and relatives along the way. Finally arriving in Florida, I moved Dave's mother. I quickly got her settled, said good-bye, and flew to Tallahassee to visit more friends before flying to Atlanta for my return trip to Brussels. Wow, what a trip.

In the fall, Mother and her best friend, Pebble Pirtle, came for a three-week visit. Pebble Pirtle was her real name. People thought I was joking, so I dropped her last name and introduced her as Pebble, saving explanations. We did whirlwind sightseeing in the Netherlands, Belgium, Germany, and France. I regretted not taking them to San Georgio, Italy, where my maternal grandmother was born and lived for fifteen years. For two seventy-five-year-old women, Pebble and Mother were very brave to make the trip to see us; however, Mother said she never wanted to travel again.

Christmas arrived and so did Todd. Bruce went to Mother's house for the holidays. If he couldn't be with us, I was content he was at his grandmother's, which also made her happy. Instead of turkey, she cooked his favorite: manicotti.

After New Year's Day, Dave, Todd, and I traveled by train to the French Riviera and stayed in the Grand Hotel in Cannes directly across the street from the beautiful, blue Mediterranean Sea. What a lovely area—until *it snowed.* First time in fifteen years! We have a picture of two doves perched on our balcony, overlooking palm trees and the Med. Two days later, we took another picture of the same two doves, standing on the snow-covered railing, their feathers fluffed, overlooking snow-covered palm trees. Fortunately, we had departed home in cold weather and had coats to wear, even in the restaurants.

The weather didn't slow us down. We rented a Mercedes, donned our coats, turned up our collars, and toured the area— Monte Carlo, Eze, Monaco (where we viewed Grace Kelly's tomb at their church's altar), Antibes, Nice—steep, winding roads through the hillsides and lots of steps to climb in the villages. Our last morning, Todd suffered from some obviously bad seafood he had eaten the night before. He was almost green. We loaded him into our "state room" on the train, and in between trips to the bathroom, he slept. I asked the train station's ticket girl to pronounce the two French cities, Caen and Cannes, because the names sounded alike to me. "Oh, no," she said, "It's very different." She pronounced them for us, but to my ears, they still sounded the same.

Todd returned to Arizona for the second semester of his junior year, majoring in parties, girls, and finance—in that order. He claimed he would be a millionaire by the time he was thirty years old. What happened? He had champagne taste on a beer budget.

The Right Stuff was playing at the movie theater at the headquarters locale. I called the American Air Force wives whose husbands were pilots, suggesting we all dress up in our husbands' flying suits and attend the movie in fighter pilot style. The husbands were out of town on a war exercise, so we were free for the evening. I sewed a sign on my back that said, "A Fighter Pilot's Wife with the Right Stuff," and on the front, I had a little patch with the quote, "Fighter pilots do it with jet propulsion." We monopolized the front row of the theater and drew some strange looks from the few theater patrons. Someone complained about the strange women in the flying suits. The report read like this:

> During the exercise week, the Alliance Theater at AFCENT ran a showing of *The Right Stuff*. I and several other NCOs

noticed this group of what appeared to be strange-looking USAF officers. Their flight suits fit a little loose, we noticed the long hair, and one was wearing cowboy boots. We became very uncomfortable and thought about calling the police on these imposters. I moved around and got close enough to read their nametags. I was shocked! Some of the names were Forgan, Eddy, and Lord. I knew this wasn't General Forgan. I suspect these ladies were officers' wives, masquerading as their husbands. It was a difficult situation because we weren't sure how to address them or whether or not to salute. I think it is unfair to the enlisted population for them to play these kinds of jokes. It confused us and made us extremely uncomfortable.

We heard nothing about this complaint until an officer in charge of complaints presented me with a copy of the complaint for posterity. We were told that the complaint was real, but the story had been enhanced. Every time I try to do something fun or out of the ordinary, I get in trouble. Because I was the general's wife, I got away with it this time.

In the spring, our good friends, Judy and Boomer Roberts, with another couple from Kansas City came to Germany for a symposium. After it was over, they rented a car and drove to our house in Nieuwenhagen. Boomer asked Dave why cars had been honking and flashing their lights at him. "Damn foreigners." We reminded Boomer that *he* was the foreigner. Dave asked if he had been in the left lane. He responded, "Yes, so what?" Dave explained that, in Europe, the left lane is for extremely fast drivers and passing only. It was a wonder Boomer didn't have a Mercedes or Porsche going one hundred miles per hour—or more—run right up his tailpipe. We did lots of sightseeing and shopping, and at the Frankfurt airport, it took three carts to haul all their luggage and European bargains.

Chuck Donnelly, our old friend from Maxwell Air Force Base and the Pentagon and Dave's boss at Torrejon Air Base, received his fourth star and became United States Air Force Europe Commander, assigned to Ramstein Air Base in Germany. We were honored to know him and proud of his success. Chuck and Carolyn Donnelly visited all the bases in his command, including AFCENT. Approximately twenty generals from the central region of NATO, representing Germany, Belgium, England, Canada, the Netherlands, and the United States, attended the dinner honoring Chuck.

During cocktails, Chuck whispered in my ear, "How would you like to come to Ramstein and be the wife of the Deputy Chief of Staff for Operations?" He smiled and walked away before I could question him. At AFCENT for almost three years, we had anticipated a new assignment at anytime. At my first chance to speak to Dave, I mentioned Chuck's comment. He looked astounded, curious, and baffled all at the same time. The AFCENT commander (a German four-star) clinked his glass for everyone's attention, welcomed General Donnelly, and turned over the floor to him. Chuck thanked everyone, gave his "glad to be here" speech, and then said, "You all know Shirley Forgan. I know her as Dobbie. Well, tonight she's going home with a fighter pilot who has been selected to receive his second star and come to Ramstein to work for me."

You could have knocked us over with a feather. The air force can certainly spring surprises. I couldn't convince anyone that we had no clue about the promotion, much less the new assignment—both of which Dave readily accepted. He would be flying again and directing all American Air Force flying operations in Europe, a dream come true. We could hardly eat our dinner while receiving congratulations from everyone and trying to get Chuck's attention for more details. He seemed to be as excited for us as we were for ourselves. After the promotion was official, Dave, in his normal, casual, and unceremonious demeanor, read the air force order that listed his date of rank, attached the additional stars to his uniform, and went to work—no ceremony, no pomp. Typical of Dave.

The month of May hit me like a ton of bricks. My fiftieth birthday. A man "sees" Abraham when he reaches the ripe old age of fifty; therefore, a woman "sees" Sara. Depressed about becoming a half century old, I didn't want any celebration, so Dave planned a quiet dinner for the two of us at a nice Dutch restaurant. Stopping by the officers' club to get some Dutch guilders at the convenient cashier, Dave said, "Come on in with me." I refused, saying I'd wait in the car and pout about being another year "over the hill." He kept insisting, so I finally gave in, slammed the car door, and walked with him into the club, muttering to myself. When we rounded the corner of a private dining room, I saw twenty familiar people with silly grins on their faces. Someone finally shouted, "Happy Birthday!" Dave had arranged a dinner party, and I had never been so surprised in my life. "Sara" in her mask, stuffed body, wig, scarf, tennis racquet, and tennis shoes was the guest of honor at the end of the table. "She" went home with me, and I gave her a special rocking-chair throne in front of our house, queen for a day. I received riotous gifts, from a heart-embroidered thong to a number fifty football jersey with two stars and a note that said:

> We all know a girly named Shirley
> Whose husband we call "Sir."
> He is tall, and he is cool.
> On the uniform of deep blue
> He wears silver stars.
> There are two!
> So we figured, Shirley,
> Who is really quite nifty,
> Should have her own stars
> Now that she's fifty!

Dave occasionally pulls out all the stops and does something special, and this was one of those occasions.

Todd came home for our last summer in the Netherlands, and he accompanied Nancy Eddy and me to the Wimbledon tennis tournament. Todd knew two girls from the University of Arizona who were spending the summer in London, so he went with us. We flew on Virgin Airways (which always got a couple of snickers) and stayed in the Royal Air Force Officers' Club in London.

The three of us went sightseeing the first day; then Todd called the girls to pick him up at the officers' club. Waiting in the lobby, he was politely, but sternly, asked to remain outside because he wasn't properly attired. He wore Bermuda shorts and a Ralph Lauren polo shirt; however, the club dress rules called for coat and tie. The girls collected Todd from *outside* the club, and Nancy and I took the train to the town of Wimbledon.-

We watched a doubles match between Australians Cash and Fitzgerald and Americans John McEnroe and Peter Fleming. McEnroe displayed his usual bad temper, and Fleming strutted around the court as if he were "King of Tennisdom." During the match, a thunder, lightning, and torrential rain storm descended upon us. We ran to the protective cover of the tunnel, which led to the seating areas. Lightning bolts and thunder boomed all around as we stood ankle deep in water. We could have been electrocuted. The tennis match continued after the storm passed. We raced over to our reserved seats at court one to see a doubles match with Martina Navratilova and Pat Shriver versus Hanna Mandlikova and Wendy Turnbull. Drenched from the rain, Nancy and I walked to the train station and were stunned to see the storm's damage—trees broken, limbs lying everywhere, signs blown over, and windows busted.

We flew back home, Todd returned to U of A, and I prepared for a short move to Germany.

Before I close this chapter, I would like to share a few fasinating stories from some Germans stationed with us—"their side" of World War II. A colonel said, "The next war, I am going to fight on the American side." When asked, "Why?" he answered, "You always win." Another German colonel shared a story about returning to his hometown after the war ended. It took him a year to find his way. I asked, "At eleven years of age, how did you survive?" He looked at me solemnly and confessed, "You must remember, Shirley, I was well trained in the Hitler Youth Corp." What a revelation.

One of the German wives told me she had lost every male member of her family—father, brother, and uncles. This same wife stood next to me at one of our American celebrations and joined us in singing "The Star Spangled Banner," saying she was proud of America and what we always did to help the world. I wish more people felt her appreciation. War is destructive, terrible, and sad, but time heals. Those who were our enemies are now our friends. We also suffered terrible losses, but our homeland and families were safe in the good ole' USA. The German four-star general who commanded AFCENT retired while we were there. He had lost his right arm during the war and did not pin up the uniform's empty sleeve. Dave said it used to drive him crazy when General Von Senger gave a briefing, loose sleeve flapping about, quite distracting. The general was a tall man, serious, and rather intimidating. However, Dave's impression was that of a good officer, a very solid man, who worked NATO issues for the good of NATO, not just for Germany. General Von Senger attended a party at our house one night shortly before his retirement, and I gathered my nerve to speak to the very formidable man.

"Hello, General, how are you tonight?"

"Fine."

Pause. "Uh, I just wanted to tell you how much Dave admires you and has enjoyed working for you."

He responded, "It's time to go." That ended the conversation—short and to the point. I quickly excused myself to take care of other hostess duties.

We had enjoyed two years and nine months in this land of friendly people, beautiful flowers, delicious cheeses, and lousy weather. It had been a swirl of social events, visitors, travels, and ski trips. Learning and enjoying the characteristics and cultures of each NATO country was very educational. To aid the packers in what was ours and what was not, I put "No" signs on all the military-issue furniture and lamps that we had been using so the movers wouldn't pack them. We were accustomed to surprises when our household goods arrived at our new stations—wastebaskets packed with trash still in them, old newspapers, used bars of soap. If it wasn't nailed down, marked, or thrown away, it got packed. This would be an easy move, just two hours down the road to Headquarters, United States Air Force Europe, designated general's quarters, ready and waiting for us.

At a farewell coffee, the air force wives gave me a beautiful Waterford dish, and Nancy Eddy read the following sweet note:

> Dear Shirley,
> For all those times you worked in the thrift shop, on committees, and on various boards and you made everyone feel so welcome—a big "Thank you." And on behalf of all the air force wives, I would like to say, *"Generally"* speaking, you're our Number One Star!
> Fondly, Nancy

They were a nice group of ladies, and I enjoyed their friendship.

On Dave's last day at work, the Ops Division personnel gave us a champagne send-off. Dave's executive officer escorted us to our chauffeured "chariot," an old, classic Rolls Royce. What a surprise. As we departed AFCENT Headquarters for the last time, all the personnel stood on the sidewalk, came to attention, and saluted as we passed. A great send-off. Thank you "Freddy Eddy."

However, we hadn't traveled more than two miles when the "chariot" went *putt-putt* and conked out. The driver made a phone call; a staff car retrieved us, delivered us to our empty house where we climbed in our own "chariots," the Mazda and Nissan (a second car Dave bought that we'd need in Germany). Without Hazel for the first time in sixteen years, we drove the short, two-hour trip to our eighteenth assignment in twenty-seven years.

Soon after we left, Dave's successor received a threatening phone call to his house (the one we'd occupied), stating, "There is a bomb in General Forgan's house that is scheduled to explode." The new general and his wife were immediately escorted to nearby Geilenkirchen Air Base, a secure, guarded base, where they stayed for several weeks until the scare was over. "Someone" didn't know the Forgans had moved on! Dave thought it was probably the Dutch kids up to some of their antics again, testing the new general on the block. Maybe so, but in those days, it was not to be dealt with lightly. After hearing this news, I was happy to be in a secure housing area on a large American base.

Tot ziens (Good-bye) to the Netherlands and
Guten Tag (Greetings) to Germany.

Ski Heil

Ramstein Air Base, West Germany
Headquarters, United States Air Force Europe
August 1985-March 1987

We crossed the nearby border into Germany and drove to Ramstein Air Base, located in southwest Germany only thirty minutes from France's eastern border. The security police checked our identification cards at the entrance gate, gave Dave a sharp salute, and we entered what was commonly called "Little America." The base was huge, providing everything that one could want or need. Rumors had it that some dependents (wives and children) never left the base. Wondering how the Germans tolerated seventy thousand Americans at various bases in the area, I discovered them to be cordial and helpful. The surrounding land had been devoted primarily to farming, but the locals employed at the U.S. military installations now prospered.

We spent the night and met the movers at our new quarters the next day. Accustomed to living in foreign countries, I taped a numbered sheet of paper over each room's door. If I didn't know the number in the local language, I held up the correct number of fingers, directing the mover to the correct room for the box he was toting. Worked beautifully. Our quarters had been renovated from two apartments into one living complex, so the place was huge—

living room, dining room, kitchen, and his and her dens (originally bedrooms) on the first floor; four bedrooms and two bathrooms on the second floor (originally a separate apartment); a bedroom, bathroom, and recreation room on the third floor. The full-size basement was laundry and storage. In the Netherlands, we had to tolerate ugly transformer boxes that converted European voltage to our 110 volt appliances all over the house; however, since the base was on 110 voltage, transformers weren't necessary.

Mother was always amazed how I found the exact spot for our furniture and accessories. Like fitting a jigsaw puzzle together, I simply placed large items where they fit and decorated around them. I was usually settled in two weeks—no time to dally. Sometimes the movers unpacked all the boxes and placed the contents wherever they could find room—on furniture, floors, shelves, tables, countertops—removing all the moving material when they left. Personally, I preferred to put things away as I unpacked the boxes myself. The downside was having to stuff all the wrapping paper into boxes, flatten the empty boxes, and discard it all.

Our next-door neighbor had been the ZAB wing commander after we left Spain. His wife, in all good humor, I hope, chastised me for initiating programs at ZAB that succeeding commanders' wives had to oversee, sarcastically saying, "Thanks a lot." I replied, "At least you didn't have to coach a tee-ball team." The first snowfall at Ramstein, she and I built a "snow lady" (boobs and all) in our front parking lot. The snow lady wore a hat and had eyes, a nose, big red lips, stone buttons on her bodice, and a "skirt" decorated with leaves—a work of art.

General and Mrs. Donnelly (Chuck and Carolyn) lived in quarters number one across the park from us. They had two full-time house aides, a staff car and driver, and bodyguards who constantly accompanied them. It was rumored that whenever General Donnelly played golf and hit into the woods, miraculously the ball reappeared on the fairway. Every golfer could use that help. Dave and I had no aides, staff car, or bodyguards. Occasionally, I observed a security policeman and his dog checking around our quarters. I didn't know whether to feel frightened or secure.

Dave's official title was Deputy Chief of Staff for Operations, commonly referred to as the DO. Responsible for all American Air Force flying operations throughout Europe, he was able to fly all the latest fighters: F-111, F-15, F-16, A-10, and the F-4. Being back in a cockpit was a real joy for this pilot who had "flown a desk" the previous eight years.

As the wife of the new general on the block, I was interviewed for the Ramstein Officers' Wives' Club monthly newsletter. A few quotes from the article about generals' wives:

> With watchwords such as adaptability, flexibility, humor, and friendship, these women have learned to make the very most of their challenging lives.
>
> Shirley Forgan is one woman who clearly thrives on the topsy-turvy life of the military wife. While discussing her experiences, her ever-present smile and spontaneous laughter make this obvious. With humor and flexibility, she has faced the many occupational hazards of military life.
>
> As a commander's wife, Mrs. Forgan believes it is her goal to improve and make life more pleasant for the families in the military community.
>
> She enjoys playing tennis and bridge and hopes to spend lots of time skiing in Austria and Switzerland while here. When not on the slopes, she wants to "meet as many of the 225 DO wives as I can."

We celebrated Christmas 1985 in Germany with both of our mothers and both sons, together for the first time in three years. Mother came with Bruce from Tulsa, and Mom Forgan and Todd arrived separately, keeping Dave busy making trips to the Frankport airport. We unwrapped our usual mega-amount of presents, the "toys" getting larger and more expensive.

Mom Forgan returned to Florida, and Bruce and Todd joined other visiting college students on a chartered bus trip to Paris for

New Year's Eve. Dave and I and my mother attended the New Year's Eve festivities at the Ramstein Officers' Club. Shortly after midnight, Dave was called out of the dining room. I observed several officers who worked for him also begin to exit. He returned a few minutes later to say that he had to leave, and he couldn't tell me anything else. He was still tightlipped after he got home in the middle of the night. After the holidays, all returned to their respective homes and tried to live up to their 1986 New Year's resolutions.

For the next four and a half months, Dave was instrumental in planning a secret mission. Only about fifty people were aware of it. In the middle of April, Dave left for England, which I thought nothing of because he was always flying somewhere. April 16, while watching CNN (our only English channel on TV), I heard the newscaster interrupt with "breaking news." Libya had been bombed by U.S. Air Force and Navy fighter planes in retaliation for a Berlin disco bombing and other terrorist activity. Suddenly the answer to Dave's secretiveness, as well as his mysterious New Year's Eve disappearance, was clear. I was glued to the TV the rest of the day. When Dave returned home several days later, I exploded with questions, which he answered as much as he was allowed.

The U.S. Air Force pilots from England bases were denied flights over France and Spain by their respective governments, forcing our pilots to fly through the Strait of Gibraltar. Without the use of European continental bases to land, the pilots had to make multiple air-to-air refuelings. Those brave pilots sat on sore butts in their fighter planes for fourteen hours for the attack that lasted ten minutes. The raid on Libya is controversial, but the crushing strikes caused a remarkable stop in Libya-sponsored terrorist activity.

Christmas in Germany with mothers and sons

Dave and I –
too many martinis??

General and Mrs. Forgan
at a formal reception

I took advantage of wonderful ski areas in Switzerland and Austria, only five to six hours away. The base recreation center chartered buses to ski destinations every weekend, departing late Friday afternoon and returning Sunday night. It was a great deal, cheap, and left the driving to someone else. On one trip, I questioned several passengers about their level of skiing and most admitted being intermediate skiers. They readily agreed to have me tag along with them. I realized I was in trouble when several of the skiers took long cords from their pockets and attached them to their skis and boots. I nervously, naïvely asked what they were for. One of the gals replied, "If your skis come off when you fall in deep snow, you can find them." *Deep snow? Oh, what have I gotten myself into?* I didn't dare fall. I skied on—without cords—doing my best to keep up, snowplowing through the white stuff. Snowy weather conditions were reducing our visibility so after lunch we returned to the bus. The next day, instead of long cords, I attached myself to some saner skiers.

One time in Austria, we were riding a chair lift alongside a mountain ridge, when I suddenly realized on three sides of me there was nothing but *air*. I almost swallowed my stomach. It was like being in an airplane seat without the airplane. At the top, the wind was blowing, and I was petrified I would get blown over the edge. I took a deep breath, gritted my teeth, and pushed my "go button." I wanted off that mountain peak quickly. I gratefully made it to the bottom, falling only once.

Another time I went to Switzerland with a couple who had reservations at a different hotel than mine. When they checked in, a room was available for me, so I called and canceled my original hotel reservation. Later, I received a bill in the mail, charging me for the entire weekend. I called and explained, but they were emphatic that I owed the amount because I canceled too late. I told them I wouldn't pay. I received another letter quoting their country's laws regarding hotels and reservations. Humbly, I went to our legal department where the head JAG was a friend. He called the hotel and, like a good lawyer should, talked them out of the charge, stating I was just a "dumb" American woman and didn't realize I had done anything wrong. He also said they should have told me that I was liable for the charges at the time I canceled, because being an American I was unfamiliar with their laws. I got out of that one. I was scared Dave might not let me go on any more ski trips.

My fabulous ski adventures took me to areas most of us have never heard of—the Zugspitze in Germany; Engelberg, Grindelwald, Wengen, Kleine Scheidegg, Jungfrau, Adelboden, Crans Montana, and Zermatt in Switzerland. In Austria, I was enchanted on the beautiful slopes of St. Anton, Lech, St. Christof, Zurs, Steuben, and nervous on the glaciers at Hinterux and Kaprun. When in the Netherlands, I had skied other unfamiliar resorts of St. Veit, Erpfendorf, Fieberbrunn, Steinplatte, and Kitzbuhel in Austria; Les Arcs in France; and the treachrous, icy slopes of Yugoslavia. Dave never accompanied me. I skied; he flew. I hit the slopes as often as I could because our next assignment might be in Texas. (Little did I know.)

After winter snows had melted and I hung up my skis, I attended a tennis camp in southern Germany, and on our return, a friend and I detoured through Austria, enjoying the beautiful Alps. Tall steeples of picturesque churches peeked over the skyline, and a profusion of flower boxes outlined the decks on houses. We were captivated by the musical cowbells and envisioned Julie Andrews coming over the next hill, arms outstretched, twirling, and joyously singing, "The hills are alive with the sound of music."

I flew back to the U.S. to spend a month visiting friends and family. Mother and I drove her car from McAlester to Tucson to see Todd, who was in summer school. He and another fellow rented a little house near the campus, and it was a mess. My motherly instincts kicked in. I wanted to clean the place, but I denied myself the questionable "pleasure." I pretended the mess didn't exist and tried to erase it from my mind to enjoy the visit. Whoever said Arizona is not hot in the summer because it is dry has been out in the sun too long. It was 110 degrees in the shade. Todd said it was the price they paid for mild winters.

From Tucson, we drove to California to visit relatives and backtracked through northern Arizona and Colorado.

In eastern Colorado, a patrolman stopped me at a speed trap. I argued that the cruise control was set at the proper speed, but the car went faster downhill. He didn't buy my story. I showed him my International Driver's License, which was unfamiliar to him, explaining that my stateside driver's license had expired while we were living in Europe. (Dave was allowed to retain a Florida driver's license because Florida was our legal domicile; however, military dependents were required to have licenses in whatever state they were currently living. Unfair.) Had the cop read the fine print on my International License, he would have seen, "This license is not legal for driving in the U.S." Besides the speeding ticket, he could have fined me for no license. I argued about a surcharge on the ticket for $19 to assist victims of crime in Colorado. Mother was cringing, fearful I would be arrested and sent to jail. My arguments not getting me anywhere, I finally just wrote a check. Mother was relieved to make our getaway. I stewed all the way to Salina, Kansas, our next stop. When I received our breakfast bill the following morning, I nearly fell out of my chair. I was charged for the milk I poured into my cereal. Feeling paranoid, I was ready to end the trip and return to Europe.

We finally arrived in Tulsa, had a short visit with Bruce, and met his new girlfriend. I wasn't impressed but kept my mouth shut and pretended to be friendly. (I've smiled through gritted teeth for numerous girlfriends squired by our sons over the years. I longed for them to get married, but the quality hadn't measured up to the quantity.) Our almost four thousand-mile journey ended in McAlester, and I returned home to Germany, thankful to be in my own bed and for no more cross-country driving.

When I wasn't gallivanting, many visitors appeared on our

Ramstein doorstep—both official and unofficial. Unofficially, the Eddins dropped by with their handsome teenager. We didn't recognize the two-year-old "key hider" we had known in Carlisle, Pennsylvania. "Bo" Boehringer discovered us when he was deployed to Ramstein for temporary duty with the California Air National Guard. This was the same "Bo" who was with Dave in his red Corvette my first day in Dallas when I drooled over jet fighter pilots twenty-nine years ago.

Mike Carns showed up at Ramstein for a conference and brought his wife, Victoria. After the conference, we joined them for a week's tour around northeast Germany. Along the East German border were frightening views of border fortifications. About two feet beyond a simple barricade was a sign reading, "*Halt! Hier Grenze.*" ("Stop! Here is the border.") The fortifications beyond the sign were unbelievable:

One hundred meter strip of cleared terrain
Double metal grid fence with electrical and acoustic alarms; the space between panels mined, guarded by patrolling dogs
Vehicle barrier ditch reinforced with concrete slabs
Six meter plowed detection strip
Patrol road
Concrete observation towers and bunkers
Row of high-powered lights
Concrete wall

The distance from where we stood to the fence on the other side was about two hundred yards. We looked at the Russian guards through our binoculars as they stared back at us through theirs. We reminded ourselves that this fortification was primarily to keep the East Germans in, not keep us out. Saturated with sightseeing— museums, parks, memorials, local culture, and architecture—we returned to our American "sanctuary" at Ramstein. Victoria and Mike flew back to their base in Hawaii.

Officially, we welcomed high-ranking officers from Israel, whose wives accompanied them. I was chosen to host the wives and invited several American wives to join us for lunch. We took them to the BX to shop afterwards. They were absolutely fascinated with the amount of items available and couldn't understand why so many different brands of the same item were offered. How does one explain, in a brief answer, our free enterprise and American economic system in which businesses compete with each other? I shrugged my shoulders and said, "Competition." They shrugged their shoulders and muttered, "Too much."

A young U.S. Congressman from Oklahoma and his entourage descended upon Ramstein to inquire about air force defense needs to help them appropriately vote in Congress. Probably because I was from Oklahoma, Dave and I were invited by General and Mrs. Donnelly to join them and other guests for the evening. While coffee was being served, General Donnelly scooted back his chair, looked seriously at Representative Mike, and asked him questions. Puzzled, Mike asked, "Are we going to discuss business now?" General Donnelly responded, "That's what you're here for, isn't it?" Chuck Donnelly wasn't about to let that young whippersnapper congressman get away with just being entertained for the evening.

I was pleasantly surprised to discover that one of the young ladies accompanying Mike on this junket was from McAlester. She told me, "I drove by your house recently and saw your mother working in her yard." "Yep, that's Mother—always working in her yard." Small world.

We were honored by a visit from retired Colonel George (Bud) Day and his wife, Doris. (Yes, her name is "Doris Day," but she claimed she did not sing.) Bud had been a POW in Hanoi for five years, seven months, and thirteen days and was touring bases for speaking engagements. Bud's thirty-year military career included action in World War II, in the Korean War, and in Vietnam. Of his more than seventy decorations, fifty are for combat, including the Air Force Cross and the Medal of Honor.

"All POWs, except maybe three or four, came to some very basic conclusions about themselves, their country, and the way we live," he said. "I learned that you can't go it alone. My mind went back to religious principles with which I was raised." He added, "Before Vietnam, my attendance at 'happy hour' was a little bit better than my attendance at church. I felt hypocritical suddenly praying again. I can say prayer didn't stop the torture, but it gave me courage, it kept my mind working, and it gave me the most important thing: faith."

Bud Day was my dinner partner at the Ramstein Officers' Club their last night, and I noticed his arm was still misshapen, the result of torture and improper healing. Doris spoke at the officers' wives' club luncheon and had us laughing one minute and crying the next—crying when we heard what she endured as a "waiting wife," not knowing if her husband was dead or alive, trying to raise their children alone, and keeping her own faith and sanity after so many years without her husband. We admired her sense of humor about some of the incidents after Bud came home. She heard doors closing, and when she investigated, she found Bud opening and closing doors, walking in and out without guards or locks. She happily let him enjoy his newfound freedoms that we take for granted. Notice how many times a day you open and close a door—something he couldn't do for over five years. She said he became very nervous when he heard keys jangling. The noise revived fearful memories of guards taking POWs to the torture area.

Hearing stories through the years from several former POWs, I found that religion played a very important part in their survival. The men were convinced their prayers were answered for the strength to stay alive another week, day, hour, or another minute. I still experience deep sorrow when I think of what those brave incarcerated men endured. They were tortured unmercifully, lacked medical attention, and barely had enough food to survive. Some didn't. May God bless those who survived and must live with memories of those horrible years.

We bumped into Colonel Don Kosovac and his wife, Bitsy, at Ramstein where they were on R & R (Rest and Recuperation) for a few days. Don was the Air Attaché in Prague, Czechoslovakia (Czechoslovakia was under communist rule at the time), and he asked if we'd be interested in visiting Prague. We said, "Of course." On Armed Forces Day, he would be hosting a formal reception for each country's attaché assigned to Prague. The U.S. Ambassador to Czechoslovakia wrote Headquarters USAFE, requesting General Forgan to be the visiting official host officer. The personal invitation read:

On the Occasion of Armed Forces Day
of the United States of America,
The Staff of the Defense Attaché Office
requests the honor of the presence of
Major General and Mrs. David W. Forgan
at a reception on Tuesday, 20 May 1986
between 1700 and 1900 hours.

We were flown in an air force C-12 to the German-Czech border where Don and Bitsy met us in their car and drove two hours to Prague. As we passed through each village, Don pointed out Russian soldiers watching us through binoculars. He said they would keep track of us all the way, making sure we were where we were supposed to be.

I thought we had a big house at Ramstein. I almost fainted when I saw what an attaché colonel lived in. It was a mansion. A local family provided a full-time cook, gardener, and housekeeper, and whatever else was needed to maintain the house and social requirements.

We met the Russian attaché at the reception. It was a little intimidating, meeting my first real communist. Don warned us that the Russian pretended not to speak or understand English. It was a friendly reception, and we met some interesting people from all over the world.

The next day, a personal guide gave us an exciting tour of the city. She took us to a local artist's home to see his pen and ink drawings of Prague. I loved his artwork and bought a large drawing of the St. Charles Bridge. The American ambassador was out of town, and we were privileged to tour his residence. It looked like a small Versailles. Gold was on everything—the bathroom plumbing, mirror frames, and crystal chandeliers. On loan from museums, huge paintings adorned the walls. My mouth gaped in total awe at the showplace. I couldn't fathom how anyone lived there in comfort.

When the Kosovacs drove us back to the border, I waved at one of the Russian soldiers watching us through his binoculars. We flew back to our comfortable four-floor duplex with chrome plumbing and brass lamps.

Dave made various official visits, and I accompanied him on several: Strasbourg (France), Heidelberg (Germany), and Bern (Switzerland). We traveled to southern Germany with three other American generals and their wives and four German generals and their wives on a three-car train: an engine, a sitting car, and a dining car. We American wives wore conservative slacks and sweaters. When the train stopped to pick up a German general's wife, she paraded onboard with tousled, upswept, bleached-blond hair, tight blue jeans tucked into stylish boots, and a red suede Bavarian jacket under a fur coat. All the German wives sported full-length fur coats; we American women were somewhat dowdy in comparison.

Following lunch in the dining car, the women adjourned to the sitting car to visit while the men conducted military business. After a day and night of sightseeing in Munich, we were driven to a Bavarian farm for lunch. It was the middle of winter, and the animals were in the barn, which was connected to the house— not a nice aroma. Wrapped in blankets, we went on horse-drawn sleigh rides; I was sitting in front with the driver when our horse lifted his tail and broke wind. Very embarrassing, but the witty German general behind me said, "This horse has jet propulsion." That defused an awkward moment. The sleigh driver didn't flinch. Living next to the barn, he was probably accustomed to the odor.

That night we enjoyed dinner at a German restaurant, and the

American generals tried to keep up with the German generals' intake of liters of beer, an impossible challenge. At the train station the next day, for the return trip, I took a different train to Innsbruck, Austria, for a glorious ski weekend at St. Anton with friends from Ramstein.

Unofficially, Dave and I traveled around Germany, driving the "Romantic Way" through Rothenburg and other old medieval cities. We cruised the Rhine and Mozel Rivers and visited Trier, Germany's oldest city. On one of our speedy drives on the autobahn, a policeman pulled in front of us, flashed his lights, and posted a sign in his rear window saying "Please pull over" in six languages. He explained that even though there was no speed limit on most of the autobahn, there was a 100k speed limit (about 62 mph) around town entrances and exits. Dave ignored those signs and pressed right on down the highway at one hundred miles per hour, resulting in a fine. We still laugh about the sign in the rear window; clever idea for speeding foreigners.

Todd notified us in the fall of '86 that he would finally receive his B.S. degree in finance in December—after four and half years and two summer schools. Before making flight reservations, I made him guarantee our trip was warranted. Bruce flew to Tucson where we attended graduation and celebrated getting another son through college. We then flew to Denver, Colorado, and drove a rented car to a condo in Frisco to spend the Christmas holiday. To decorate our tree, we improvised. Bruce created a snowman chain from folded and cut paper; Todd stuck marshmallows on the branches; I hung candy canes; and after we opened our gifts, we hung the bows on the tree. Cute. We skied and joined the Cafferys at their house for Christmas dinner. Their daughter and one son were home for the holidays. Because our kids hadn't seen each other in twelve years, it was a fun reunion for them too. Great snow, blue skies, and sunshiny days made for perfect skiing.

Todd returned to Tucson to job hunt, Bruce returned to his Tulsa job, and Dave and I flew to Toronto to spend New Year's with Frances and Jim LaVigne. We drove to Niagara-on-the-Lake, often called the loveliest town in Ontario, where we had a festive celebration New Year's Eve at our hotel. Midnight prompted kisses for everyone and toasts for Auld Lang Syne. It had been twenty-seven years since we met the LaVignes in Panama City, Florida. Old friends sometimes die, but the memories never fade away.

We had some great parties at Ramstein in addition to the usual "hail and farewells," promotions, holiday and birthday festivities—any excuse for more camaraderie. A "Fifties Fling" was staged in a hangar, and someone found two old classic cars that enhanced the decorations and atmosphere. Two of us wives dressed as drive-in car hops. We each wore a short black flannel skirt and vest (with our name embroidered in red), a white blouse with red tie, a little white apron, a waitress headpiece crafted from a white paper doily, and indoor roller skates. We carried a tray on which a hamburger, a paper cup of Coke, and a plate of French fries were glued. Most participants wore blue jeans, long shirts, letter jackets, and sweaters; therefore, we were the hit of the evening.

We hosted an Operations Division party at our house called "Come as Your Secret Desire." I dressed with *big* (plastic) boobs under a tight, white turtleneck shirt. One guest appeared as a big Mac truck driver, complete with dangling keys hanging from his belt, a "Keep on Truckin'" T-shirt, a long hair wig, and a CAT hat. A dapper "yachtsman" paid a visit dressed in white pants and shirt, blue blazer with pocket crest, red ascot, white cap, and the required sunglasses. But the prize for the best costume went to Dave dressed as an air force wife.

I bought a large dress for him at the thrift shop and asked the sales girl at the BX, "What is the biggest size you have in pantyhose?" When she answered, "Queen," I said, "No, I need them bigger than that." She looked me up and down quizzically, and I quickly explained, "Oh no, they're not for me; they're for my husband." I left her standing there, flustered, with her mouth open.

Completing "Mrs. Air Force Wife's" ensemble were earrings, a necklace, and a black wig. He/she carried a handbag full of foreign exchange, a bridge book, a golf club, a tennis racquet, and several plastic shopping bags. I did his/her extremely impressive makeup with blue eyeshadow, mascara, rouge, and lipstick.

He/she offered and received lots of hugs and kisses from the men at the party. When a newly-assigned colonel and wife came to our front door, "Mrs. Air Force Wife" greeted the officer with a hug and a kiss on the cheek. The man started backing away, wide-eyed and stunned. If this was Mrs. Forgan, *she* was worried, and if this was General Forgan, *he* was even more concerned. Everyone roared with laughter. I don't think the new couple knew whether to laugh or cry.

That successful party came back to haunt us. One evening, we were at Chuck and Carolyn Donnellys' with several couples for cocktails and dinner, honoring a visiting navy admiral. Dave told the story of our "Secret Desire" party, and Carolyn did not think it was funny that Dave portrayed an air force wife in such a frivolous manner and told him so. All Dave could say was, "Carolyn, when did you lose your sense of humor?" I wanted to crawl under the table.

In February 1987, General Donnelly's secretary called our house to say the general would stop by for a drink after work. Dave thought, *Uh-oh, what have I done now? Am I in trouble for my AF wife impersonation? Whose toes have I stepped on?* We nervously welcomed the general into our quarters, Dave made us drinks, and we chatted about inane things until finally, Chuck dropped the bomb. He said, "Dave, you're going to Sheppard Air Force Base as the commanding general. The Change of Command will be

March 31." We couldn't believe our ears; we had been at Ramstein only seventeen months. I told Chuck, "I can't be there March 31 because I'm going to Russia on a wives' club trip." He looked at me and sternly stated, "No, Dobbie, you are going to be in Wichita Falls, Texas, on March 31." Well, shut my mouth. Dave had mixed emotions. Being Sheppard's commanding general was an honor, but jet fuel runs in the veins of fighter pilots; all they want to do is fly. Chuck departed, and Dave tried to answer all my questions and gather his wits. He didn't want to leave this ideal assignment at Ramstein, flying all the latest fighter planes. Was this good news? Was it bad? One never knew for sure. Promotions and new assignments came in surprise packages.

Disappointed, I immediately canceled my Russian trip; however, complicating matters, Frances LaVigne and I had plans to ski in Austria and Switzerland and visit Portugal in March. She had made all the arrangements, and all was paid. Since Dave and I would still be in Germany in March, I didn't see a way out. It would be a hectic month.

We wrote the boys about our new assignment. Bruce was still working in Tulsa, and Todd was still working at getting a job, selling kitchen knives in the meantime. We called our mothers, who were both excited that we were coming home. Mother was especially thrilled because Wichita Falls is only three hours from her home in McAlester. After our second five-year tour in Europe, I looked forward to being on American soil again with green money, common language, and familiar culture. I was certain Daddy was cheering from his grave. His daughter was going to live in Texas where he was born and raised.

I attempted to get organized before the move across the big pond again. Then another wife and I rendezvoused with Frances at Interlaken train station in Switzerland. We spent several days skiing the slopes at Grindelwald and Wengen. We had beautiful weather, good snow, and Barb and I did our best to keep up with "Gold-Medalist Frances."

Returning to Ramstein, we took a couple days' breather before

Frances and I drove to St. Anton, Austria. It was stop and go in bumper-to-bumper traffic in a nasty snowstorm for twelve hours rather than the normal five. We were exhausted when we finally arrived at our destination, my knuckles white from gripping the steering wheel. Because we hadn't eaten, our hostess at the gasthaus where we were staying prepared a little supper for us, and we hit the sack.

Frances and I skied the next few days at St. Anton, Lech, St. Christof, and Steuben. Frances especially liked a mogul run at Steuben that I had difficulty with, so I said, "Be my guest. I'll wait right here until you get back." I was content at the bottom of a chairlift for what I thought would be about fifteen minutes. Time passed; I kicked off my skis and sat on the snow. When it started snowing, I got a chairlift blanket, wrapped up in it for warmth, and sat back down on the snow. Now I was beginning to worry. Where was she? Was she lost? Was she hurt? Had she run off with a ski instructor? How long should I wait before trying to find my way back without her? European ski area boundaries are not well marked, and neither of us was sure how to get back to St. Anton. I was beginning to worry about myself. I could be lost, frozen, and not found until spring.

An hour later, in a haze of falling snow, four skiers appeared. Thank God, one of them was Frances. In the poor visibility, she had had a hard time finding her way, so she tagged along with an instructor and his two students. She started laughing when she saw me sitting on the ground, covered with snow, saying I looked like a "white Buddha." I did not think it was funny, but I was thankful we were together again. The instructor pointed us in the direction for St. Anton. Hampered by heavily falling snow, we followed tall metal sign poles planted alongside the ski run. We made it to a lift that would get us to our destination, but it was closed. We rode a shuttle bus to St. Anton, my legs grateful.

We drove back to Ramstein, in the normal time, dumped our ski gear, and regrouped for our next escapade to Portugal. Dave drove us to Frankfurt where we caught a plane to Lisbon. We rented a car, took up temporary residence at the beautiful Lisbon Ritz Hotel, and toured the city and part of the coast. Driving into central Portugal then heading south, we drove past gypsies in colorful one-horse, two-wheeled wagons and went around a sheep herder, guiding his sheep down the narrow two-lane road. Wine vineyards, cork tree forests, and fruit orchards dotted the hillsides.

At the Atlantic Ocean coast, we located our rental apartment at Lagos on Praia du Luz (Beach of Light) where we settled for a few days. We bought groceries, and Frances had a problem at breakfast. She wanted toast. Never one to be thwarted, she created a bread holder from a clothes hanger and held it over the gas stove in the kitchen. *Voila*. Toast. We toured villages, admired the huge coastal rock formations and beaches, and watched a fisherman's wedding. Fishermen working on their boats and nets provided charming photo opportunities.

Leaving the beaches to the fishermen, we followed directions on a street corner sign that read Faro, Lisboa, Sagres, with an arrow pointing to a one-way street out of town. Because Faro is east, Lisboa (Lisbon) is north, and Sagres is west; it amused and confused us. Following the correct highway north to Lisboa, we drove up the west coast.

Driving to the airport on our final day, we got lost in the countryside. I stopped a farmer and, using my limited Spanish (similar to Portugese), asked him where the "*aeropuerto*" was. He understood me, and I hoped I understood him. We followed his directions and found the terminal. Dave retrieved us in Frankfurt and carted us home. (Poor fellow, he certainly made lots of round trips to the Frankfurt airport.) We were tired and hungry for American food, especially toast from a toaster.

Frances stayed with us the rest of the week, attending a special dinner I had planned for General and Mrs. Donnelly, who were retiring in the summer. The plans had already been made before we knew we would be leaving sooner than the Donnellys. Chuck always held to the tradition that fighter pilots eat flowers. (Dave claims to have invented the silly ritual.) I planned my entire dinner to be cooked or decorated with flowers. My soup course was decorated with daisy petals in the shape of a daisy. I chopped Nasturtiums into the rice, a very delicious peppery flavor. Dessert was a Rosé wine-flavored ice cream with pieces of rose petals in the ice cream. The guests thought the dinner was spectacular and enjoyed every flower petal. Frances, a gourmet guru, confessed that it was a first for her.

Dave took Frances to Frankfurt (by now, he could make the trip blindfolded) for her return flight to Toronto, and I raced around the house, frantically organizing for the movers who were coming two days later. Dave and I moved into the base VIP guest quarters to await our flight to Texas.

In our honor, the Operations Division hosted a lovely farewell dinner and presented us with two framed, beautiful wood-inlayed landscapes, unique in that no two are ever made the same.

An engraved brass plaque on the back reads:

Maj. Gen and Mrs. David W. Forgan
HQ USAFE DCS FOR OPERATIONS
1 August 1985 to 25 March 1987
To a Fighter Pilot and
His Lady—THANKS
for the Leadership

Dave received his final flight in the F-16, grateful for having flown the latest advanced fighter planes. What a glorious nineteen months it had been for him, challenging and rewarding. To wrap up our farewells, the generals and colonels, with their wives, hosted a dinner, where General Donnelly presented Dave the standard gift: a wood base with a cut crystal ball placed over a USAFE crest. My two tennis buddies gave me a new tennis racquet bag. I didn't own one, and they thought it was about time I at least looked like a tennis player.

Because we wouldn't have numerous bag drags this time, Dave "allowed" me to pack two large pieces of luggage and my carry-on. We sold our two cars and were driven to Frankfurt for the last time in a staff car. I was ready to shut my eyes and relax for the next ten hours. I basked in the quiet time and good memories of living in Europe again for five years. I realized that Bruce and Todd had experienced no crises for the past nineteen months. What a reprieve. In the furture, their problems would be fewer but bigger.

We flew to Texas nonstop, giving me time to think about being the commander's wife, first lady of Sheppard Air Force Base. I had read an article that stated, "A commander's wife is a paradox for she is an active individual and a solitary one. She has to attend countless civic affairs, speeches, innumerable military functions, club meetings, and dinners; yet many nights are spent just worrying or waiting because something or someone has priority on her husband's time." I became a little apprehensive thinking about this. Did I have enough experience and expertise to fill the shoes? I had no doubts about Dave, but as his wife, I knew that I must also exhibit leadership qualities besides my normal "friendly good ole' girl."

Auf Wiedersehn, Deutschland (Good-bye, Germany).
Howdy, Texas.

Final Salute

Wichita Falls, Texas
Sheppard Air Force Base
Air Training Command
March 1987-July 1989

We landed at the Dallas-Ft. Worth Airport under clear blue skies and were blasted with heat and humidity, and it wasn't even summer. Met by Dave's new executive officer, we loaded our tired bodies and overused luggage into his car and aimed northwest for the two-hour ride to Wichita Falls. I asked the exec about the fields of beautiful blue flowers, and he said, "That's the first thing you should know about Texas; those are bluebonnets, the state flower." Thanks to Lady Bird Johnson's efforts, Texas is covered with wild flowers in the spring. They provide photo ops for families, children, pets, and brides. So I had my first Texas lesson.

The exec delivered us to the base VIP guest quarters where we hung our hats for several weeks until our household shipment arrived. The quarters had a nice living room, a desk for Dave, a kitchenette, and a large bedroom and bath. We unpacked, rested, and walked across the street to the officers' club for dinner. The first thing I noticed as we walked out into the Texas evening was the zillions of stars in the clear sky. It took me by surprise because Europe was overcast most of the time. "The stars at night are big and bright, deep in the heart of Texas." The popular words and music struck a chord.

We called our mothers and sons to let them know we were back on U.S. soil. We drove around to acquaint ourselves with the base and prepared for the Change of Command (C of C). The protocol office had sent formal invitations to our close friends and relatives who began arriving the day before the C of C. I arranged a private dinner party at the officers' club for our guests the night before, providing opportunity to visit without time constraints; the next day would be too hectic.

We awoke to frigid weather, and the C of C was changed from the parade grounds to a hangar. Thank goodness because I was prepared to dress for Texas heat. For the ceremony, a packed house of mostly air force blue-clad spectators heard welcoming remarks from Dave, the new Sheppard Technical Training Center (STTC) commander, a farewell from the outgoing STTC commander, and high praises for both generals from the Air Training Command commander stationed at Randolph Air Force Base in San Antonio. He called General Forgan "the perfect one to take command of the technical training center." I don't know where his speech writer got that idea because Dave had not been in the Air Training Command since he entered the air force thirty-one years before.

After the C of C, a reception with coffee, tea, and cookies was held at the officers' club. Not my idea of a very imposing affair, but no one had asked for my input. Welcoming us were key officers from the base and pertinent civilians from town. In the receiving line, I noticed a Wichita Falls pin on a man's lapel and said, "I need one of those." He grinned, pulled a handful of pins from his pocket, and gave each of us one. Good timing, Shirley, and great PR.

When we finished "gripping and grinning," Dave went to his office, ready to take the reins. (His official picture later—at his desk with the American, the air force, and his personal two-star flags behind him—portrays a dashing and distinquished figure.)

Our personal guests and I received a tour of the headquarters building and then were escorted to the flight line for a tour and briefing of the T-37 and T-38 jet-fighter training program. Bruce and Todd sat in the planes' cockpits, playing "fighter pilot." I was sad that Dave's father was not alive to celebrate his son's success. He would have been so proud. After everyone returned home, Dave went to work, and I received my first "schedule of the week" from the secretary. Oh boy, was I going to be busy.

My first commitment as the new commander's wife was to address the Wichita Falls Women's Forum. We had been on base a week, and I knew nothing about the town or the women's club. I composed my speech while driving to the forum luncheon. Using my native southeastern Oklahoma accent, I told a little of my background and family history. I concluded by sharing that my father grew up in Granbury and Fort Worth, so I was sure he was shouting in his grave, "Way to go, girl! You have finally become a *Texan* like your daddy." That brought forth a round of applause, and I was cordially accepted.

We were quickly involved in welcoming events. The mayor of Burkburnett (nearby town) introduced us to their pertinent people at a small reception at the library. Burkburnett is the town featured in the 1940 movie *Boom Town*, starring Clark Gable and Spencer Tracy. There are hundreds of oil rigs around the town, some still in operation. In addition to other welcoming events for both of us, the officers' wives' club honored me at a lovely tea, where I tried my best to put names with faces. I studied names before each function and reviewed them afterwards to help my memory.

The weekly schedule of events provided by the secretary was a godsend; I needed someone to keep me thoroughly informed and tell me when and where to go. "Just point me in the right direction." The meager wardrobe I'd brought with me was getting multiple uses. At least I wore matching shoes as I had so carelessly not done at my welcome coffee at AFCENT. We received many requests for interviews. I relied on the article in the officers' wives' club newsletter to boost my morale whenever I felt unappreciated.

A few quotes:

Welcome, Mrs. Forgan
The ease with which I was able to conduct my first personal interview is testimony to one of the outstanding qualities you will discover when you meet Shirley Forgan. Her warm, friendly smile and pleasant personality made our conversation very relaxed and enjoyable. Mrs. Forgan extends an invitation to each of us to meet and talk with her. Take it at your earliest opportunity; you will find it a very pleasant experience.

Dave's interviews had been formidable and professional until the *Wichita Falls Times* May 3 Sunday edition. I opened the paper to see a large, color picture of Dave on the front page with the headline "STTC Commander Joined Air Force to Avoid the Draft." I woke Dave and shoved the paper under his nose. He thought it was funny; however, others, including me, didn't see any humor in it. When asked why he joined the air force, Dave told the reporter that while attending the University of Colorado on a football scholarship, the coach advised all the players to sign up for ROTC so they wouldn't get drafted into the Korean War. The reporter failed to explain this. The article was well written and complimentary, just a shame journalism relies on such attention-getters. The next week, a letter to the editor chastised the paper for the cheap shot and suggested several headlines more complimentary to the new commander. Newspaper personnel called Dave and apologized. The publisher became our friend, but Dave, in all good humor, never let him live down the headline.

The base newspaper's interview had the more favorable headline "GENERALLY Speaking, Plane Talk About Loving the Air Force." Clever. Following are some excerpts:

The general—tall, handsome, and graying—relaxes in a comfortable chair opposite his wife of 29 years, Shirley, who is sparkling, pretty, and vivacious. They seem settled and comfortable after their four months here.

The couple is warm and easygoing. They are quick to laugh and share humor and seem to exemplify their claim that "we always have fun wherever we are."

Does he have to act like a "tough guy" to be a general? "I can be a friendly guy," he says, "within the constraints of I'm the general and no one else is." He laughs.

Entertaining and dinner parties are a regular duty. "Our social calendar is full," Mrs. Forgan says. "With the NATO flight training school located here, we entertain many European visitors." She had just finished making a Gran Marnier parfait for 28 people.

Whatever jobs await the Forgans, they both seem to tackle each with a positive attitude—even their many moves. "It's a tough but exciting life," Mrs. Forgan concludes.

He (Dave) looks down at his breast where his wings are pinned. "I'm just as proud of my pilot wings today as 30 years ago." And he seems qualified to instill that pride in thousands of young men and women from all over the world, training under him at SAFB.

Our welcomes and interviews came to a halt; our household goods arrived from Germany; and we moved into quarters number one—the few inevitable scratches and dents but no major damage. Replacing our sons' predictable moving curse, I had an accident of my own, taking a big hunk off my shinbone. At the ER, a tech washed the wound, realigned the flap of skin, and sewed it all back together. Ouch, ouch. He had received his training at Sheppard, and I hoped he made an A in sewing and would take extra special care of the new commander's wife.

Although much smaller than our last three houses, the quarters were adequate and flowed well for entertaining. The house sat on a fenced acre of yard with a nice patio under the shade of a large Texas oak tree, and I decked out the guest powder room in Texas décor. (I left it that way for our successor, stating I'd never be back to Texas again. Ha! Little did I know.)

This command authorized us to have two aides, one from the office who kept Dave pointed in the right direction. He and his beautiful, blonde Norwegian wife were a delightful young couple who took to their roles with ease and seemed comfortable around us.

The other aide, a lookalike for actor Morgan Freeman, was assigned to our house weekdays plus weekends if we were entertaining. He mowed the yard, did household chores, took Dave's uniforms to the cleaners, and did the general's ironing (he was not allowed to do mine). He was surprised to learn I disliked big cocktail parties, so he would have to cook, serve, and clean up for sit-down dinners. I created menus A, B, and C with three courses each: soup or fish appetizer, entree, and dessert. I prepared a grocery list for each menu and showed him how to cook the food and serve the guests at the table. For example, I requested him to prepare menu A for eight people, and he took it from there. The first dinner party went well until I heard him in the kitchen, loading the crystal, silver, and china in the dishwasher. I went to the kitchen and told him everything had to be handwashed and dried. He was not a happy camper, but I figured he paid in labor at our dinner parties for the lack of work during the week. After the initial shock, he did a great job. He also assisted me with daytime functions at home—coffees, brunches, luncheons. His help made my commitments tolerable and more enjoyable.

Dave's office personnel also included his secretary, a vice commander and secretary, and executive officer. Protocol handled official social needs—plans and invitations, and Public Affairs took care of publicity and speech writing. Seemed to me he had ample help for all his duties. Once again, I bought a new mop.

We braced ourselves for the many social commitments: "hails and farewells," promotion ceremonies and parties, retirement ceremonies and parties, graduation ceremonies and parties, receptions with two-hour long receiving lines, annual military balls, annual NCOWC (non-commissioned officers' wives' club) Charity Balls, Fortieth Air Force Anniversary Ball, European dignitary entertainment, civilian events, officers' wives' club events, coffees, luncheons, dinner parties (mine and others), community appreciation dinners, Boy Scout affairs, Special Olympics, Junior League training tours, and holiday parties. The schedule of events never slowed down. Sometimes I changed clothes five times a day.

We eagerly invited Tom Danaher for dinner. He was a distinguished pilot from World War II and the Korean War, who continued to be an avid aviator, living in a small apartment above his own private airport in Wichita Falls. Tom did all the flying scenes in the movie *Out of Africa*. In *Empire of the Sun*, a Steven Spielberg movie, Danaher commanded the squadron of Japanese Zero pilots and had a cameo role as an American colonel.

Tom invited Dave to his airport for a spin with him in a small, old French trainer. When Dave looked into the cockpit of one of Tom's airplanes, there was *no* instrument panel. In its place was taped a piece of paper with instruments drawn on it. The old warrior just filled the gas tank, kicked the tires, checked the rudders, and went off into the wild blue yonder.

Two important events took place while we were at Sheppard. The first was called "Operation Texan." The air force commanding generals of thirteen NATO nations visited the Euro NATO Joint Jet Pilot Training (ENJJPT) program at our base, which trained selected pilots from all the NATO countries. (Several Dutch pilots in the program bought two old classic 1950s cars, painted them the colors of the Dutch flag, and sliced off their tops, creating convertibles. They were a sight to behold, garnering a great degree of attention. I doubted the vehicles' legality, but the townspeople were very tolerant of the foreign officers. In fact, a program was created whereby civilians sponsored some of the student pilots, including them in social events, in their homes, ranches, ski resort homes, and on vacations. It produced wonderful relationships between the town and our foreign students. The concept was simple; the results tremendous. Other good relationships were formed when town girls pursued some of those darling foreign fighter pilots.)

For the first event, members of the civilian community hosted a western-style barbeque at a local ranch. Rigid security was a primary concern, as the military "stars" almost outnumbered those in the Texas sky. Twenty-four World War II airplanes participated in a flying demonstration, prompting many "oohs and ahhs" on the ground below. A precise demonstration by two Japanese fighters motivated a visiting general to say, "That was so realistic, I started looking around for a foxhole." Not on the program, but definitely entertaining, was a small herd of longhorn steers being driven to the spectator area. Just before arriving at their destination, the longhorns bolted through a small clump of trees, "flushing out" two Sheppard AFB SWAT members in camouflage, with rifles, from their hiding place. The cowboys guided the steers back to the party, and the security guards returned to the trees. The NATO generals were impressed and appreciated the big Texas welcome.

The second important event was a moving ceremony held on base to honor all POWs and MIAs (Prisoners of War and Missing in Action). Dave dedicated a granite monument inscribed with the words "Eternal Vigilance for Your Return," and said, "I urge you to pass by this monument, look at it, and reflect on its meaning from time to time." One of our flight training squadrons did a T-38 flyby in the missing man formation. Dave presented new congressionally-approved POW medals to sixty-three former POWs from the Wichita Falls area who represented service in three wars. Family members received the medals for those no longer living. One hundred-fifty balloons were released, symbolizing the one hundred-fifty Texas MIAs. A luncheon followed the dedication, and retired Air Force Colonel Conrad Trautman, a six-year North Vietnam POW, was the guest speaker. "Connie" and his wife, Angela, lived in Wichita Falls. I admire his bravery and her strength in raising their children with no father during those lonely, dreadful years. I was disappointed in myself that I did not think to ask Angela to join me when I placed a red ribbon on the memorial at the ceremony. She was more deserving of the honor than I! Ceremonies like this bring us together to thank and honor those who have given so much for their country. "Lest we forget!"

I had a big surprise in store for Dave on Father's Day. I met a family moving into base quarters with two big sheepdogs, ten new puppies, a black Lab, and several children. They couldn't get rid of the children, so, in order to live in smaller base housing, they had to decrease the number of dogs. Sizing up the pack of canines, I immediately decided against the sheepdog hair-shedding machines. The poor Lab hid under the coffee table to escape the children and the sheepdogs. I enticed her from her hiding place, she put her head in my lap, and I was adopted. I hung a Father's Day card around her neck, and with her tongue hanging out and her tail wagging, she eagerly met Dave for the first time. Eighteen-month-old Cleopatra of Hunter's Glen (Cleo for short) happily found a new home where she no longer had to compete for attention. She was beautiful and sweet with only one bad habit: chewing things. She chewed several of my cookbooks, the corners of coffee table books, a dried flower arrangement, and Dave's plastic bridge-playing calculator. These episodes occurred only when we were gone—"Leave me alone, I'll show you."

Cleo's "baby" was a stuffed, black Lab puppy. She licked it, curled up with it, and carried it around the house. Her "best friend" was Toby, a golden retriever from two doors away who had play dates with Cleo in our large, fenced-in backyard. They ran around until they were exhausted and then rested under the shade of the large trees bordering the yard. After several visits, the dogs eagerly anticipated their playtimes. The phone ringing at four o'clock was Toby's signal to go to his back door to be let out. I opened our gate and stood out of the way to avoid being mowed down by the one-hundred-pound golden streak on a mission as he raced from his house into our yard. One time Toby showed his ingenuity by raising the latch on the chain link gate with his nose, releasing Cleo for a twosome romp around the neighborhood.

That first summer, we joined the townspeople to celebrate an event they had been eagerly promoting for many years. Billed as the "biggest turn-on" in Texas, city officials unveiled the newly-constructed waterfall in Wichita Falls on June 5, 1987. Thousands of people attended the celebration. The city newspaper reported,

> Major General David W. Forgan spoke briefly at the ceremony, citing the strong friendship between Sheppard and the Wichita Falls community. Michael O'Laughlin, mayor of Niagara Falls, New York, attended the dedication, bringing a 2,500 pound rock over 300 million years old and a keg of water from Niagara Falls. The rock was placed at the bottom of the falls and water from the keg was poured over it, initiating the dedication.

A national television station did a broadcast from the falls site. It was exciting for the local community to finally bring the "falls" to Wichita Falls, after many years of trying to explain why they had none.

All the family arrived for our first Christmas at Sheppard. Bruce drove from Tulsa, picking up Nonna on the way. Todd flew from Tucson where he was *still* job hunting a year after graduation, selling kitchen knives and telemarketing in the meantime. Grandma Forgan flew in from Sarasota, Florida. We had our usual extravagant gift-giving and traditional formal dinner (with Bruce in his usual informal attire). After a couple days, I kept the grandmothers separated because Grandma Forgan complained that Nonna hogged the newspaper. All returned to their respective homes, and Cleo and I collapsed, exhausted.

Following the holidays, we attended a city social function

where someone suggested that Todd attend Midwestern State University in Wichita Falls and work on his master's degree. I liked the idea. Since we resided in Texas, Todd was eligible for in-state tuition. Dave liked that idea. I called Todd with the suggestion, and six days later he arrived, pulling a U-Haul trailer with all his belongings. He had survived a snow storm in New Mexico; however, the Camaro suffered a bashed fender. The doorbell rang at 7:30 p.m., and when I opened the door, Todd staggered in and collapsed facedown on the foyer rug. A little dramatic, but he was exhausted from the rough trip. He registered for classes the next day and hit the books two days later.

In the meantime, he mailed 250 resumes to Texas banks. With an undergraduate degree in finance, he wanted to pursue a career in the banking business; unfortunately, forty-eight Texas banks closed their doors that year due to the savings and loans crisis. I didn't think Todd had a snowball's chance in Hades to get a banking job. Even the postman was compassionate when he handed me Todd's daily stack of rejection letters, always inquiring if there'd been any good news. To be frugal, he sold his Camaro and bought a little Volkswagen GTI. And thus, Todd returned to the nest.

Every August, Wichita Falls sponsors the "Hotter 'n Hell Hundred," a one-hundred-mile bike ride over hills (yes, there are some hills in west Texas), down straights, and around curves in hot, windy weather. Todd decided to be one of the 12,500 participants. He had bicycled a lot in Arizona, but competing in this race without training was unthinkable. The winner finished in three hours and fifty-nine minutes. Todd clocked in at six hours and thirty minutes, but he finished. It added some family excitement to our busy schedule.

I planned a surprise for our thirtieth wedding anniversary in October 1988, asking the secretary and vice commander to free Dave's schedule. I made a reservation at the local Hilton and left this note at the house for Dave to read when he came home from work: Meet me in the bar at the Hilton, bring your dopp kit, and be prepared to remain overnight. He followed my instructions; we enjoyed a nice dinner at a local restaurant and then returned to the hotel. Slinking out of the bathroom in a sexy, red nightgown, I was greeted by Dave's "holy cow" exclamation, and the rest of the evening was x-rated.

The next morning, Dave paced around the bedroom until I said, "Oh, for heaven's sake, get dressed and go to work. I'm going back to sleep." Leaving the hotel in civilian clothes, tie rolled up in his pocket, he bumped into a young man I shall call Joe arriving for a United Fund breakfast. Dave had been scheduled to attend the event, but unbeknown to Joe, the vice commander was substituting. Joe asked, "Are you coming to the breakfast this morning, sir?" Dave replied, "I don't see why not," turned around, put on his tie, and went to the breakfast. The vice commander wondered what Dave was doing at the breakfast, and Dave didn't explain, probably too embarrassed to tell anyone he'd spent the night with his wife at the hotel. He never explained to Joe why he was exiting a hotel at seven in the morning dressed in civilian clothes. To this day, Joe is probably still gossiping about the general.

Adding a little more spice to our many activities, the vice commander's wife, Rosie, and I pulled a daring stunt. The Air Training Command commander, a three-star general from Randolph AFB in San Antonio, was the guest speaker at a Sheppard "Dining-In," a formal dinner for military officers and non-commissioned officers to promote camaraderie. I don't know what possessed us, but Rosie and I decided to crash the affair. Rosie dressed in tattered overalls and flowery blouse, was barefoot, had painted freckles on her face, and wore a straw hat with a big flower sticking straight up. My appearance was just as ridiculous: a plaid skirt, a clashing plaid shirt with one side tucked in and the other hanging out, red knee-high hose, blue sneakers, painted freckles, two blacked-out teeth, a large-brimmed white hat atop a long, black wig, and a pitch fork in hand.

Rosie and I barged into the dining room about the time the general started his speech, which abruptly came to a halt. Stomping around the room, we exclaimed loudly, "What's going on here and who are all these people? Why weren't we invited to this here dinner affair?" There was laughter and bewildered stares. Dave lowered his head, and the general looked startled. Rosie gave Dave a big kiss, and I smacked one on the general's cheek. We ran out of the room and went home, prepared to pack our bags and depart before our husbands arrived and grounded us. Rosie was recognizable in her costume, actually looked rather "farm-cute." On the other hand, I did not look cute and hoped no one recognized the other "kook." When asked, I denied everything. We escaped punishment and harsh words from our husbands, but I certainly laid low for a while and minded my manners.

Rosie and I in our daring party-crashing attire

Todd was forced to leave Midwestern State University after the spring semester and summer session due to eligibility complications. He had completed twelve credit hours with As and Bs; we always knew he was capable. He continued to job hunt and work part time on the computer at a beer distributor. One evening, noticing the beautiful female news anchor on local TV, Todd remarked, "Now I would stay in Wichita Falls for her." Through contacts and conniving on my part, they met for drinks at Bennigan's and began dating.

Dave and I met them at the Wichita Falls Country Club one night for dinner, and shortly after he and I were seated, a hush came over the crowd as all heads turned toward the dining room entrance. Entering the room was a striking couple: tall, svelte Diana in an ankle-length Kelly-green coat, her gorgeous copper-colored hair in an upsweep, perfect makeup complementing her blue eyes, and her radiant smile accenting her deep dimples. The dinner guests probably recognized her from TV. Todd, her six-foot two-inch escort, looked handsome in coat and tie, stylish haircut, and *his* dimples. The crowd probably wondered who *he* was. What a pair. Even I was speechless. A former participant in two Miss Texas competitions, Diana knew how to make an entrance. She was vivacious and friendly, and we immediately liked her.

Todd was finally hired as an operations analyst in the operations division of First Interstate Bank in Dallas. Hooray, a job. Even the postman was happy. Only Diana was not thrilled, and she immediately looked for a TV position in Dallas. Todd rented an apartment near his office, and the highway between Wichita Falls and Dallas became hot and heavy with Diana/Todd traffic.

In the meantime, Bruce became unenamored with his Tulsa postion and found a job in Dallas. The two brothers moved into an apartment together. I thought it intriguing that after thirty-one years, our two sons lived in Dallas where Dave and I had started our journey together.

We celebrated our second and last Christmas at Sheppard without Grandma Forgan, who didn't feel up to the trip. Nonna joined us, happy to have the newspaper and family all to herself. After our usual paper and ribbon gift-opening mess, I served a champagne brunch followed later with our traditional formal dinner. Bruce honored us in a coat and tie. When everyone departed, Cleo and I again collapsed from the rigors of the base and family holiday festivities.

Dave's mother was not doing well and occasionally didn't have "both oars in the water." She called me, really disturbed about an announcement in the Sarasota newspaper of a nurse's engagement to an air force F-16 pilot at Ramstein Air Base in Germany. Confused, she related the F-16 and Ramstein with Dave because of our previous assignment and was upset that *David* would dump his family for some nurse. I told her Dave was still at Sheppard AFB in Wichita Falls. She mailed the article to me, and I returned it with the F-16 pilot's name circled, convincing her it wasn't Dave.

As predicted, the move to Texas didn't offer many skiing opportunities; however, I managed to don my long underwear and ski togs for two trips to Crested Butte and one to Taos, New Mexico. Most of my travels involved several trips to California to take care of the needs of elderly relatives. Dave's Aunt Grace in Sun City lost her husband and her sister, Aunt May, and was being cared for by several certified nurses assistants, one a male. Aunt Grace gave him full power of attorney and lent him money, so the Forgan family became concerned about her care and finances. I volunteered to fly to California to check on her and also my Aunt Jane in Hemet, thirty minutes from Sun City. It became a nightmare. Aunt Grace became bedridden for eight years, frozen into a fetal position the final four years. The male caretaker disappeared after I confronted him about his $30,000 debt to Aunt Grace, and she eventually was moved into a trusted caretaker's home. I had the undesirable task of selling her house and disposing of her belongings. Aunt Grace died with $750 remaining in her bank account.

Aunt Jane became incapacitated soon after her third husband died, and after she sold her house, I moved her to an assisted-living care facility and later to a nursing home. She became the victim of a scam, a fraudulent insurance man taking her $167,000 savings; however, with perseverance and determination to see justice done and my aunt's money returned, I collected enough evidence to have him arrested. He was sentenced to three years in California's Chino Prison. We sued the insurance company that had an employee contract with the conman, and Aunt Jane retrieved $99,000 in settlement. We invested the money with a Hemet firm, it profited, and she was financially sound the rest of her days, leaving me a nice little inheritance for my trouble. Thank you, Aunt Jane. Caring for the aunts had been time consuming and nerve wracking, but I assured their quality of life was sustained in their final days.

Having sold our Fairfax, Virginia, house when we were stationed overseas, we had two years after returning to the U.S. to invest the money in another house to avoid capital gains tax. The deadline of June 22, 1989, was sneaking up on us. It made no sense financially to own a home somewhere and let it sit empty. Therefore, the situation presented itself to buy a house and retire. The big question was where? This was the first time *we* got to decide where to "hang our hats." None of our previous locations appealed to us, but it was necessary to be near military medical facilities until we reached age sixty-five and qualified for Medicare.

We quickly decided on Colorado Springs—several military installations for shopping and medical care, plus taxes were low. In April, I prepared to drive to "The Springs" to meet with a real estate agent. The night before I left, the agent called and said,

"Bring your skis, and we'll take a ski day while you're here." The next morning, I waited until Dave left for work before sneaking my ski gear into the car. I didn't want a lecture about house hunting, not skiing.

Looking at houses for one week, I became very discouraged. Nothing appealed to me until we came upon a house south of downtown, located in Cheyenne Mountain's foothills at 6,500 feet altitude. I said, "Now this is more like it." An open floor plan with glass windows all across the back made it bright inside. I liked the neighborhood—lots of pine, aspen, and scrub oak trees. Now I had to convince Dave of my choice.

Saturated with house viewing, I took the suggested ski day with the agent and her friends. It was refreshing to concentrate on something else—like keeping up with those good skiers. We took a warm-up run on a black diamond slope, and I immediately knew my mind was not going to be on a house. My focus was on getting down the mountain in one piece without looking like a dork.

Dave flew a T-38 jet trainer to Peterson Air Force Base in Colorado Springs, and we began the "parade of homes." I had selected six houses for Dave to consider. We fought over two and finally settled on my first choice, the house south of town. Up the hill, situated in the mountain, was NORAD, the command post for the air defense of the United States. Dave looked at it from the deck of the house and said, "Well, we're at Ground Zero and won't feel a thing."

The happy real estate agent had a sale, Dave flew back to Sheppard, and I drove home. In June, the loaded Mayflower truck left, we transferred into base VIP guest quarters, and then drove to "The Springs" to meet the moving van at our new retirement abode. We spent a few days unpacking some boxes, and I organized the kitchen, expertly and quickly after many years of practice.

Returning to Wichita Falls, we geared up for the retirement festivities. Dinner invitations piled up, and our calendar got filled. A farewell luncheon for me included all the colonels' wives and selected ladies from surrounding communities. They showered me with gifts, including appropriate Texas mementos. I responded, "We gather again for more farewells. So many good-byes have been said, most of you probably think, *Wish she would just shut up and go*." Directing most of my remarks to the civilian guests, I praised military wives. My request for all the colonels' wives to stand brought a round of applause. The luncheon was to honor me, but I wanted to acknowledge those special ladies. I expressed my thanks to all, my appreciation for the civilian friendships, and read parts of the "Air Force Wives" poem.

Other farewell luncheons were hosted by the non-commissioned officers' wives' club, the Wichita Falls Ladies Forum, and the wives of the headquarters staff. The officers' wives' club hosted my big farewell luncheon. Dessert was a beautiful red, white, and blue cake decorated with a Texas flag, an American flag, red, white, and blue flowers, and "farewell" in twelve languages. I had suggested only *one gift*, preferably a Hermes scarf. After checking the price, Rosie gave me a Hermes catalog with *pictures* of scarves; however, I was given several lovely gifts in spite of my request.

I wanted my farewell response to be meaningful, especially to the young wives. Outlining Dave's thirty-four-year career—serving in nine different commands, including fighter pilot, scope dope, educator, Fort Fumbler, student, tactical planner, commando/spook, diplomat, and commander—I elaborated on both positive and negative aspects of military life. I praised and encouraged participation in wives' clubs and paid special tribute to Angela Trautman in the audience, whose marriage survived the six years her husband was a POW in North Vietnam. In conclusion, I said, "Being the wife of the only general on base can be a lonely existence, so thank you for letting me be a *part* of you, not *apart* from you." I quoted the poem by an unknown author:

> Like flowers in a garden
> And blossoms on a tree,
> I couldn't count the lovely things
> Each friendship means to me.
> For each new friend adds a blossom

To the beautiful bouquet
Of warm and special memories
I gather on life's way.

I said, "Thank you for adding to my bouquet of memories."

I wished them happy, successful, rewarding years with their husbands, enjoying the moments, forgetting the disappointments, and relishing the good memories, and stated, "I am honored to have served with my husband and am proud to be an air force wife."

A very special card from a Sheppard air force wife contained this message:

Dear Shirley,

I truly do feel so lucky to have had these two years together and to have learned so very much from you. You have a rare quality of being fun, silly, and "one of the girls" while radiating leadership and poise as a perfect lady and role model for the young wives.

Being involved with the student wives gave me the opportunity to see the impact you are making on the wives of the air force's future leaders. I so often heard them say how terrific it was that a general's wife is so warm and friendly to them and really cares about their personal needs. We will miss your smile, your warmth, and your fun personality. I do consider it an honor to have known you and am very, very proud to have you as a Kappa sister. I'll miss you.

She expressed exactly what I wanted as my legacy of a good air force wife and helped me believe I had contributed to the betterment of our military community. Dave received medals and promotions. I received compliments and treasured words of appreciation.

On the fifteenth of July, the base honored us with a memorable dinner party at the officers' club. Many out-of-town friends and relatives arrived for the affair. Dave's former executive officer at AFCENT in the Netherlands and his wife drove from Florida, and Frances and Jim LaVigne flew in from Toronto.

The evening's program read:

> The men and women of Sheppard Technical Training Center wish to take this opportunity to express thanks and fond regards to Major General Dave and Shirley Forgan. Their leadership, support, and dedication have been an inspiration to all who have come in contact with them.
>
> The culmination of General Forgan's distinguished career deserves an evening of reflection, reverence, and even some good natured fun. General Forgan has dedicated nearly thirty-four years of service to the United States Air Force. These years have been rewarding not only to him but also to the many lives he has touched. General Forgan, Shirley, please accept our sincere "Thank you" from an appreciative Center, a thankful community, and a grateful nation.
>
> Safe flying and happy landings.

Following dinner, we were entertained with several musical performances. A male quartet sang "What Can You Do with a General" (when he retires) from the Bing Crosby movie *White Christmas*. I requested that a wife sing Kenny Rogers's "Through the Years," dedicated to Dave from Shirley. It ended with "As long as it's okay, I'll stay with you...through the years." Tears rolled down cheeks, and muffled sniffles could be heard around the room.

Dave was presented with many thoughtful and generous gifts. He especially liked the glass-topped table that enclosed his two-star general flag and a leather flight jacket from ENJJPT. Dave made his final flight with them the previous week, getting hosed down from a fire truck and celebrating with champagne.

The next night we took our out-of-town guests to the Wichita Falls Country Club for dinner. I gave Dave a retirement gift: a framed and blue-matted cross stitch of the air force seal. I had secretly worked on the project for months, so it was a complete surprise.

After we returned to our temporary quarters for the last night, Bruce, Todd, and I found a screwdriver and removed and confiscated the *VIP Parking* sign outside our quarters. What could they do to us if caught? Make us retire? As I climbed into bed, there was a knock on the door. I cautiously asked who was there, wondering who could possibly want us at that time of night. A husky, male voice said, "Excuse me, Mrs. Forgan, this is the security police, and I understand that someone here has the VIP Parking sign." I nervously responded, "Oh, all right, I'll return it tomorrow." Hearing giggles, I jerked open the door, and there stood Bruce and Todd about to collapse with laughter. They got me. The future site of the VIP sign was on our new garage wall in Colorado Springs.

July 17, 1989, was the big finale, and I had mixed emotions, tired and a little burned out. However, I would miss the camaraderie. We would no longer be VIPs, and Dave would not be saluted. Everyone gathered at the parade field, where Dave and I were chauffeured by staff car and escorted to the reviewing stand. The highlights of his career faded into the shadows as I heard ruffles and flourishes (drum rolls and trumpet played simultaneously preceding the music "The General's March") in Dave's honor for the last time. The color guard presented the colors, and SSgt. Michael A. Merrill, in beautiful baritone, sang the national anthem. General Oaks pinned the Air Force Distinguished Service Medal on Dave's shirt and read the retirement orders. I wept at the finality of it all.

Then came my turn. I was escorted to Dave's side where General Oaks gave me a certificate of appreciation and a dozen yellow roses and spoke words of thanks on behalf of the air force. When he bent to kiss me on the cheek, I thought, *Does he recognize me as one of the "incognito broads" who crashed the formal Dining-In affair and kissed him on the cheek?* He never mentioned it, and it was too late for me to care.

Following the new commander's remarks and Dave's farewell speech, the troops paraded by in review for the final salute. A flyby of ENJJPT's T-38s climaxed the event, and Dave and I were escorted to the staff car for our departure. As the car door was opened for me, I waved good-bye to everyone in the reviewing area. Then I lost it, and the tears flowed. I think I heard only a deep sigh from Dave.

We returned to our VIP quarters where Dave handled some last minute details while our out-of-town guests gathered for coffee and snacks and said their farewells. We kissed everyone good-bye and departed for Colorado Springs to begin a more relaxed lifestyle.

Dave had "descended from the wild blue yonder, made his final approach to the runway, and landed his plane for the last time. He parked, shut down the engine, and closed the hangar door." My thirty-one-year journey in the military with an air force fighter pilot was finished. Thank you, Dave, for marrying me and providing this adventure. More tears fall as I write this final chapter, remembering special moments to cherish the rest of my life.

As one door closes, another opens...

The Final Salute

Air Force Wives

Author Unknown

Who said that variety is the spice of life?
No doubt it was first said by an Air Force Wife!
For the poor woman never knows just where she's "at."
"At home" is wherever he parks his hat.

She moves every year into new sets of quarters.
And when she's not moving, she births sons and daughters.
She packs up to move to the plains of Nebraska—
Orders are changed, and they go to Alaska.

She wrangles empty boxes and finds the beds,
Makes curtains of sheets last used for spreads.
And during each move—now isn't it strange?—
The kids catch the measles, the mumps or ptomaine.

She knows the traditions, the songs, and the lore
And how fast she learns how he won the war!
She waltzes with some who are a little bit glamorous,
Dances with others who are just a bit amorous.

She drinks all concoctions of gin, whiskey, beer—
But moderately, Honey, she'll wreck his career!
He insists on economy, eyes each check stub.
Yet her house must be run like a hotel or club.

She entertains at all hours, both early and late,
Any number of people, from eighty to eight.
The first of the month there is plenty of cash,
So she serves ham and steak—the last week it's hash.

When it's all said and done,
She still is convinced the Air Force is fun.
She has loved every minute, in spite of the grief,
She'd have been bored with a banker or merchant chief.

But there's one fancy medal,
Lots of Air Force men wear it,
It's their wives who should have it—
That Legion of Merit!

Legion of Merit

Epilogue

After retiring, we lived in Colorado Springs for fourteen years, where I was mostly on the tennis courts (indoors in winter and outdoors in summer) or skiing in the beautiful Colorado mountains. Indulging my passion for the two sports, I became proficient at both. We attended Air Force Academy football games every year, in the blaring sun, drenching rain, or freezing snow. Renewing military friendships and creating new ones, I discovered our social life still centered around the military. To quote an unknown veteran,

> After a lifetime of camaraderie that few experience, it remained as a longing for those past times. We know in the military life there is a fellowship that lasts long after the uniforms are hung up in the back of the closet. This is what we were yesterday, are today, and will be forever.

An additional non-military contingent included Dave's fraternity brothers from the University of Colorado, my tennis acquaintances, our neighbors, and our avid bridge players.

Our dear and longtime Canadian friend, Jim LaVigne, died of colon cancer, and many of our military friends passed away. We lost Cleo, our faithful and loveable black Lab. Bruce married and divorced; Todd is still single, but they provided us with two grandsons—the loves of my life. Shortly after Dave's retirement, Mom Forgan died at the age of eighty-nine, and in 1995, I moved Mother to a retirement community in Colorado Springs. Two fall injuries the first year forced her to move from independent living, through two hospital stays and two rehabs, into assisted living, spending her final three years in a nursing home. We lost her on December 27, 1999, two months after her nintieth birthday. I still shed inherited Italian tears when I think of her, a devoted, protective mother and adoring grandmother.

In May 2001, I was shocked with a breast cancer diagnosis, thinking they made a mistake and would discover their error. Finally accepting the diagnosis, I proceeded with immediate surgery and radiation followed by five years of antiestrogen therapy. I was deluged with support from friends, and my Kappa sorority sisters composed, sang, and taped a "fight song" for my recovery, a big morale booster.

The year following my surgery, I decided to move to Texas. If the cancer returned, I wanted to be near our sons and grandsons, and if I were fortunate to be a survivor, I would not regret relocating. In February 2003, we moved into our Texas home, which I designed and had built. Dave's heels were dug in all the way; he still hasn't forgiven me for uprooting him from his golfing buddies in Colorado Springs.

We enjoy quality time with grandson Spencer, playing cards and board games, dining out, and attending his many sports games and school activities. He and Pa Pa share a love of orange sherbet. Thirteen years old, he still holds my hand (if no one is looking) and gives me hugs and kisses. He calls me the Huggy Monster. I want him to be a lawyer because he is good at arguing. I've offered to send him to Harvard Law School.

Our other grandson, Jacob, is a very compassionate young man, a graduate of Victory Bible Institute in Tulsa. I hope he finds his way in the world to help others as he is destined to be one of God's disciples. I wish we'd had more time with him through the years, but, thankfully, a special bond exists between us.

As a six-year cancer survivor in 2007, I participated in the Dallas 3 Day-60 Mile Walk For the Cure of Breast Cancer. I consider it the greatest achievement of my life—besides defeating the cancer, which I figured was in someone else's hands. I trained for eight months, walking four days a week and doing strength training twice weekly at the gym, gradually building my endurance. I was totally dedicated. I chalked up 695 training miles, completed the entire sixty-mile event, and personally raised $11,985.45 for the Susan G. Komen Foundation. The amount placed me in the top ten fund-raisers out of approximately 2,400 registered walkers. I was blessed with very generous, supportive friends and family.

It is now 2010. Dave is fighting emphysema and bladder cancer, and Todd continues to expose us to his myriad of girlfriends. Bruce has moved to the British Virgin Islands where he purchased a sailboat and charter business. We have lost more friends, but I guess that's to be expected as we reach our seventies. I still love to travel, exploring many faraway places: Peru, South Africa, Russia, Asia, and Europe. My little seven-year-old West Highland Terrier, Biscuit, gives me all the love he can possibly muster and entertains us with tricks. He also keeps me on a walking regimen, dragging his leash in his mouth to the front door, wagging his little white tail, eager to explore the neighborhoods.

The following sentiment, I copied from an e-mail, author unknown, expresses my philosophy:

> Life should not be a journey to the grave with the intention of arriving safely in an attractive and well-preserved body but rather to skid in sideways, chocolate in hand, body thoroughly used up, totally worn out and screaming, "Whoo Hoo, what a ride!"

Since 1957, I have moved twenty-four times; therefore, unless I relocate again, I would like my tombstone to read: "My 25th and final move!"

About the Author

 Shirley grew up amidst the rolling hills of southeastern Oklahoma in McAlester (Choctaw Indian Nation, cowboy country, and home of the famous "inside the walls" prison rodeo). She is a graduate of Oklahoma State University in 1957 with a degree in elementary education and is a member of Kappa Kappa Gamma sorority. Not enamored with the teaching profession, she made her way to Dallas to find a more exciting lifestyle.

Shortly after her arrival in Dallas, a jet fighter pilot swept her off her feet, and they had a short, but intense, two-month courtship. She married him a year later after he had been away on assignment in Japan. Thus began her incredible journey in the air force with her husband and their two sons, making the transition from a first lieutenant's girlfriend to general's wife. They lived and traveled all over the world for the next thirty-one years.

After the general's retirement in 1989, their home was in Colorado Springs, Colorado, for the next fourteen years. In 2001, Shirley was struck down with breast cancer, and after successful treatment, *she* decided they would move to the Dallas-Ft. Worth metroplex to be near their two sons and two grandsons. She has been married to her "unemployed fighter pilot" for more than fifty years.